Unwinnable Wars

ALSO BY DAVID CALLAHAN

Dangerous Capabilities:
Paul Nitze and the Cold War

Between Two Worlds:
Realism, Idealism, and American Foreign Policy After the Cold War

State of the Union

UNWINNABLE WARS

AMERICAN POWER AND ETHNIC CONFLICT

DAVID CALLAHAN

A TWENTIETH CENTURY FUND BOOK

HILL AND WANG
A DIVISION OF FARRAR, STRAUS AND GIROUX
NEW YORK

Hill and Wang
A division of Farrar, Straus and Giroux
19 Union Square West, New York 10003

Distributed in Canada by Douglas & McIntyre Ltd.
Printed in the United States of America
Designed by Debbie Glasserman
First published in 1997 by Hill and Wang
First paperback edition, 1998

The Twentieth Century Fund sponsors and supervises timely analyses of economic policy, foreign affairs, and domestic political issues. Not-for-profit and nonpartisan, the Fund was founded in 1919 and endowed by Edward A. Filene.

The Library of Congress has catalogued the hardcover edition as follows:
Callahan, David, 1965–
   Unwinnable wars : American power and ethnic conflict / David
Callahan. — 1st ed.
      p.   cm.
   "A twentieth century fund book."
   Includes bibliographical references and index.
   ISBN (invalid) 0-8090-3064-2 (cloth : alk. paper)
      1. United States—Foreign relations—1945–1989.   2. United States—
Foreign relations—1989–   3. Ethnic relations—History—20th
century.   I. Title.
E840.C335   1998
327.73—dc21   97-27912

*For Peter
and
Perry*

CONTENTS

CHAPTER FOUR: INTERVENTION 132

CHAPTER FIVE: TOWARD THE FUTURE 200

ACKNOWLEDGMENTS

THIS BOOK WOULD not have been written without backing from the Twentieth Century Fund. Richard Leone supported this project from its inception and generously invited me to take up residence at the Fund. Later, he provided useful feedback on the book as it evolved into final form. Trustee member Brewster Denny was also very supportive of this project and offered many astute suggestions for strengthening the manuscript. Other help at the Fund came from Michelle Miller, who championed the project at its earliest stage; from Greg Anrig, who helped me sharpen my arguments and proved to be a good friend and ally in myriad ways; from Beverly Goldberg, who marketed the manuscript; and from Carol Starmack, Kathie Young, and Laurie Ahlrich. Judy Miller and Ellen Chesler, both Fellows at the Fund, were a source of much enriching conversation.

During the early stages of my research, Paul Bonk shared with me his considerable expertise on ethnicity and ethnic conflict, lending me books and articles, listening to my ideas, and offering advice. As the project neared completion, I received helpful comments on the manuscript from Morton Halperin, Richard Ullman, and Michael Klare. My editor at Hill and Wang, Lauren Osborne, did an excellent job of editing the book and was a pleasure to work with in every way. Her assistant, Susan DeCarava, smoothly shepherded the manuscript through production.

Finally, my friends and family were, as always, enormously supportive. In particular, Perry Ann Turnbull Callahan has brightened my life with a charm that grows ever more beguiling.

by Richard C. Leone

ETHNIC CONFLICT IS a modern catch-all for one of the oldest scourges of humanity. It encompasses a wide variety of struggles, often involving hatred without reason and warfare without rules. Absent the clarity provided by the cold war, the world's leading statesmen often seem confounded by the ambiguities of such hostilities. Contemporary ethnic conflicts can be very difficult to understand and considerably harder to resolve. Indeed, while inaction is routinely subject to criticism, there are few general guidelines for effective action.

Recent events in Bosnia and Africa, especially, have focused attention on the issue of intervention by the great powers, but without a clear understanding of the consequences. We are still learning. David Callahan's book is, in part, about the attempt to move beyond the obvious "damned if you do, damned if you don't" character of national policy in this area. The search for firm guidelines for both civil and military action will be a long and painstaking process.

Even before completing his doctorate at Princeton University, Callahan had written two books on U.S. foreign policy—*Dangerous Capabilities: Paul Nitze and the Cold War* and *Between Two Worlds: Realism, Idealism, and American Foreign Policy After the Cold War*. More recently, he branched out into fiction with the publication of his first novel, *State of the Union*. He did the research for *Unwinnable Wars* while a visiting scholar at the Twentieth Century Fund.

The structure of this timely volume reflects the hard lessons learned by political thinkers and leaders over the past several years. Many thought that the world was evolving into a more peaceful and stable place. Even the bipolar standoff of the cold war was, with notable exceptions, something short of open warfare. But the reassertion of old animosities and the proliferation of outright violence has, at least in the short run, given the lie to that optimistic view of human development.

Yet Callahan believes that there can be generally consistent and effective U.S. strategies for defusing or deescalating ethnic conflicts. This positive view informs much of his prescriptive material and shapes his judgments about how the United States has performed in the recent past.

He explores in considerable detail the growing importance of self-determination movements in the post-cold war world and offers criteria for the United States to use when judging appropriate responses. Some of these factors are straightforward (for example, whether a nation's groups or states have a real commitment to democracy and human rights). Others depend on a realistic assessment of the prospects for legitimacy versus the potential for simply generating new divisions or a new political line-up.

Callahan also assesses how well the United States has done in the nuts and bolts of predicting and understanding critical and significant conflicts over the past decade. He discusses in some detail examples such as Yugoslavia, Rwanda, Burundi, and the Kurdish rebellion. He also analyzes specific cases of American leadership in military interventions, war crimes indictments, and direct mediation, concluding overall "that uncertainty and frustration are permanent features of post-cold war internationalism."

Perhaps the most thought-provoking aspect of this book is Callahan's speculation about the future. He discusses the prospect of a more orderly and routine collective response by such agencies as the United Nations and NATO, and considers the constraints imposed by American public opinion and domestic politics. Specifically, he considers reform of relevant institutions, particularly the State Department, as an essential component of improving the United States' ability to become more effective in this new world. Finally, he argues that a slow and steady approach, while it will never completely eliminate ethnic strife, has great potential to reduce the number of deaths and the level of violence generated by such hostility. On behalf of the Trustees of the Twentieth Century Fund, I thank him for his contribution to national policy and global affairs.

Richard C. Leone, President
The Twentieth Century Fund
June 1997

Unwinnable Wars

Introduction

IN EARLY MAY 1972, the central African country of Burundi descended into mass murder. After an uprising by Hutu extremists, the Tutsi-dominated army unleashed a reign of terror. As many as a thousand Hutu a day were massacred over a four-month period. The killers worked mainly at night, moving from house to house in rural areas. The houses were far enough apart that Hutu families knew nothing of the fate of their neighbors until it was too late and the killers were at the door. In the major towns and in the capital city of Bujumbura, roadblocks were set up and Hutu were pulled from their cars. Educated Hutu males were especially targeted. By the end of the summer, more than a hundred thousand Hutu would be dead.

The U.S. embassy kept Washington posted about events. Thomas Patrick Melady, the ambassador to Burundi, cabled the State Department on May 10 to report that the massacres were akin to "selective genocide."[1] Melady and his colleagues didn't have to investigate very hard to reach this conclusion: trucks piled high with bodies were passing the embassy and Hutu embassy employees feared for their lives, telling of murdered relatives. The brutality of the killing campaign stunned the U.S. diplomats. "Many Hutu are being buried while still alive," stated one cable to Washington. "Leadership elements have been slaughtered. The rest are docile and obedient. They are digging graves for themselves and are thrown in afterwards."[2]

Despite such reports, the U.S. response to the mayhem in Burundi was muted. There was no outraged public protest to the Burundi ambassador to Washington. There were no condemnations by high-level officials at the White House or the State Department. Even as the massacres continued week after week, hardly anything was said at all. Instead, the United States pursued a quiet effort of modest pressures. On May 5, shortly after the killing began, Ambassador Melady had met with Michael Micombero, the Tutsi strongman. Melady implored him to stop the violence and reestablish political control peacefully. President Micombero, who sat in his office with a machine gun on the desk and a pistol strapped to his waist, assured Melady that "there would not be unnecessary bloodshed."[3] He was lying. The Tutsi death squads had only begun their work.

The United States turned next to the Organization of African Unity (OAU) and to individual African leaders. The State Department asked the OAU to intercede to stop the killing in Burundi, and the U.S. Senate demanded the same. But the OAU did almost the exact opposite. In late May it pledged its full support to Micombero. With the OAU avenue closed, the State Department wired its ambassadors in Africa with instructions to make their concerns about Burundi known. Through the summer, U.S. ambassadors called on African leaders, urging them to use their influence with the Burundi government to stop the killing. This effort, too, came to nothing.[4]

Over the next several years, U.S. officials defended their inaction to those few Americans who pressed for answers. "Direct unilateral intervention was out of the question," wrote Thomas Melady. "It would have been contrary to our policy of nonintervention in the affairs of African states; it would have reactivated fears of American imperialism in world affairs. Finally, it is doubtful if the American people would have approved of any kind of direct intervention, unilateral or multilateral."[5] Herman Cohen, director of the State Department's Office of Central African Affairs, stressed to a congressional committee in 1973 that there was little that the United States could have done even if it had wanted to take action: "Our overall influence on that government had never been more than minimal." While it was true that 80 percent of Burundi's coffee exports went to the United States and coffee sales accounted for 65 percent of the country's foreign-exchange earnings, Cohen dismissed the option of a coffee embargo. "We felt that a threatened boycott would not have influenced the immediate problems of ethnic violence," he said. A boycott would only have hurt average citizens in Burundi. It would have "been an inhuman response."[6]

The carnage in Burundi caught U.S. officials off guard and, as they saw it, with few good options. But the crisis should not have been a surprise. Nor should disoriented officials have had to jury-rig a policy under duress. After all, warning signals about the potential for major violence between Hutu and Tutsi had been emanating from Burundi and neighboring Rwanda since the two countries had gained independence in 1962. Rwanda had exploded in 1962–63, and Burundi had been the scene of massacres in 1965, 1966, and 1969.[7] President Micombero's rule had been consolidated amid wide repression of Hutu, and in the several years preceding the massacres, tensions between the two ethnic groups had been rising. However, planning for a genocidal explosion in Burundi was not high on the list of U.S. national-security priorities in the late 1960s and early 1970s. The cold war with Soviet Russia and the hot war in Vietnam were more important.

The slaughter of more than a hundred thousand Hutu over a four-month period in 1972 did nothing to help U.S. policy makers craft long-range policies for heading off future violence in Burundi and Rwanda. There were more killings in 1973, and in August 1988 Burundi again turned into a zone of genocide, with up to twenty thousand Hutu losing their lives in just a few weeks. Once again,

U.S. officials expressed surprise at the mayhem. Once again, they said that the United States could do little to alter the situation. Representative Gus Yatron of Pennsylvania said: "I am concerned that the administration has not spoken out publicly or done enough privately in response to the latest massacres." Yatron also criticized the State Department for not anticipating the violence.[8] Word for word, his comments could have been made sixteen years earlier. Word for word, these comments could also have been made in response to a new wave of violence that followed an aborted coup in 1993. By 1996, nearly all observers agreed that Burundi was teetering on the brink of an explosion that would be even greater than that of 1972—the kind of violence that had swept Rwanda in 1994, leaving more than a half million dead. And, once again, there was widespread disappointment that the United States was not prepared to take decisive steps to stop this development. Preventing mass slaughter in other lands, U.S. officials made clear, was not an important enough national interest to risk the lives of U.S. soldiers.

THE FUTURE OF ETHNIC CONFLICT

During the cold war, ethnic conflicts exploded often and sometimes with unspeakable levels of inhumanity. At times, such as in Biafra and Lebanon, these conflicts ended up on the front page of newspapers and briefly occupied the attention of high-ranking U.S. policy makers. More commonly, as in Burundi, they went largely unnoticed. They were the province of State Department desk officers and deputy assistant secretaries. They generated grisly embassy cables that were never read by top decision makers. Ethnic conflict was heavily studied by academics, but largely by scholars of comparative politics interested in the causes and internal dynamics of ethnic rivalry.[9] Scholars of international affairs and foreign policy rarely interested themselves in ethnic conflict.[10] They studied nuclear strategy, crisis management, civil wars that pitted left against right, and other trendy issues of the day. American policy makers received more advice than they needed on how, for example, to achieve "escalation dominance" in a limited nuclear war. They received little guidance on how to approach internal conflicts fueled by ethnic differences.

With the end of the cold war, it was commonplace to hear ethnic conflict described as one of the most puzzling and unfamiliar challenges of the new era.* The "new tribalism," as the *Los Angeles Times* called it, promised to deliver to U.S. policy makers a steady stream of agonizing dilemmas.[11] In part, the rediscovery of ethnic conflict was hype from a media and foreign policy establishment whose attention had previously been focused on the cold war. Ethnic conflict is, of course, an age-old problem. But even if the problem was not new, its dimensions were far larger following the collapse of Soviet power—a force that had kept myriad nationalist passions at bay for decades. "History is not over. It has simply been frozen and now is thawing with a vengeance Americans ignore at their peril," Robert Gates, director of the CIA, said in December 1991.[12]

To some observers ethnic conflict stands as the overshadowing threat of the future. "The defining mode of conflict in the era ahead is ethnic conflict," said Senator Daniel Patrick Moynihan in 1993. "It promises to be savage. Get ready for 50 new countries in the world in the next 50 years. Most of them will be born in bloodshed."[13] Even as sober a person as Secretary of State Warren Christopher proclaimed the potential for nearly limitless turmoil and violence. "If we don't find some way that the different ethnic groups can live together in a country, how many countries will we have?" Christopher asked at his confirmation hearings before the Senate Foreign Relations Committee. "We'll have 5,000 countries rather than the hundred plus that we now have."[14]

The savagery of ethnic conflict in recent years has staggered the

---

* For the purposes of this study, ethnic conflict is defined as conflict between groups that view themselves as culturally distinct as a result of tribal affiliations, national heritage, religious beliefs, linguistic traditions, or shared territorial background. For an examination of the foundations of ethnic community, see Anthony D. Smith, *The Ethnic Origins of Nations* (Oxford: Basil Blackwell, 1986), pp. 21–46.

imagination and appeared to confirm the most pessimistic predictions for the future. The 1994 attempted genocide in Rwanda claimed more lives in a month than the Arab-Israeli wars have claimed over forty years. Bosnia-Herzegovina was the scene of the most horrendous atrocities to take place in Europe since World War II. Elsewhere in Eurasia, the Chechen secessionist effort spawned a protracted and brutal war; there was terrible bloodshed in Georgia, where both the Abkhazia and South Ossetia regions sought to secede; Azerbaijan and Armenia fought for control of Nagorno-Karabakh; and the Dniester region sought violently to secede from Moldova. In the Middle East, there was continuing violence in the 1990s between Kurds and both Iraq and Turkey. In South Asia, the volatile Kashmir dispute escalated in the early 1990s, while the continuing civil war in Sri Lanka took a deadly new turn when Tamil insurgents began to favor suicide bombings. The disintegration of Zaire in 1997 was accompanied by brutal tribal violence that claimed the lives of thousands of refugees.

Simple math tallying up the vast number of ethnic groups in the world against the limited supply of states has been used often to underscore predictions of an ever-growing circle of nationalist furies. This calculus is misleading. In reality, the world is probably now at the tail end of the third great wave of state fragmentation during this century and can expect a limited number of new ethnic conflicts in the near future. The first wave accompanied the breakup of the Austro-Hungarian and Ottoman Empires at the end of World War I. The second wave was triggered by the dissolution of the great empires after World War II. The third wave, with crescendos in the early 1990s, came about as Communism collapsed in the Soviet Union and Eastern Europe. Much of the ethnic violence in recent years has been an outgrowth of this transformation. Most other recent ethnic struggles—such as those in Burundi and Kurdistan—are continuations of ones that have been flaring up sporadically for decades and are not part of a broader trend. It would thus be wrong to imagine that an endless stream of ethnic groups will be vying for statehood in the coming years. Most of the thousands of ethnic groups around the world do not aspire to their own states, and they are not likely to in the foreseeable future. Native Americans, for example, are not about to secede, nor are the Huaorani Indians of the Amazon lobbying for their own state. There are hundreds of tribal groups in Africa that have never challenged the state borders drawn up by colonialists. Communal bloodletting and nationalist aspirations receive much media attention, but most ethnic minorities in the world do not seek to overthrow the status quo.

The record of recent ethnic violence, in fact, offers some grounds for optimism. The list of post–cold war ethnic conflicts is tragically long, but it is not nearly as long as it might be. For every ethnic rivalry that has exploded into violence, others have been resolved or have at least remained nonviolent. In the early 1990s the leaders of Albania were talking ominously about the virtues of a "greater Albania," raising the specter of a war over the autonomous Serbian province of Kosovo (which has a majority Albanian population) and generating tensions with Macedonia, which also has many Albanians. By 1995, that rhetoric had been considerably toned down, and ethnic tensions in Kosovo and Macedonia had decreased. In Romania, it appeared that the end of Communism might soon be followed by a serious internal conflict or a war with Hungary, as Romania's ethnic Hungarians strove for greater autonomy and nationalist passions soared. But cooperation between Hungary and Romania defused this crisis and led to an agreement in 1994 that addressed many of the demands of ethnic Hungarians in Romania. Nearby, the breakup of Czechoslovakia into two states was accomplished with a minimum of animosity and no bloodshed.

To be sure, the former Soviet republics in the Caucasus have been a cauldron of violence, with ethnic conflicts in Moldova, Georgia, and Nagorno-Karabakh. But ethnic tensions in central Asian states like Kazakhstan, Turkmenistan, and Kyrgyzstan have not erupted into major violence in recent years. In Ukraine, despite predictions by U.S. intelligence to the contrary, the presence of millions of ethnic Russians has not fractured the country.

The Baltic states of Lithuania, Latvia, and Estonia have also avoided violence. In the early 1990s these states passed or debated citizenship laws that undermined the rights of ethnic Russians. Leaders in Moscow issued vague but threatening statements about protecting Russians living in the "near abroad." There was talk that Russia would not remove its troops from the Baltic states in 1994, as scheduled. Yet this situation never escalated into a full-blown crisis. Russian troops did pull out on schedule, and the Baltic states responded to Western pressure to ease repression of ethnic Russians. Within Russia itself, there are dozens of separate ethnic groups. But, with the exception of the Chechens, few of these groups have pressed separatist demands so far that armed conflict is a possibility.

The post–cold war record in Africa and South Asia is also not nearly as disturbing as it might be. The mass slayings in Rwanda cast a shadow over the entire continent of Africa, and in neighboring Burundi ethnic extremists have created a killing field of major dimensions. Yet Burundi has managed to avoid a catastrophe of the scope that many feared, and other ethnic flash points in Africa—Nigeria, for example—have not ignited. The two major ethnic war zones in South Asia, Sri Lanka and Kashmir, have seen significant yet contained outbreaks of violence. And India, one of the leading multiethnic experiments in the world, has remained relatively stable (apart from Kashmir).

The purpose of this brief global roundup is to place today's ethnic conflicts in proper perspective. In some parts of the world, such as the Balkans and portions of Africa and the former Soviet Union, ethnic rivalries will indeed be at the center of international security questions. Elsewhere, like in South America or East Asia, ethnic conflict will be only a minor element in regional politics. Without question, ethnic conflict has emerged as a greater problem for U.S. policy makers than ever before. In the future, new ethnic crises are sure to arise and ethnic wars now simmering will almost certainly boil over. Terrible choices will have to be made. It would be wrong, however, to exaggerate the centrality of ethnic conflict in international affairs. Ethnic conflict is just one among many threats that U.S. policy makers will confront, along with the dangers posed by weapons proliferation, interstate rivalries, political civil wars, humanitarian crises, environmental degradation, and the like. Clearer thinking about U.S. policy toward ethnic conflict is nevertheless necessary; outlining such thinking is the goal of this book.

FAILED IDEALS

Perhaps one reason political thinkers and leaders have been so fixated on the threat of ethnic conflict in the post–cold war era is that the increased number of such conflicts has confounded long-time predictions about how international affairs would evolve. From the eighteenth century onward, the most powerful minds in political theory predicted a world in which nationality and nationalism would become less important. In the Marxist outlook, class solidarity would supplant national identity as the central organizing concept in world affairs. Workers would come to realize that they had far more in common with their oppressed brethren in other countries than with the ruling elites of their own nationalities. Only capitalist propaganda could bring workers to slaughter their natural allies from other countries, as happened in World War I, and in time that propaganda could be expected to disappear along with capitalism itself. At the internal level, Communist rulers in multiethnic states sought to blot out ethnic differences, often through repressive means, and held that over time these fault lines would become insignificant.

Liberal theorists were also optimistic about the demise of nationalism, but for different reasons. In the liberal imagination, the persuasive power of the market would check a range of unprofitable instincts, including nationalist bloodletting. The common search for prosperity would transcend state borders and create a world of open trading. Growing economic interdependence would lead to a breakdown of cultural divisions, producing greater understanding between different peoples and thus a more peaceful world. The other pillar of the liberal future, democratic freedom, was also invested with magic healing powers. Democratic peoples would naturally respect the rights of minorities in their midst and the populaces of other countries. The chauvinist impulse, so central to nationalist scheming, could be expected to wither in the face of a democratic ethos that counseled self-determination and an end to arbitrary rule.

During the cold war, Marxists and liberals could both be heard claiming that their predictions had been confirmed. In the Communist mythology, scores of nationalities lived peacefully together in the Soviet Union, putting aside old grievances to work together on the most ambitious collective project of all time. In reality, of course, it was the old-fashioned glue of imperialism that sustained a harmony that was often mere façade.[15] The multiethnic state of Yugoslavia was a more benign empire, but an empire nonetheless, with ethnic grievances simmering for decades just under the surface of official solidarity and proclamations of national unity.

The liberal story of nationalism also was oversold. During the cold war, the advanced democracies did create a community of states where unprecedented levels of cooperation were the norm. Two countries with the most dangerous nationalist tendencies— Germany and Japan—were integrated into this community as peaceful trading states. A variety of international regimes were established that helped manage conflicts among the advanced democracies. The creation of this community was made possible partly by the exigencies of the cold war and the resulting hegemony of the United States over its Western allies. To prevail over the Soviet Union in a global contest for power, the United States urged the democracies to put aside historic rivalries and band together for survival. And even without the Soviet threat, it is likely that common democratic values, painful memories of war, and a shared stake in a world of free trade would have worked to reduce nationalist excesses in the West. In this sense, some of the central elements of the liberal story are deeply compelling.

Yet it has always been a story with limited applicability. High levels of democracy and economic interdependence exist in only a few regions of the world; on a global scale, their dampening effect on nationalist passions is not great. Also, the liberal story has been geared toward the dynamics of relations between states, not within them. Factors that help reduce tensions between states may do nothing to better ethnic relations within a state. Democracy, as numerous scholars maintain, probably does make states less nationalistic and warlike toward other states, especially toward other democracies.[16] And usually it produces greater tolerance toward minorities inside a state. In some cases, this tolerance can defuse secessionist energies. In other cases, however, liberalization can open the floodgates of ethnic nationalism, providing the political space for ethnic groups to organize around their common identity.[17] It was precisely the collapse of authoritarianism that led to the self-determination bids of so many ethnic groups in the former Soviet bloc.

The bankruptcy of Marxist claims in relation to nationalism was evident well before the cold war's end, but liberal optimism has been dislodged less easily. Triumphalists in the West talked about the end of history and the final victory of the liberal democratic system. A swift victory in the Persian Gulf War accentuated the illusion of a world in which a purposeful democratic community could vanquish threats to the global order. For a brief time in the late 1980s and early 1990s, the less attractive aspects of the new era were obscured by euphoria. It took the carnage in Bosnia, complete with images of Nazi-like barbarism, to make the truth undeniably clear: history was alive and well in many parts of the world, with nationalism as its central driving force. Liberalism's victory was anything but complete.

TOWARD A U.S. STRATEGY

Because it came as something of a shock, the surge of ethnic conflict in the post–cold war era has generated much confusion. In the United States, policy thinkers both in and outside government have been slow to analyze what this new violence means and what the United States might do about it. Washington has had a few successes in handling ethnic conflicts; more often, U.S. policies have been inconsistent at best and disastrous at worst. This maladroitness must be viewed in the broader context of a U.S. internationalism that has not been successfully reconfigured for post–cold war times.

Throughout the twentieth century, U.S. internationalism has centered on ambitious responses to clear-cut challenges. After the catastrophe of World War I, Wilsonian internationalism sought nothing less than the reordering of world politics. The cold war internationalism that followed World War II aimed to thwart Communism and avoid a repetition of German and Japanese aggression by creating a community of liberal states bound together by shared political ideals, economic interdependence, and U.S. power. Since 1990, however, U.S. internationalism has lacked its previous clarity and vigorous sense of purpose. There has been consensus on the need for continued U.S. leadership of NATO and other central organizations of the Western community and of the web of bilateral alliances in East Asia; widely recognized, too, is the need for U.S. leadership in containing rogue states like Iraq and North Korea. In addition, promotion of U.S. economic interests has gained new salience during the Clinton years. But none of these missions has the grandeur or freshness of Wilson's vision or that laid out by the architects of containment. Instead, the principal objectives of post–cold war internationalism have been the product of incrementalism and adaptation. There has been no agreement on how to cope with a variety of ambiguous challenges and secondary threats to international security. The confusion here has been about ends as well as means. Not only has there been disagreement in identifying national interests outside the traditional areas of U.S. concern but there is no clear understanding of what kinds of public support and financial resources can be tapped successfully to deal with challenges in peripheral areas. For forty years, U.S. foreign policy on the periphery was formulated and explained in the context of the cold war struggle. During the 1990s, with the disappearance of the cold war measuring cup to assess threats and justify sacrifices, U.S. foreign policy on the periphery has become a series of ad hoc adventures.

In the former Yugoslavia, the United States committed a series of missteps in the early 1990s that reflected its lack of clear goals. When the country was first fragmenting, U.S. diplomats called for continual unity yet also came to acknowledge the merits of self-determination bids by the Yugoslav republics. Thus, Washington may have encouraged the independence efforts of Slovenia, Croatia, and Bosnia while seeming to sanction Serb violence aimed at squelching those efforts—the worst of both worlds. Then, when the war in Bosnia was under way, the United States vacillated between backing a victory by the Bosnian government and backing a compromise solution that would accept Serb gains won by aggression. It could not decide whether to bring Serb leaders to trial as war criminals or to bring them to the negotiating table as statesmen. In 1995, the United States negotiated a highly fragile end to the war. At no time has the United States articulated a long-term vision of a new political order in the Balkans that might eventually bring stability, and by 1997 dangerous tensions endured.

In the Caucasus, the United States has failed to lay out a well-defined policy for dealing with ethnic conflicts. It has been reluctant to intervene, while fluctuating between backing an active Russian policing role and criticizing Russian meddling. Beyond denying that the United States has recognized a Russian sphere of interest in the Caucasus, U.S. officials have been vague about U.S. interests and intentions. Washington's passive policies toward Russia may have been one reason Moscow felt free to use excessive force in Chechnya. In the mid-1990s, the ethnic wars in the Caucasus began to die down, but there is every possibility that they will flare up again. Again, U.S. policy makers have left unaddressed long-range questions about the kind of regional order that can be created to prevent future instability.

The attempted genocide in Rwanda delivered a powerful shock to official Washington and to many outside government. Erupting with even greater suddenness than in Bosnia, the conflict in Rwanda graphically illustrated the insanity of ethnic rivalry. Still, the policy world seems to have learned few lessons from Rwanda. After the massacres, U.S. diplomats did take energetic steps to prevent similar violence in neighboring Burundi, but these emergency measures were not part of a broader strategic framework for avoiding tribal violence in Africa. In the Middle East, the United States found itself in the strange position of protecting the Kurdish citizens of Iraq from the armies of Saddam Hussein at the same time as it provided arms to Turkey for its brutal war against the Kurds.

American foreign policy has not been wholly bereft of strategic thinking in regard to ethnic conflicts, even if that thinking has been applied only selectively. In the post–cold war era, U.S. officials have put new emphasis on the preventive component of foreign policy and have thus generated some prescient policies in ethnic hot spots. The Clinton administration saw the potential for disaster in the Baltic states and pressed leaders there for better treatment of ethnic Russians. Both the Bush and the Clinton administrations recognized the danger inherent in Albanian calls for a greater Albania and used a burgeoning U.S. relationship with the Albanian government to temper such ambitions. (Unfortunately, Washington didn't also press hard for internal reforms in Albania, an action that might have headed off the upheaval there in 1997.) In 1993, President Clinton ordered a small detachment of U.S. troops to Macedonia to deter Serbian ethnic cleansing in neighboring Kosovo. Under both Bush and Clinton, the United States has at least offered to play a mediating role in the dispute in Kashmir, even as its offers have been consistently rebuffed. Burundi has been the focus of substantial U.S. concern since the massacres in Rwanda. And before the Rwanda crisis the United States was engaged in an effort to defuse the mounting political crisis in that country.

The U.S. government has also made efforts to improve responses to ethnic conflict. The politics and logistics of peacekeeping and humanitarian missions have received much attention, which will improve U.S. policy toward all internal conflicts, with obvious and far-reaching applicability to ethnic conflicts. American policy makers have sought to formulate guidelines about when, why, and how to intervene; with whom to intervene and under what command arrangements; how to conduct operations while intervening; and how and when to extricate U.S. forces. This planning work came together most clearly in Presidential Directive 25, a May 1994 document that lays out U.S. policy guidelines for participating in U.N. peacekeeping operations. In addition, U.S. military operations in Rwanda, northern Iraq, and Bosnia have yielded an enormous number of lessons, both large and small, that the policy world is struggling to digest.

American political and military thinking about ethnic conflict has unquestionably come a long way since the end of the cold war, but it still has far to go. A document like PD-25 raises as many questions as it answers, and evidence abounds of half-learned lessons and forgotten insights. Overall, the project of developing guidelines for U.S. policy toward ethnic conflict remains in a nascent stage. Without more successful planning efforts, botched U.S. policy toward ethnic conflicts will continue to be commonplace.

Responding to ethnic conflict must be part of a broader strategy for reinvigorating U.S. internationalism. Since the days of Woodrow Wilson, the case for an internationalist foreign policy has always rested on a simple idea: that sustained U.S. engagement to nurture peace and stability would lower the chances of war, that it was better to pay less now than to pay more later. This preventive thinking has remained at the center of post-cold war foreign policy toward the industrial areas of the world. In calling for a continued primacy in the West, U.S. leaders have repeatedly invoked the lessons of past isolationist neglect. While recent internationalist policies for preserving the Western community have often been unimaginative and incrementalist, they have nonetheless won bipartisan support in Washington and among the U.S. public.

What has been missing in recent years is a vigorous application of such internationalist logic to foreign policy problems outside the core areas of U.S. concern. Preventive efforts in peripheral regions have been lacking on three levels. First, U.S. policies to address long-term causes of instability like poverty, overpopulation, and environmental degradation have remained poorly developed and funded, despite growing awareness of them. Second, U.S. support for stronger collective-security mechanisms that could promote stability in peripheral regions has been inconsistent. In addition to opposing many credible proposals to strengthen U.N. capabilities, the United States has often failed to play an active part in reducing conventional arms transfers, ensuring human-rights accountability, and instituting new regional collective-security measures. Third, the U.S. record of short-term preventive diplomacy in crisis situations has been decidedly mixed; many dangerous situations have failed to make it onto Washington's radar screen, preventing opportunities for constructive U.S. engagement.

The reasons for this stunted internationalism are obvious enough: there is no consensus over which of the myriad problems in peripheral areas the United States should care about; U.S. policy makers have their hands full with major challenges in the core areas; and rising isolationism after the cold war has been manifested chiefly through opposition to engagements in situations that do not affect vital U.S. interests. Each of these obstacles must be overcome if the United States is to formulate better policies toward ethnic conflict.

If U.S. policy makers want to take all possible steps to prevent nightmares like Bosnia and Rwanda, they must creatively adapt the preventive logic of internationalism to challenges that will rarely be clear-cut. Consensus about which countries the United States should pay attention to is less important than agreement that certain types of nascent crises deserve U.S. attention—those that are likely to destabilize entire regions or generate humanitarian catastrophes of a scope that will inevitably generate demands for action in the West. The chief priorities of U.S. policy makers will always, and rightly, lie in stabilizing the core areas, but this focus cannot be allowed to blot out other concerns. By habit, U.S. foreign policy leaders are most comfortable in arenas they have worked in throughout their professional lives. Recent events, however, demonstrate the need for U.S. officials to venture off the beaten track. It is always easier to make another jaunt to Brussels or Geneva or Damascus to nurture long-standing projects than it is to make new investments of diplomatic capital in places like Burundi, Moldova, or Macedonia. Similarly, working on traditional foreign policy problems like alliance management and interstate mediation is safer and more familiar than meddling with nasty tribal rivalries or creating multilateral institutions where none have existed. Warren Christopher was the quintessential example of a foreign policy official who clearly preferred to practice internationalism of the most traditional kind, even as some in his department (like Undersecretary Timothy Wirth) pushed him to expand his thinking. Partly as a result, the State Department made scant progress during Clinton's first term in developing comprehensive preventive policies to deal with instability in peripheral areas. With her U.N. background, Madeleine Albright may press for a change in thinking, but if she does she will have to confront powerful traditions in U.S. diplomatic style.

The constraints imposed by a rising isolationism in the United States are, of course, very real. It is bitterly ironic that this development should occur at precisely the time when the United States needs an ever-greater level of internationalist creativity to deal with threats to global stability. Republicans in Congress have cut the international-affairs budget across the board and sought to limit U.S. involvement in U.N. operations. The public is skeptical of military ventures abroad that are not justified by threats to vital interests and of many kinds of foreign aid. Nevertheless, there remains room for crafting new policies of U.S. engagement abroad. The president and his highest political appointees have considerable capacities for education and persuasion in the foreign policy arena. While there is never any guarantee that the public and Congress will follow where an administration leads, there are numerous examples of presidents who have successfully altered the terms of the foreign policy debate by sheer force of leadership. Compelling, passionate arguments by highly visible public officials always carry weight in the discourse over policy, even if they often do not carry the day.

There is, moreover, much that the executive branch can do with a minimal level of congressional acquiescence. The Clinton administration has, for example, greatly elevated the attention given to global environmental issues. It did this by creating a new undersecretary for global affairs and by having a vice president, Albert

Gore, who regularly shone a spotlight on environmental concerns. The result was a turnaround in U.S. policy, with the United States taking a far more active role in global environmental issues.

A dramatically stepped-up emphasis on preventive U.S. engagement in peripheral areas would also alter the terms of foreign policy discourse. In 1995 and 1996, Warren Christopher belatedly began to draw on the rhetoric of preventive engagement in defending the international-affairs budget in Congress. Albright is even more comfortable with such language. The ongoing dramas in Burundi and Kosovo have provided textbook examples of why preventive engagement matters, and they are often cited by top U.S. officials. Preventive engagement has also become a major interest of policy analysts and a wide range of leaders in nongovernmental organizations (NGOs). Preventive engagement today may be what arms control was in the early 1960s: a relatively new concept, but one destined to occupy a central place in U.S. national-security doctrine.

To accelerate this process, strategies of preventive engagement —especially toward ethnic conflicts—need to be further refined. The goal should not be the sweeping vision of a containmentlike concept, for there is no silver bullet with which to stop ethnic extremists. The vast differences in the nature and circumstances of ethnic conflicts make it hard to develop overall guidelines for policy. Rigid strictures will be useless or worse than useless. Each situation has its own peculiarities, and it can be risky to generalize from one conflict to the next. Nevertheless, there are at least three tasks that policy thinkers can work through in seeking a more coherent strategy.

First, we must establish a more consistent standard for evaluating both the merits of self-determination efforts and the degree to which these efforts affect U.S. interests. Second, we must analyze the wide array of policy instruments used to respond to ethnic conflict to determine what works and what doesn't, and why. Finally, we must answer larger questions about how the United States can help build political orders that will promote lasting stability in conflict-riven parts of the world; what role collective-security mechanisms can play in managing ethnic conflicts; and how U.S. national-security organizations must change to handle this kind of challenge.

For the combatants, most ethnic conflicts are unwinnable wars that only guarantee future cycles of violence. The United States will never be able to end these wars entirely, but it can help to make them less common and, when they do occur, to reduce both their intensity and their duration.

CHAPTER ONE

Ethnic Conflict
and U.S. Interests

MOST ETHNIC CONFLICTS in recent times have been fueled by a group's bid for greater autonomy, full national independence, or affiliation with a neighboring country. The principle of self-determination is, of course, hardly a new concept. The central difference between the new nationalism and its anticolonial fore-runners, however, is that it has generated fissures along far more troublesome territorial lines. Much of the process of decoloniza-tion earlier in the twentieth century allowed large and distinct countries to win their independence from distant masters of an entirely different color, economic status, and cultural background. In today's struggles, peoples who often share many common traits are in conflict with one another as a result of nationalist efforts to carve out states that never previously existed or to rewrite regional maps to reunite ethnic groups across borders. There are plenty of real grievances fueling some of these efforts. In other instances, the case for a group's self-determination is less clear and compelling.

All this has created great confusion for U.S. policy makers.[1]

This, too, is not new. Historically, Americans have approached questions of self-determination with both stridency and uncertainty. The very concept of the United States, as it emerged in the late eighteenth century, was premised on the notion that all peoples with a sense of national distinctiveness had a right to self-governance. Early U.S. leaders were often self-righteous in espousing this idea as a global ideal; indeed, their liberal outlook was teleological: democratic self-governance, they suggested, was the way of the future.[2] Less than a century after the drafting of the Declaration of Independence, however, the U.S. government fought a bloody war to stop the South from seceding. The government also destroyed Indian tribes that considered themselves sovereign nations and, at the turn of the century, acquired colonial holdings as a result of the Spanish-American War.

Woodrow Wilson's embrace of the concept of self-determination after World War I was marked by controversy and ambivalence. Some U.S. elites were disturbed by his call for the creation of many new states to represent the yearnings of ethnic groups that had been ruled by the Ottoman and Austro-Hungarian Empires. The president's own secretary of state, Robert Lansing, was among the skeptics. "Will it not breed discontent, disorder, and rebellion?" Lansing wrote of the self-determination proclamation. "The phrase is simply loaded with dynamite. It will raise hopes which can never be realized. It will, I fear, cost thousands of lives. . . . What a calamity that the phrase was ever uttered! What misery it will cause!"[3]

Like much else in Wilson's Fourteen Points, his views on self-determination had rhetorical staying power, but they failed to muster a consensus for action in the 1920s and 1930s. The plight of the Kurds, for example, was taken up by U.S. officials after World War I long enough to secure a treaty guaranteeing that they would get an independent state. Later, when Turkey changed its mind, U.S. statesmen did not raise a protest on behalf of one of the largest ethnic groups in the Middle East.[4]

After World War II, as the vast empires of the European powers crumbled, the principle of self-determination was embraced by

U.S. policy makers with an eye toward geopolitical gains. It was used as a cudgel in the cold war arena, wielded in uncounted U.S. protests at the fate of states under Moscow's rule. American diplomats also showed support for the concept in the developing world, where many new countries were coming into existence. The political allegiance of these countries was up for grabs and the United States invoked its own anticolonial heritage to establish its credentials as a sympathetic great power. Of course, it also sometimes undermined these efforts, backing, for example, the French effort to hold on to Vietnam. For the most part, however, the United States found it relatively easy to support the principle of self-determination as it related to decolonization. A factor that further simplified U.S. policy was a 1960 U.N. resolution, the Declaration on the Granting of Independence to Colonial Countries and Peoples.[5] By backing decolonization efforts, the United States allied itself with the consensus of the international community and the trajectory of history.

On only one occasion during the cold war did the United States recognize the independence of a region that had seceded from a state with long-established postcolonial borders: in 1971, when East Pakistan, separated from West Pakistan by a thousand miles of Indian territory, proclaimed its sovereignty. In other notable cases—Biafra in the late 1960s and Eritrea in the 1970s and 1980s—the United States was steadfast in its support of the territorial status quo. This tendency reflected the view of other major powers and the thrust of international law. While the U.N. and regional organizations of states backed decolonization, they also consistently rejected any right of secession from already independent states and, as a 1970 U.N. declaration stated, condemned "any action aimed at the partial or total disruption of the national unity and territorial integrity of any other state or country."[6]

As the breakup of the Soviet Union became likely in the late 1980s, U.S. policy makers reacted with considerable caution and at times evinced a preference for continued unity. For good reason they feared the potential instability that could follow the disintegration of so vast an empire. When that disintegration became inevitable, however, it presented few conundrums for policy makers. The breakup was akin to the decolonization processes earlier in the century, with large and distinctive nationalities winning independence from imperial overlords who spoke a different language and governed from far away. In its broad contours, the Soviet breakup was an easy case for U.S. policymakers: there was no question about the legitimacy of new states such as Ukraine, Armenia, and Kazakhstan.

Yet harder cases have also emerged from the wreckage of the Soviet empire and from the former Yugoslavia as well. These have included the quest by the Armenians of Nagorno-Karabakh to secede from Azerbaijan, the effort at secession from Georgia by Abkhazia and South Ossetia, and the conflict over the Dniester region of Moldova. In Yugoslavia, an independent Slovenia was easy enough to support, given the ethnic homogeneity of Slovenia and its distance from Belgrade. Croatian independence was a more dangerous proposition because of Serbian pockets in Croatia and the history of violence between Serbs and Croats. The creation of a separate state of Bosnia was the most dubious venture of all, as it attempted to unite three distinct ethnic groups: Muslims, Croats, and Serbs.

SELF-DETERMINATION: CONFLICTING CLAIMS

It is impossible to predict the number of new secessionist efforts likely in the future. But whatever the number, it seems inevitable that some of these efforts will present agonizing choices for U.S. leaders. If recent history is any guide, U.S. policy makers will be unprepared to deal well with future dilemmas. There is, consequently, a need to lay out the conditions under which the United States will support or oppose secessionist efforts—or simply remain neutral.

At the broadest level, crafting a policy on self-determination requires adopting clear preferences as to the optimal size of states and degree of heterogeneity within them. It also means weighing the risks to international stability of a policy that tends to favor the status quo as against a policy that indulges nationalist aspirations. Is there really anything wrong with fragmentation that yields many small new states, or are there intrinsic virtues to larger and more ethnically diverse states? Does supporting some secessionist movements risk setting off a dangerous chain reaction of ethnic dominoes falling throughout the world?

These questions have been the subject of much debate in recent years and no clear consensus has emerged in the U.S. foreign policy community.[7] The case for a policy favoring the status quo has generally been the most powerful, resting on several arguments. First, there is the sentiment Warren Christopher expressed at his confirmation hearing: that in a world consisting of thousands of ethnic groups and less than two hundred states, fragmentation would increase to enormous levels if left unchecked. Most new states would still contain stranded minority groups and these groups would begin their own quests for autonomy. If there were a true right to ethnic self-determination, the international system would likely be in permanent turmoil as this right was exercised in one state after the other.

A second argument in favor of the status quo is that largeness and diversity are good things. Amitai Etzioni suggests that "in most states of the world, further fragmentation is likely to imperil democratic forces and endanger economic development." Ethnic breakaway states, Etzioni contends, tend to be highly nationalistic and intolerant of minorities within them. They are predisposed toward creating monolithic national cultures that undermine the kind of social pluralism democracies thrive on.[8] To the degree that such newborn states remain in conflict with the states from which they have seceded, the resulting garrison atmosphere might also serve to weaken democracy. Economically, too, Etzioni and others argue, small states tend to be worse off than larger ones. At a time when advanced industrial states are seeking to expand free-trade zones and collaborate on high-tech ventures, smaller economic units are at a disadvantage. Secession will thus often hurt rather than help the economic prospects of an ethnic group. Quebec, for example, would be better off remaining part of Canada.[9]

Those who support the status quo qualify their argument by pointing out that much can and should be done to protect the rights of minorities. International leaders should try to keep Pandora's box firmly shut while nurturing democratic pluralism and ethnic tolerance around the world. They should also consider creative solutions to meet ethnic demands for greater autonomy and unity among groups separated by national borders.[10] Under this strict approach, secession would be a very last resort. It would be supported only in rare cases that involved egregious oppression of a minority and a lack of other alternatives.

Opposing these arguments are those observers who downplay the dangers of fragmentation and believe that the United States should side with minority groups seeking to control their destiny. Michael Lind, for example, suggests that there is little chance of ethnic dominoes toppling uncontrollably since there are not more than a dozen or so ethnic groups that have both the cohesion and the ambition to form their own states. In any event, the international system has accommodated a sudden spurt of new states gaining independence before and can do so again.[11] Even twenty or thirty states entering the system over the next decade or two would not be historically unprecedented. Moreover, the disruption that accompanies the creation of new states will often be less great than the instability caused by ethnically riven states. As in a marriage gone sour, divorce can be the best of all possible solutions.

Furthermore, the argument that ethnic pluralism strengthens democracy is far from universally accepted. Every year human-rights groups document a wide array of abuses of ethnic minorities living in democracies.[12] Ethnic divisions have not destroyed democracy in states like India, Turkey, and Israel, but neither have they strengthened it. Democratic rule has not guaranteed the rights of minorities in these countries. Historically, the strongest arguments in support of secessionist movements have rested on human-rights claims. Many observers have argued that persistently abused minorities should be given international support if they make a bid for independence—assuming that selected other criteria are met as well. What faith, for example, can the Kurds of Iraq have that democracy will come anytime soon to Iraq or that it will truly change their plight if it does, given the oppression of Kurds in Turkey? Americans know only too well from their own history that minorities are not necessarily safe in a democratic system.

Finally, some analysts counter the claim that small states are less economically viable. In the past hundred years the average size of states has been steadily shrinking. There is no solid evidence that this has been a bad trend, either for smaller states themselves or for the international economy as a whole.[13] There are plenty of examples of small states that are very prosperous—Taiwan, Singapore, Switzerland—and of larger states that have economic problems Brazil, France, Turkey. A state's size is not the determining factor behind economic success. Sometimes secession will have negative economic consequences, but sometimes it is a boon: Slovenia and Croatia rightly saw that they would be better off if they were separated from Yugoslavia, since these areas were more prosperous than the rest of the country.

Disagreement exists as to whether a world with a greater number of smaller states would be less stable. More international borders mean more potential for territorial disputes, while more separate defense establishments mean more potential for military rivalries and arms races. Conversely, smaller states tend to be more interdependent with their neighbors and with the international economic system as a whole. Often they cannot produce even basic necessities like food and energy and arms; they are more likely to be landlocked or dependent on supply routes that run through other countries. "Trade or die" is the maxim they must live by. With that maxim comes a foreign policy imperative: Don't disrupt the peace that is required to keep economic ties functioning. By this logic, the international system is less stable when it contains many large and self-sufficient states that can endure economic isolation from the rest of the system during times of war.

SECESSION AND U.S. POLICY

The mixed consequences of secessionist efforts suggest that the
U.S. government should avoid sweeping edicts supporting or opposing a further fracturing of the state system. If U.S. policy makers make blanket statements in favor of the territorial status quo,
they might encourage state leaders to think that the United States
will tolerate the repression of ethnic secessionist movements. Such
repression, in turn, might only fuel the push for secession and
undermine prospects for settling internal conflicts without war and
the breakup of states. At the same time, U.S. leaders should be
wary of general statements supporting secessionist efforts. Such
rhetoric is capable of giving false encouragement to secessionists
whose movements are doomed or lack merit and of helping insti-
gate or prolong violence. They can feed the impatience of secessionist leaders and damage efforts to resolve disputes within the
framework of existing states.

A case-by-case approach to secessionist movements should be
founded on guidelines for judging their merits and assessing the
alternatives. A skeleton of such guidelines already exists. During
the breakup of Yugoslavia and the Soviet Union, U.S. policy
loosely held that Washington would not recognize new states unless they were democracies that respected the rights of minorities,
had come into existence as a result of a peaceful referendum process, and had the status of some kind of republic or centrally governed entity before attaining independence. This policy was clearly
articulated, as well, by the foreign ministers of the European Community when they agreed in December 1991 on guidelines for recognizing the new states in the former Yugoslavia.[14]

Neither the United States nor its Western allies consistently
followed these guidelines. Different Western countries recognized
the seceding republics at different times and for different reasons.
Occasionally the guidelines were blatantly ignored and new states
were recognized prematurely. Some of the new states of the former
Soviet Union and Yugoslavia were only marginally democratic and
showed little interest in safeguarding minority rights. In Bosnia,

the referendum for independence was boycotted by many Serbs.

Nevertheless, however roughly defined and inconsistently followed, the guidelines that the United States and its allies set in the 1990s serve as a useful foundation on which to build a more sophisticated approach to secessionist efforts. Work by analysts outside government can inform such an approach as well.

Territorial and historical issues constitute the most obvious starting point for assessing a secessionist claim. For the United States, the independence bids of most of the Soviet republics were the "easy" cases because many of these republics had some previous history of independence. Most of these states, moreover, had clear borders and centralized administrative capacities that facilitated the step to independence. The same was true of new states in the former Yugoslavia. The federal system in that country gave each of the republics distinct borders and significant capacities for self rule. Some of these republics had a history of either outright independence or substantial autonomy. Croatia was an independent state earlier in the twentieth century. Macedonia had a long history of seeking independence and was an autonomous republic in Yugoslavia, its people recognized as a separate nationality. Slovenia was never formally independent, but its territorial situation—it is far from Belgrade and shares international borders with several countries—enhanced its viability as a separate state.

Outside Europe, territorial and historical issues have also influenced U.S. policy. The desire of East Pakistan to secede struck many in Washington as intrinsically defensible because of its great distance from the rest of Pakistan. In recognizing Eritrea's independence in 1991, the United States acquiesced for the first time to a major change in Africa's postcolonial borders, but Eritrea's lack of a deeply rooted historical tie to Ethiopia made independence seem sensible, as did its geographic position, which gave it both access to the sea and its own international boundaries. By contrast, the state of Biafra had deep ties to Nigeria and no history of independence. The Ibo tribe, which formed the ethnic core of Biafra, had previously been well integrated into Nigerian economic and political life.

Territorial and historical issues should remain an important part of the calculus that U.S. officials employ in considering the merits of secessionist movements. These issues, it must be granted, are more practical than normative: they tell nothing about whether a state would be a benign entity. Ultimately, therefore, the democratic credentials of a secessionist movement are what U.S. policy makers should examine most closely. However, because avoiding failed states and the disruption of the international system are paramount goals of U.S. policy, the ease with which a stable state can be established is a crucial consideration. In general, new states will be more viable if they have long-established and natural borders, if they are distant from the center of the state from which they are seceding, if they have a history of independence or autonomy, and if they have a strong capacity for self-governance.

While the republics of the former Soviet Union and some of the republics in the former Yugoslavia represent the easy cases, places like Kurdistan and Kashmir represent the hard ones. In these regions people feel little kinship with those who rule them from the center, yet there is no clearly delineated governing entity that could be the basis of a new state. Moreover, while there is some historical record that gives credence to demands for independence, there is no record of a state or autonomous region actually existing in recent times. As the largest ethnic group in the Middle East, the Kurds have, in principle, a solid case for statehood. Past promises of a state are recognition of this fact. An independent Kurdistan has never existed, however, and creating one would mean carving up at least two existing states. Many in Kashmir would probably be willing to forgo full independence if they could at least merge with Pakistan. Yet such a move would mean a redrawing of international borders in a way that India finds unacceptable. Altering borders is also the only solution in many other areas where an ethnic minority in a state seeks formal union with a neighboring state in which its group is in the majority.

The United States must exercise extreme caution in approaching the hard cases. Supporting the creation of states with a thin territorial and historical basis can be disastrous even if the claims of ethnic nationalists have great moral merit. It would be folly, for example, for Washington to endorse the cause of Kashmiri separatists. Such encouragement could lead the rebels to escalate their war with India and eschew any compromise settlement. The result could be heightened tensions in South Asia that would bring India and Pakistan to the brink of war or beyond. Encouraging the Kurdish separatists would also be unwise. The United States already has blood on its hands from its covert support for the doomed Kurdish insurgency of the mid-1970s. These great losers of history are not likely to win statehood in the foreseeable future and it would be cruel to cater to any illusions they might harbor. In retrospect, we can see that those states that encouraged the Biafran secessionist bid in the late 1960s only helped prolong a war that Biafra was destined to lose. The United States was right to remain neutral in that conflict.

Overall, the United States will always have little choice but to evaluate secessionist movements on the basis of their likely success, and territorial and historical factors are inescapable elements of this calculation. Issues of economic viability are also relevant; the creation of new states that have no natural resources or manufacturing facilities or other means of self-sustenance is obviously not a good thing.

Nevertheless, hard-nosed calculations regarding viability should not be allowed to dominate U.S. policy. A more idealistic outlook also should inform judgments about secessionist efforts. Long-oppressed minorities and democratically inclined secessionists present a better case for independence than do nationalists who seek statehood for chauvinistic reasons and offer no guarantee of democracy. There is little appeal in backing the creation of new states that are likely to be authoritarian. Few problems are solved if an ethnic minority creates its own state and then proceeds to oppress other minorities trapped within the new borders. The United States must make clear that it will not even consider supporting secessionist efforts or recognizing new states unless a number of criteria are satisfied, most of which were laid out by U.S. and European officials during the early 1990s.

First, a putative new state must promise to put in place the structures of democratic governance, including an elected parliamentary
body, a chief executive with checked power, and an independent
judiciary. It must have a plan for free elections and a willingness
to allow international observers to monitor those elections. It must
be ready to place all armed forces under civilian control, to rein in
or disarm paramilitary groups, and to ensure that police agencies
are professional organizations and not bastions of irregular power.

Second, a secessionist group must pledge to respect human
rights generally and minority rights specifically. This means guaranteeing a free press, an independent judiciary, and professional
police. It also means affirming the commitment to human rights
that comes with membership in an international organization like
the United Nations and in regional organizations like the Organization for Security and Cooperation in Europe (OSCE). Cooperation with human-rights monitors from these organizations, as
well as with those from groups like Amnesty International and the
Red Cross, is an important indicator of a state's intentions. A secessionist group or new state must make clear its tolerance of minority rights by refraining from discriminatory actions. These
include language requirements for citizenship, property laws that
disadvantage minorities, educational arrangements or curricula
that disparage minorities, and travel or immigration restrictions
that clearly target a given group. If significant ethnic pockets exist
within its borders, a putative new state must show a willingness to
engage in a dialogue with minority groups about safeguarding
rights and expanding autonomy. If there are irredendist issues
involving an ethnic group and a neighboring state, a secessionist group must indicate its openness to discussions with both
parties.

Third, a secessionist effort must be judged not simply by its
democratic credentials but also by the process that it pursues to
achieve independence. Trouble is likely in a new state if a large
number of its inhabitants never wanted it to secede in the first place
and felt that their views were ignored. During the breakup of Yu-

goslavia, the United States and its allies held that they would not recognize new states that were not born through popular referendums. This condition made sense, but referendums are only one part of a workable process for moving toward independence. Hasty referendum votes often represent a tyrannical majority's grab for power, especially if they are orchestrated by a nationalist movement in an atmosphere of rising ethnic tensions. The referendums in Bosnia and Croatia did little to reassure the Serb minorities in those countries that their rights would be respected. In Bosnia many Serbs boycotted the referendum and never recognized the legitimacy of the Bosnian government. In mobilizing Bosnian Serbs for war, Serb nationalist leaders exploited fears that the Serbs would be a persecuted people under a Muslim tyranny.

The European Community and the United States should have insisted on a slower and more elaborate process of independence for the states of the former Yugoslavia. By contrast, the path Canada took in weighing Quebec's secessionist claim is a good model for future policy. The referendum of October 1995 was scheduled far in advance to allow for a drawn-out debate within Quebec. Had the secessionist proposal passed, Quebec would have entered into negotiations with the government of Canada about the exact timing and arrangements of independence. Overall, the process allowed for ample reflection and the tempering of nationalist passions. Mechanisms that allow for a cooling-off period can reassure minorities and may sometimes cause a rethinking of the entire secessionist enterprise.

Secessionist efforts are often creatures of a fast-moving and euphoric moment. The breakup of the Soviet Union and Yugoslavia, for example, left U.S. leaders scrambling just to keep up with events. Calls for dialogue and gradual change were repeatedly made, only to be ignored. In future situations, too, the U.S. government will often have little more than marginal influence over the policies that secessionist leaders pursue. It will find itself pushed to the sidelines, its counsel and demands unheeded. As in the past, the United States will be confronted by the de facto existence of new states that may or may not be territorially viable, may or may not be democratic, and may or may not be respectful of minorities.

Despite these realities it makes sense to think through the criteria for supporting secession and to state those criteria emphatically. If nothing else, these criteria are internally useful for U.S. policy makers, giving them a tool with which to evaluate secessionist movements and achieve intragovernmental consensus on how to handle specific ones. And in the instances when the United States does have some leverage, the criteria may emerge as important instruments of diplomacy. Not all new states are born in a frenzy. In situations that move more slowly and dispassionately, nationalist leaders will take into account the views of the United States and its allies. They will worry about how their state will secure from the West aid, trade, arms, and loans. If they know that their secessionist effort cannot meet the criteria set out by the United States and that their new state will face isolation, they may think twice about pursuing full independence. If they are close to the criteria, they will be able to identify the steps necessary to win the backing of the United States. In theory, at least, clearly stated U.S. criteria for backing secessionist efforts can help nix ill-conceived efforts and democratize deserving nationalist movements.

EXPLORING SEMISOVEREIGNTY

With the great empires dead, only a small number of nationalist movements will clearly deserve U.S. support in the foreseeable future. More common will be the hard cases: efforts that have some merit but not nearly enough. To avoid stark choices between either backing secessionist efforts or supporting the status quo, the United States must develop creative policy approaches that explore the political space between these extremes. It must find ways to support the rights of ethnic groups without inadvertently encouraging them to strive for full independence. The most obvious of these ways is to follow a human-rights regime that punishes state governments that repress minorities. Some secessionist efforts probably would not develop at all if ethnic groups felt well-treated within a unified state. The Ibo of Nigeria, for example, probably would not have created Biafra if they had not been subject to repression culminating in massacres in 1966.

While better treatment of minorities might stop some secessionist efforts, it would have no effect on others. There will always be regimes that carry out repression, whatever the international costs. And there will sometimes be ethnic groups that are not repressed yet still want their own state. There is thus a need to consider more dramatic measures that address minority demands without redrawing borders. It has been suggested, for example, that special regimes be developed through international mediation for recognizing the "historical homeland" of certain ethnic groups.[15] Such homelands may lie completely within a single state or straddle two or more states. Homeland regimes could ensure cultural rights and some level of governing autonomy and would allow members of ethnic groups to undertake collective efforts even across international boundaries.

For example, a Kurdish homeland regime would assure the eighteen million Kurds of Iraq, Iran, and Turkey of their right to speak their own language, establish their own educational and cultural institutions, and create centralized Kurdish associations with representatives from all three countries. Kurds would be able to travel easily across international boundaries to participate in this quasi-national life. A historic homeland for the two million Hungarians of Romania and the 600,000 Hungarians in Slovakia would have some similar features. It would assure ethnic Hungarians of linguistic and cultural rights, along with some freedom to govern their own affairs. Most important, it would allow these Hungarians to associate freely with their brethren in Hungary proper. The concept of an autonomous Serb republic within the state of Bosnia, devised by U.S. diplomats during peace negotiations in 1995, bore some resemblance to the homeland regime idea. In that case, of course, the creation of a parallel political entity was won by the

Serbs after a military campaign. It is possible, however, to imagine the Bosnian war's having been avoided altogether if a Serbian homeland had been a condition of Bosnia's independence. Similarly, the creation of a Palestinian homeland in the West Bank and Gaza has rightly been seen as a prerequisite to any kind of lasting peace in the Middle East. Considerable bloodshed might have been avoided if Israel and its neighbors had begun to focus seriously on this goal after the 1967 war.

Another way to satisfy the demands of ethnic groups is to grant them a measure of international recognition.[16] Such recognition might mean allowing groups to establish their own diplomatic relations with foreign countries, granting them observer status in international organizations like the United Nations and the OSCE, and giving them a voice within international lending institutions like the International Monetary Fund and the World Bank. In the past, U.S. officials have often refused to meet with the representatives of secessionist movements, fearing that to do so would grant such movements legitimacy and fuel their quests for complete independence. Even in the immediate aftermath of the Gulf War, some of Iraq's Kurdish leaders received the cold shoulder in Washington. Diplomatic contacts with nonstate ethnic leaders would be more palatable if placed in the context of broader semisovereign arrangements. If the Kurds were granted a historic homeland and they ended efforts at outright secession, receiving Kurdish leaders in Washington or other national capitals would not mean venturing onto a slippery slope.

The same holds for international institutions. Sovereign states are unlikely to grant recognition to groups with urgent secessionist ambitions. After all, there will always be members of such states who have their own secessionist groups to worry about, and they will avoid any action that might provide encouragement. There is far less reason, however, for international organizations not to grant some recognition to ethnic groups that have clearly proclaimed their respect for international boundaries. Ethnic minorities would welcome membership in such organizations, which would provide them forums to air their grievances against state rulers. An ethnic group that had observer status in the OSCE, for example, could use that position to press for investigations of human-rights abuses, electoral fraud, or other kinds of repression. In particularly egregious cases, ethnic groups could use their position in international organizations to appeal for sanctions against state governments. The existence of such recourse, however limited, could help dampen the common complaint that only nationhood can ensure an ethnic group's protection under international law.

The idea of giving ethnic groups a voice in international economic institutions also has considerable logic. It is a modest measure to address a central grievance of many secessionist efforts—that central state leaders are unresponsive to the economic needs of a given region or ethnic group. In recent years, there has been a growing recognition that when economic aid is channeled through central governments it often does nothing to relieve poverty or patterns of inequality. As a result, there has been a new emphasis on the part of both bilateral and multilateral donors to channel more aid through nongovernmental organizations that are committed to change at the grassroots level. Allowing ethnic groups to have a voice in international lending institutions would be consistent with this trend, since minorities and regions furthest from the center are often extremely poor and are the least likely to get a fair share of international aid.

Thus, for example, as Serbia is rehabilitated and seeks loans for postwar economic development, the Albanians of Kosovo will rightly want a way to influence the lending process so that some international funds end up in their province. In addition, they may also want a way to bypass the Serb government altogether in seeking economic assistance. Creating such arrangements, and others like it elsewhere, can help defuse at least some of the resentment that ethnic groups often feel toward state governments that hog economic resources.

Schemes for semisovereignty are far easier imagined than implemented. Many obstacles are obvious. State leaders may fear that concessions of greater autonomy to ethnic groups will only spur demands for independence. Repressive leaders like Iraq's Saddam Hussein may balk at making any concessions to longtime enemies, while well-meaning leaders may be reluctant to take steps that undermine policies aimed at assimilating ethnic minorities into the national life of a unified state. Also, the presence of an armed militant faction in an ethnic group can easily torpedo arrangements that grant greater autonomy and free travel across borders. Moderate ethnic leaders may be happy with autonomy as a final end even as militants move to exploit such new liberalization to step up the struggle for full independence. A few terrorist attacks can lead to retightened borders and increased policing. The security problems that have surrounded the creation of a Palestinian state in the Occupied Territories are testimony to the potential intractability of these issues. Violent political divisions among the Kurds of Iraq in the 1990s also illustrate how difficult it can be for a long-repressed people to govern themselves and control their more radical elements.

Despite these hurdles, U.S. policy makers have little choice but to emphasize arrangements that lie between the extremes of secession and the status quo. When such arrangements are workable they can defuse rising tensions. Enhancing the number of nonsecessionist alternatives available to unhappy ethnic groups would add an additional criterion for U.S. policy makers to consider in assessing the merits of an independence bid: Has the breakaway movement exhausted other options? Where the answer is no, a secessionist effort can rightly be seen as impetuous and illegitimate. Clearly, the Ibo of Nigeria did not make a sustained effort to see if they could live with autonomy arrangements before moving forward to create Biafra. In contrast, the Kurds of Iraq have seen promises for greater autonomy broken on more than one occasion. They have no reason to believe that Saddam Hussein will keep his word in the future. Just as the United States should avoid coddling impatient nationalists, it should extend special sympathy to groups that have been betrayed repeatedly by treacherous central governments.

CONFRONTING ETHNIC CONFLICTS:
U.S. NEEDS AND WANTS

Clear thinking about the phenomenon of self-determinism can help make the world a more peaceful place. Along with its allies and with international organizations, the United States can play a role in stopping some secessionist efforts from leading to war. In many, if not most, situations, however, U.S. influence will be limited. Secessionist movements and state governments often will not care what Washington and the rest of the international community think and will ignore threats of punishment or promises of rewards. Also, some ethnic conflicts do not revolve around secessionist goals at all and thus cannot be defused through agreements on territory or autonomy. The rivalry between Hutu and Tutsi in Rwanda and Burundi is one example; the tensions in Lebanon that led to the civil war are another. These types of strife can be particularly frustrating to policy makers.

Understanding the circumstances of an ethnic conflict is obviously pivotal in assessing whether it is amenable to outside resolution. Still, for U.S. policy makers the question of whether a conflict can be resolved will almost always be secondary to the issue of whether the United States has an interest in working toward this end. When the U.S. government has perceived a strong interest, it has made major efforts to stop or mediate seemingly intractable ethnic conflicts: in Bosnia, Lebanon, Northern Ireland, the Middle East. Otherwise, it has mostly remained detached, even in those instances when its influence might have made a major difference. It has played a very limited role, for example, in seeking to resolve the conflict between Turkey and its Kurdish population, and it has stayed out of the ethnic conflicts in the Caucasus.

Despite the proliferation of ethnic conflicts in recent years there remains much confusion in the United States as to how they bear on U.S. interests abroad. American policy makers have never spelled out when and why the United States should intervene. There is, for example, no presidential directive that offers guidelines in this area. The Clinton administration's guidance on peacekeeping, PD-25, only partly addresses the problem of intervening in ethnic conflicts. It states that the United States should join peacekeeping operations only if international security is threatened or a major humanitarian calamity requires outside intervention, but it doesn't offer much discussion of national interests beyond this. Mainly it is concerned with command and funding arrangements, the clarity and feasibility of the mission, and exit strategy.[17]

Discussion of intervention has become ever more muddled since the early 1980s. Following the disastrous marine deployment to Lebanon in 1982–83, Defense Secretary Caspar Weinberger decreed that U.S. troops should never be deployed overseas unless vital interests were at stake, there was a clearly defined and feasible mission, Congress supported the mission, and there was a viable exit strategy.[18] Weinberger's views, however, never represented a consensus view in the American government. Secretary of State George Schultz even went so far as to dispute them in public speeches. During Colin Powell's tenure as chairman of the Joint Chiefs of Staff between 1989 and 1993, the Weinberger criteria metamorphosed into the "Powell doctrine," as Powell repeatedly argued that the United States should not become militarily involved in murky internal conflicts. Powell favored the use of force only in situations where it could be applied massively and decisively. Panama and Desert Storm were his models of desirable wars. Powell's views, though influential, have never been dominant, and other government officials, including some in the Pentagon, have argued for a more flexible approach.

This lack of consensus about the use of force is only part of the general lack of clarity regarding the gravity of threats posed by ethnic conflicts and the proper response. During the Bosnian war, U.S. officials were inconsistent on the question not just of whether to use force but also of whether the conflict threatened vital U.S. interests and, if so, which interests. The Kurdish exodus after the Gulf War and the aftermath of the Rwanda massacres generated much loose talk about U.S. interests and the alleviation of humanitarian tragedies. These lapses into incoherence are nothing new. Sharp arguments about the national interest also eluded U.S. officials faced with conflicts in Nigeria and Lebanon during the cold war era.

To be sure, it is difficult to generalize about ethnic conflict and U.S. interests, given the range of situations around the world. Nevertheless, it is possible to establish a useful framework. A first step is to understand the kinds of threats ethnic conflicts pose to vital U.S. interests. Vital interests include the protection of American lives and territory, the security of core democratic allies, the health of the global economy (including the free flow of oil from the Persian Gulf), and the overall stability of the international system. To borrow a phrase from Robert Tucker, these four vital interests can be considered "needs"—they are requirements for the continued well-being of U.S. citizens.[19] Historically, ethnic conflicts have not threatened the first three of these needs. The overall stability of the international system, however, has been threatened by ethnic conflicts, and while the threats have not been very serious in the past, they could become more grave in the future.

During the Biafran secession, U.S. officials worried that success could produce a wave of fracturing states throughout Africa. Many analysts were rightly skeptical of this prediction, and it did not concern the United States enough for the government to aid the Nigerians against Biafra. During the Lebanese civil war, Washington feared that continued conflict would drag in outside players and produce a major Middle East war. Syria and Israel did end up battling each other in Lebanon, but their conflict in 1982 was confined to a skirmish. The threat to U.S. interests from renewed regional instability was considered serious enough for the deployment of marines but not serious enough to keep them there once the going got tough. Though significant, the interests at stake were not vital. In the Balkans there has been considerable worry that, if Kosovo were to explode, Albania and other outside states might be drawn into a wider regional war. During the Bosnian war, many analysts also worried about reverberations from damage to the credibility of the United States, NATO, and the United Nations.

But there was never a consensus that these dangers were sufficiently great to warrant putting significant numbers of U.S. troops into a situation where many might have died. Again, the interests were seen as less than vital.

Ethnic conflicts have often threatened the stability of a particular region but not the security of the international system as a whole. This could change. Clashes between Ukrainians and ethnic Russians, for example, could draw Ukraine and Russia into a major war that would disrupt the entire European continent. The collapse of India's multiethnic state would destabilize the South Asian subcontinent. A serious secessionist effort by Tibet could destabilize China and put it on a collision course with the West.

Some observers have talked about the international system as having zones of stability and zones of instability. This is a useful, if somewhat crude, means of measuring progress toward greater global security. Zones of stability are characterized by democracy, economic prosperity, and peace. Zones of instability are plagued by authoritarian rule, economic uncertainty, and armed conflict. The larger the zones of stability in the world, the more stable the international system as a whole. In a world of widening stability, U.S. policy makers can focus on consolidating ties with other democracies, increasing trade, safeguarding the environment, and working toward other long-range goals that will enhance quality of life for U.S. citizens. In contrast, if the zones of instability expand or multiply, the international system will be disrupted more often by the effects of crises in those areas. U.S. policy makers will increasingly find their attention diverted to problems of short-range crisis management. The collapse of political stability on the South Asian subcontinent, for example, could put the lives of millions of people at risk and raise the prospect of a regional nuclear war—hardly a situation the United States could ignore.

The cumulative threat to international stability is reason alone to devise better policies for dealing with ethnic conflicts. More immediate, however, are the secondary U.S. national interests that are often at stake in ethnic conflicts. These interests—or "wants" —represent goals that are important to U.S. leaders and citizens but not essential to the well-being of the country. They include the desire to stop mass slaughter, starvation, or egregious human-rights abuses; the desire to support models of democratic multi-ethnic states; and the desire to prevent wars that might spread into other countries. When the Kurds of northern Iraq came under attack after the Gulf War and fled into Turkey and Iran, humanitarian impulses rather than vital interests compelled the United States to intervene and set up a safe haven to protect the Kurds. When Rwanda exploded into genocidal violence, U.S. officials didn't worry about the geopolitical implications of the huge refugee crisis; they responded viscerally, along with the public, to horrific scenes of suffering. The war in Bosnia concerned Americans for many reasons, but central among these was the appalling spectacle of a multiethnic democracy being crushed by nationalist thugs. In the late 1960s the Biafran crisis was only a peripheral concern of U.S. policy makers until it turned into a humanitarian disaster, at which point it became a major foreign policy issue.

In the post–cold war era, secondary interests have achieved a new salience in U.S. foreign policy. The United States has more freedom to gratify its wants now that its needs are largely satisfied. It would be wrong to characterize current foreign policy as idealistic overall, but it is clearly more idealistic today than it was during the cold war. The large-scale humanitarian missions to northern Iraq and Somalia, for example, have no precedent in cold war history.

Various pressures are likely to keep wants near the top of the U.S. foreign policy agenda. First, even as the U.S. public has become more isolationist it continues to demand action to deal with humanitarian calamities abroad. Graphic media images of international suffering are now transmitted faster and more widely than ever before, and these images often fuel public demands for action. There is also a small but vocal sector of the public that is deeply committed to liberal internationalist causes, such as the protection of human rights and the survival of democratic states like Bosnia. These sentiments are even more widespread among leadership and opinion-making elites.

Second, a consensus is emerging among the major democracies that a sustained collective effort must be made to deal with humanitarian crises and failed states. U.S. policy makers have taken some steps toward embracing this agenda, placing it within the context of responsibilities incurred as the world's leading power. Finally, with the core industrial regions of the world secure from outside threats for the first time in fifty years, it is natural that wars on the periphery gain more attention. Although such wars do not threaten vital interests, they can produce continual minor crises that draw the United States in. More so than any other entity in the world, the U.S. government is viewed by warring parties around the world as an acceptable mediator. This role has emerged as a defining characteristic of U.S. leadership in the new era and is not easily sidestepped. That reality alone is likely to drive U.S. involvement in future ethnic conflicts.

Because resolving specific ethnic conflicts will seldom be a vital interest of the United States, the national resources devoted to this problem will rarely be enormous in scope. The United States is unlikely ever to risk significant military casualties or to spend billions of dollars in foreign aid to prevent or end ethnic conflicts. Nor should it. Instead, it should be prepared to make far more modest commitments of political, military, and financial resources. The size and nature of these commitments should depend on the wants at stake, as they have historically. Crises that affect all the main secondary interests enumerated above should attract the greatest commitment of resources. The United States made an enormous effort to stop the war in Bosnia because it produced a humanitarian disaster, jeopardized the survival of a multiethnic democracy, and destabilized an entire region. It made a major effort in Lebanon for much the same reasons. Crises that affect none or only one of the secondary interests should generally receive less attention. The United States made virtually no effort to stop the ethnic conflict in Sri Lanka because none of its wants was at stake.

Two other factors should determine the scope of American involvement in future ethnic conflicts. First, the feasibility of successful mediation must always be at the forefront of U.S.

calculations. As Richard Haass and others have argued, the United States should avoid meddling in conflicts that are not "ripe" for settlement.[20] Since the resources available for crisis resolution are relatively scarce, U.S. policy makers must expend them carefully, concentrating on areas where they are most likely to make a difference. At times, considerations of feasibility should outweigh calculations of interest. It can make sense to become involved in a crisis that affects few U.S. interests yet lends itself to effective U.S. mediation.

Historical ties between the United States and countries in conflict also must be taken into account. It is impossible to avoid the reality of domestic ethnic influences over U.S. foreign policy, and policy makers fool themselves when they try. The conflict in Northern Ireland barely affects U.S. wants at all, yet it has been a high priority of U.S. leaders at several points in the last two decades because of intense interest on the part of Irish Americans. The Israeli-Palestinian conflict has loomed large on the U.S. diplomatic agenda for similar reasons. In future ethnic conflicts in Eastern Europe, the degree of U.S. involvement may also be related to the influence of ethnic groups in the United States.

AMERICAN POLICY TOWARD ethnic conflict involves a dizzying array of calculations. Judgments must be made about the merits of nationalist movements, their chances of creating viable states, and the available alternatives to statehood. Policy makers must step back and look at the international system as a whole, assessing how ethnic struggles might affect global stability. And, most difficult of all, the United States must determine what national interests are at stake and find policy instruments commensurate with those interests. None of these tasks is made easier by the wide variation among ethnic conflicts and the seeming uniqueness of each situation. Applying the lessons of one conflict to other conflicts might, therefore, appear a daunting, if not altogether misguided, exercise. But as I will show in subsequent chapters, there is enough sameness in a diverse range of ethnic conflicts around the world to justify policy generalizations. Nearly all ethnic conflicts pass through three stages (rising tensions, onset of violence, and lulls or stalemates). At each stage the United States has a standard array of policy tools it can use to predict, prevent, and resolve the conflict. The nature of the conflict and the degree of U.S. wants at stake determine the most appropriate tools, ranging from those that demand only modest commitments of resources to those that require significant commitments. In the next chapters, a survey of the historical record will illustrate the ways these tools have been employed in the past, showing what works and what does not.

CHAPTER TWO

Prediction

DURING THE FIRST DAYS OF MARCH 1991, in the immediate aftermath of the Persian Gulf War, the Kurds of Iraq rose in arms against the Baghdad government. In the city of Sulaymaniyah, civilians spontaneously attacked the dreaded Iraqi security headquarters where numerous Kurdish dissidents had been imprisoned and tortured. Kurdish guerrillas, emerging from their mountain hideouts, launched assaults on other government installations throughout northern Iraq and for a brief period the insurgents held sway in their historic homeland. Saddam Hussein's regime, however, was quick to recover the upper hand. After crushing an uprising by Shiite guerrillas in southern Iraq, Baghdad shifted those military forces that had survived the Gulf War to the north. By mid-March the Kurdish uprising was in tatters. The small arms of the Kurdish guerrillas were no match for the tanks, artillery, and helicopter gunships of the Iraqi army. Fearing a repeat of the genocidal violence that Saddam had unleashed against the Kurds in 1988, some two million civilians began fleeing for the Turkish and Iranian borders.

Although the U.S. government had encouraged the Iraqi people to topple Saddam Hussein during the Gulf War, it was wholly unprepared for the civil war that erupted in 1991. The Bush administration had given little thought to the question of whether to help the Kurds militarily but quickly decided such action would be unwise. Even shooting down the Iraqi helicopters attacking the insurgents was ruled out lest U.S. forces be drawn into the civil war. The Kurds and Shiites were left to their fate.

In addition to being unprepared for the civil war, U.S. officials were astonished by the scope of the humanitarian crisis that followed the collapse of the Kurdish uprising. Although over a hundred thousand Kurds had similarly fled Iraq in 1988, the United States had no plans for responding to the current mass exodus. Following an emotional visit to Turkey by Secretary of State James Baker, the U.S. government threw together a humanitarian relief operation, but officials were not prepared for the international discussion that surrounded the crisis. Resolution 688—the call by the Security Council on April 5, 1991, to allow international relief organizations to aid the Kurds—was not devised by the United States. The subsequent U.S. and allied military intervention in northern Iraq to create a safe haven for the Kurds was justified by new international legal arguments, and U.S. officials were clearly on unfamiliar ground.[1]

As it happened, these officials muddled through and U.S. actions ultimately saved the lives of thousands of Kurds. Yet the failure of prediction should never have happened in the first place. For seven months the United States had focused enormous intelligence resources on the situation in Iraq and Kuwait. It had considered the strength and goals of the different dissident groups in Iraq and pondered various scenarios for internal conflicts after the war's end. There should have been some expectation that the Kurds might use the opportunity of an Iraqi military defeat to press their perennial campaign against the hated Baghdad government. And there should have been some consideration that their effort would fail and that a refugee crisis like that of 1988 might ensue.

Although this is an egregious example, U.S. officials have frequently been caught off guard by outbreaks of ethnic conflict. Americans were stunned by the mayhem in Burundi in 1972 and 1988 and by the genocidal hurricane that devastated Rwanda in 1994. The U.S. government anticipated the breakup of Yugoslavia but did not foresee the savagery that accompanied that process in Bosnia. The intractability of the conflict in Northern Ireland came as a shock, as did the unrelenting pace of the marathon civil war in Lebanon.

Prediction is among the most important tasks of national-security policy and yet it remains among the most perplexing. During the cold war, vast resources were devoted to monitoring the West's Communist adversaries and guessing their likely next move. This work took the form of a variety of traditional intelligence and diplomatic tasks: assessing the geopolitical goals and strategic doctrine of foes, studying military deployments, collecting tidbits about near-term intentions and plans, and tracking troop movements and arms shipments. There were some notable failures of prediction during the cold war—the invasion of Korea and the placement of Soviet missiles in Cuba, for example. For the most part, however, these failures were not due to any shortage of effort or confusion about how to undertake the basic tasks of prediction. They stemmed instead from incorrect judgment calls. The failure to predict the Iraqi invasion of Kuwait in 1990 can also be seen in this way: while the United States had plenty of information that pointed to a possible invasion, most top officials simply did not think Saddam would make such a move.

Predicting ethnic conflicts is a challenge of double difficulty. It, too, involves hard judgment calls, yet there is much less basis on which to make them. Secessionist movements and ethnic insurgents tend to be less predictable than state governments. Often led by committed ideologues, they are less likely to feel bound by treaties or conventions. The passions that fuel such efforts can be dif-

ficult for outsiders to comprehend and they differ from the
calculations of national interest that usually underpin state actions.
Reliable information about nonstate ethnic actors can be scarce.
Often nationalist groups emerge suddenly and little is known about
the personalities of their leaders or the nature of their governing
organizations. There is no past track record by which to predict
future performance. Intelligence agencies have to struggle to obtain basic details about internal debates. Insurgent movements, in
particular, often have very secretive governing processes designed
to thwart penetration by agents of the central state.

The decision-making apparatus of state governments is invariably located in national capitals, close to foreign embassies, foreign
press offices, and foreign business headquarters. Information about
the thinking of state leaders leaks out to all these nearby institutions. In addition, these institutions provide cover to foreign
intelligence agencies monitoring state governments. Ethnic movements, in contrast, are often centered far from national capitals, in
remote and even inhospitable regions. It is harder for embassy officials and intelligence agents to gather information in these places.
Information from open sources is less plentiful because journalists
have little incentive to visit remote regions until wars are already
under way.

Nonstate actors also have fewer means to communicate their
motives and plans to foreign governments. U.S. officials tend to
be deeply hesitant about meeting with leaders of self-determination
movements, for fear of seeming to lend them encouragement and
angering national governments. Also, most nonstate actors do not
have much of an apparatus to represent themselves abroad. The
well-oiled diplomatic and propaganda machine of the PLO was
exceptional. More common are small offices in London, New York,
or Paris. The lack of contacts, both official and unofficial, between
the United States and self-determination movements denies policy
makers an important source of intelligence.

Despite these obstacles, U.S. officials have not always failed to
predict ethnic conflicts. The Johnson administration had advance
warning of the Biafran secession and U.S. policy makers rightly

believed that East Pakistan would make a bid for independence. In the Balkans, they foresaw that Kosovo could blow up and took preventive steps to ensure that it didn't. Following the violence in Rwanda, officials believed that Burundi could turn into a similar killing ground and participated in efforts to defuse tensions in that country. And well before the war exploded in Yugoslavia, the violent breakup of that country had been predicted within the U.S. government.

I will cut at the problem of prediction in two ways. First, I will examine the range of conditions and warning signs that point to potential ethnic conflicts. Although many observers have pronounced such conflicts primal and inscrutable antagonisms, the factors that produce them have become more clear in recent years. The breeding ground for ethnic violence is by no means uncharted territory.

Second, I will examine failures and successes in a range of ethnic conflicts, exploring why U.S. officials were caught off guard by some conflicts and not by others. Occasionally, reliable information about brewing conflicts has been scarce for the reasons discussed above. In other situations, plentiful warning signs have been missed or ignored. In still others, even close monitoring has failed to predict the timing and nature of a crisis. At times, however, U.S. officials have drawn on early warnings to shape policies of preventive action, and these are the episodes that stand as models for future policy.

PREDICTING FACTORS

Not every ethnically diverse state is a powder keg. Conversely, a state that appears stable may in fact be quite fragile. Developing an analytical capacity for distinguishing between high-risk and low-risk states is an important first step in crafting policies to prevent ethnic warfare. There are three chief factors that point to the possibility of such warfare: a history of state repression of an ethnic minority or encouragement of violence toward a minority; a history of violence among ethnic groups; and the existence of ethnic pockets within newly independent states. None of these conditions guarantees violence and it is impossible to devise a wholly reliable formula for predicting ethnic warfare. Instead, the presence of these conditions—especially in combination—serves only as a tip-off that trouble is likely.

State Repression. It is commonplace for Western media to depict ethnic violence as a product of ancient animosities and irrational antipathies. Often, though, there is a less deep-seated cause: government repression of an ethnic minority that triggers a backlash. States around the world repress ethnic minorities in a number of ways, from actively killing and persecuting members of a particular group to encouraging such abuses and failing to bring the guilty to justice. Motives may vary. A ruling ethnic group may use repression to maintain its grip on power and to weaken the strength of its ethnic rivals. A state government may practice wholesale reprisals against an ethnic group that has spawned a guerrilla movement or terrorist operation, persecuting an innocent majority for the crimes of an extremist faction. For political reasons, moderate leaders of a state may not take action against ethnic extremists from their own group and may tolerate an environment in which thugs and paramilitary groups conduct a reign of terror.[2] Finally, of course, a state apparatus may be in the hands of nationalist ideologues who use repression in pursuit of a chauvinist agenda.

For many repressed ethnic groups, even a doomed armed struggle may seem preferable to the status quo. The Kurdish insurgent movements in Iraq and Turkey have never had a chance of success; both movements have their roots in state repression. In Iraq, the Kurds have endured generations of savage abuse and broken promises. They have repeatedly indicated a willingness to settle for partial autonomy arrangements that guarantee their cultural rights and political participation. Iraq's refusal to grant such arrangements or its reneging on agreements has helped spark rebellions in each of the past three decades. As for the future, new violence is likely between the Kurds and Iraq's central government as long as Saddam Hussein or another repressive leader remains in power.

The intensification of the armed Kurdish struggle in Turkey during the early 1990s is also a development that was preceded by a pattern of state repression. The dangerous new tempo of that war came as no surprise to close observers. Since the end of the Ottoman Empire, Turkey has treated the Kurds as second-class citizens. Kemal Atatürk, the founder of modern Turkey, refused even to acknowledge the existence of the Kurds, referring to them as "mountain Turks." This attitude persisted through the 1980s, manifested most notably in criminal penalties for using the Kurdish language in certain situations and prohibitions against most teaching of Kurdish. Mounting disaffection with such cultural repression helped spawn an insurgency in 1984 that continued well into the 1990s. The tactics of the Turkish government in waging this war only exacerbated Kurdish resentment. Putting Kurdish regions under emergency control, the army razed and evacuated hundreds of towns and engaged in systematic human-rights abuses.

This campaign was stepped up after Prime Minister Suleyman Demirel took office in November 1991. "Kurds in Turkey have been killed, tortured and disappeared at an appalling rate," said a March 1993 report by Helsinki Watch. "In addition, many of their cities have been brutally attacked by security forces, hundreds of their villages forcibly evacuated, their ethnic identity continues to be attacked, their rights of free expression denied and their political freedom placed in jeopardy."[3] These actions encouraged growing numbers of militant Kurds and hordes of recruits for the Kurdish Workers Party (PKK).[4] By 1994–95, the war had escalated to the point that the Turkish army used air strikes against Kurdish positions and launched a major incursion into Iraq to attack PKK bases. Thanks to state repression, a Marxist-led insurgency with limited popular appeal had snowballed into a war that spread over international borders and attracted worldwide attention.

The war in East Pakistan is another example of the explosive consequences of unfair rule by an arrogant central government.[5] During the 1960s, the government of Pakistan was dominated by Punjabis, as was the army. The majority of East Pakistan's seventy-five million people were Bengalis. Punjabis are taller and fairer-skinned than Bengalis, and many harbored feelings of racial superiority. For the most part, repression of the Bengalis of East Pakistan did not take the form of human-rights abuses. Instead, East Pakistan was economically exploited. Its agricultural exports generated 50 percent of Pakistan's foreign currency, yet it was a region of staggering poverty and underdevelopment. Had the Bengalis been treated with more respect, had they received an equitable share of Pakistan's wealth, the pent-up frustrations that produced calls for independence might have developed far more gradually.

In Sri Lanka, blatant acts of state repression led to a Tamil uprising that began in 1983 and lasted into the 1990s. The Tamil minority in that country had become dissatisfied with the Sinhalese-dominated government as early as 1958, after anti-Tamil riots had swept the country and there had been little official response. In 1972, conditions for Tamils deteriorated markedly when a new constitution declared Sri Lanka a Sinhalese Buddhist republic and deprived Tamils of many basic rights. Even moderate Tamil leaders became increasingly radicalized. Many talked of a separate state in the traditional Tamil homeland in the north and east of the country. There were more anti-Tamil riots in 1977 and 1981, again with complicity on the part of the government, and in 1983 the country was plunged into civil war as Tamil guerrillas began responding with force.[6]

In the Balkans, Kosovo was highly unstable from the late 1980s onward because of systematic repression of ethnic Albanians by the Serb government in Belgrade. Slobodan Milosevic deliberately inflamed the situation in Kosovo because the region was a symbol of Serb nationalism and it served his political purposes to insist on Serb prerogatives there. Milosevic's campaign of repression in Kosovo not only incited the Kosovo Albanians but also aroused the passion of their ethnic brethren across the border in Albania proper.

State repression has been an important factor in numerous other ethnic conflicts. During the early 1970s, the Muslims of Lebanon felt underrepresented and, at times, ill-treated by a Christian minority that refused to acknowledge the country's changing demographic reality. In the years before Biafra was formed, the Ibo of Nigeria had come to believe that their security and political rights could not be protected by the Nigerian government. The Eritrean independence movement was fueled by assorted grievances against a repressive Ethiopian government. The 1987 Palestinian Intifada in Israel's Occupied Territories arose after twenty years of Israeli rule that left a huge population of people politically disenfranchised, economically impoverished, and subject to various forms of harassment and abuse by Israeli security. The disturbances in Northern Ireland escalated into an intractable conflict following widespread abuses by the British forces who intervened in the area. The Muslims of Kashmir have long been subjected to harsh treatment by Indian security police.

History of Ethnic Violence. State elites and their henchmen are not, of course, the sole purveyors of ethnic disharmony. The world would be a more manageable place if they were, for governments can be punished in a variety of ways and sometimes even nonrational state leaders can be brought to their knees. Unfortunately, animosities at the popular level drive ethnic conflict as well. State elites who seek to exploit ethnic differences for their own gain will be more successful in an environment where tensions are already acute. Countries in which these tensions have produced violence in the past are good candidates for explosions in the future. Where blood has been shed once it can more easily be shed again. Conversely, multiethnic states with no history of communal violence have a better chance of remaining peaceful, even if they break apart.

Rwanda and Burundi top the list of violence-prone countries. Ethnic massacres have occurred in these two countries in 1959, 1962–63, 1965, 1966, 1969, 1972, 1988, and every year between 1991 and 1996. The animosities between the Hutu and Tutsi may not be "ancient," but memories of mayhem now span more than two generations and produce fertile ground for new violence. Some theorists have posited that the more densely intermingled ethnic groups are, the greater the risk of violence.[7] The experience in Rwanda and Burundi lends credence to this proposition. The Hutu and Tutsi in these countries live together without segregation and both groups speak the Kirundi language. Because of intermarriage and similar diets, Tutsi are no longer much taller than Hutu, as they were when Belgian colonial administrators elevated them to a position of authority. Most Hutu and Tutsi are farmers and there are no great disparities in wealth or land ownership in the two countries. However, Rwanda and Burundi are among the most densely populated countries in the world and the land plots of farmers are extremely small.[8]

In the three most significant outbursts of conflict in Rwanda and Burundi—1972, 1988, and 1994—state leaders directed the violence. In Rwanda in 1994, for example, the genocide was planned by key figures in or close to the government, radio broadcasts were used to disseminate anti-Tutsi propaganda in the months leading up to the killings, and both the army and the civilian administration choreographed the orgy of bloodletting. At times, the army coerced Hutu into participating in the killings.[9] Nevertheless, it would be wrong to conclude that what happened in Rwanda was made possible only by the adept manipulativeness of state elites. Rwandan leaders mobilized large numbers of Hutu civilians to join voluntarily in the killing of defenseless Tutsi civilians. As one reporter wrote: "Neighbors hacked neighbors to death in their homes, and colleagues hacked colleagues to death in their workplaces. Priests killed their parishioners, and elementary-school teachers killed their students."[10] It is hard to imagine that such savagery could have been unleashed in the absence of a rich tradition of violence and ethnic hatred. In another country with no such tradition, elites with genocidal ambitions might not have had such success. In Rwanda more than a half million people were killed in just a few months.

Stable democratic governments in Rwanda and Burundi would vastly decrease the chances of new genocidal violence, but even then, the legacy of past violence would place Rwanda and Burundi at greater risk than many other countries. The situation will be exacerbated in the future by overpopulation and environmental degradation. According to U.N. predictions, tiny Burundi alone will have twelve million people by the year 2015.[11] If one were to draw a map of the world that predicted twenty first-century ethnic violence, the Great Lakes region of Africa would be at its center.

The violence in Sri Lanka, too, is deeply rooted. The developments that led to the civil war cannot be blamed solely on state actions. The anti-Tamil riots of 1958 that launched the country on its long path toward disintegration were a mass action by Sinhalese nationalists, as were many acts of violence in subsequent years. At times, the Sri Lankan government played an active role in persecuting the Tamil population, especially in the 1970s and early 1980s. These actions were cynical power plays, but they also reflected chauvinist sentiments that were widespread among many Sinhalese. Even had the state proceeded differently, the acting out of these sentiments might in themselves have made Tamil life in Sri Lanka sufficiently miserable to spur demands for an independent state and an armed movement bent on advancing those demands. The apparent defeat of the Tamil Tigers in 1995 is likely to end the civil war and lead to some sort of political accord. Given widespread Tamil atrocities during the war, however, Sri Lanka now has a legacy of violence in which both Sinhalese and Tamils consider themselves to have been victims. This does not bode well for the future.

The history of violence between Serbs and Croats was an important cause of the war that accompanied the breakup of Yugoslavia. Serb and Croat nationalist leaders stoked the fires of ethnic passions that had long smoldered in both cultures. Slobodan Milosevic, in particular, would not have been so successful had he not had good historical material to back his crusade. The history of conflict between the Serbs and the Croats stretches back hundreds of years. Each nationality has an oral tradition that highlights its persecution at the hands of the other. During World War II, Serb civilians were massacred in vast numbers by Croats collaborating with the Axis powers. Ante Pavelich, ruler of the Axis Croat puppet regime, was a fanatical nationalist and Serb hater who zealously boasted of the atrocities of his Ustashi forces. "A good Ustashi," he reportedly told his men, "is he who can use his knife to cut a child from the womb of its mother."[12] Croat civilians also suffered during this period at the hands of Serb Chetnik guerrillas, who exacted ample revenge for the violence visited upon Serb communities.

With this history, it is no wonder that both Serbs and Croats felt deeply apprehensive about being ruled by governments of the other group. Serbs, especially, felt that their communities, including those in Bosnia, could not be safe unless they were part of Serbia. When Yugoslavia broke up, the propaganda of nationalist Serb leaders helped turn many Serb civilians into sadistic murderers and rapists who preyed on their longtime neighbors. The propaganda was effective largely because it tapped into deep-seated fears. The 1995 peace agreement has, for the moment, delivered the former Yugoslavia from war. Yet from that war was born a new persecuted group: the Muslims of Bosnia. And they, too, will not soon forget what they endured.

In the absence of a history of violence, ethnic tensions are more likely to be played out in the political arena and even the fracturing of states may occur without bloodshed. The Quebec independence movement has been characterized by an absolute minimum of violence. Whatever their claims regarding cultural identity, the Quebecois have never seen themselves as a violently persecuted people. They have always been allowed to take part in the political life of Canada. There is no set of past grievances that can be played up enough to lend moral legitimacy to violent acts by proindependence activists. As a result, the debate over secession, which unfolded in an atmosphere unpoisoned by extremist actions, ultimately climaxed in a popular referendum in 1995. The same reasoned approach prevailed in Czechoslovakia. Here, too, there was no significant history of violence. Czechs and Slovaks had gotten along reasonably well in Czechoslovakia and there was no fear that Czechs who lived in the Slovaks' new state would be slaughtered, or vice versa. The breakup of Czechoslovakia thus proceeded in an ordered and democratic manner—a "velvet divorce."

Because of these nonviolent traditions, U.S. policy makers were unconcerned about possible wars in either Quebec or Czechoslovakia. But they guessed wrong about Ukraine. In the early 1990s many believed that the twelve million ethnic Russians in Ukraine, 22 percent of the population, would find life under Ukrainian rule intolerable and seek to join Russia. This irredentist movement never came to pass, and a major reason that Russians feel comfortable in Ukraine—and Ukrainians feel comfortable having them there—is that there is no historical legacy of violence and distrust between the two groups (with the exception, of course, of Stalin's war on the Kulaks in the early 1930s, a war characterized more by ideological extremism than by ethnic hatred). As Barry Posen observes, "There is no record of Ukrainian persecution of resident Russians. The Ukrainians and the Russians living in the eastern part of the country have had amicable relations for a great many years. A majority of Russians voted for Ukrainian independence. There are no reports of Ukrainian nationalist gangs operating against Russians."[13] An exact opposite set of points could have been made about Serbs living in Croatia on the eve of the Yugoslav war.

Existence of Ethnic Pockets. During the 1990s numerous new states came into existence in processes free of violence. Most of the states of the former Soviet Union have been at peace since gaining independence. Two of the new states in the former Yugoslavia—Slovenia and Macedonia—have been more or less peaceful as well. Those states that have been plunged into ethnic strife share a common trait: they contain ethnic minorities who would rather be affiliated with a neighboring state. This desire may stem from fear that a violent past will repeat itself or simply from a nationalist preference to live in a country dominated by one's own people. Either way, the existence of ethnic pockets is an important predictor of conflict. And conflict of this kind can be particularly explosive because it has the potential to draw two states into war.[14]

Several of the wars in Central Asia have been sparked by an

ethnic group's quest to affiliate with a neighboring state. The South Ossetians of Georgia wish to join the Ossetian region of Russia. The Armenians of Nagorno-Karabakh in Azerbaijan believe they should be part of Armenia. In the Balkans, problems of ethnic pockets have been the chief cause of war. Many of the Serbs in Croatia and Bosnia opposed the independence of those states and wanted to remain part of Serbia. Guarantees by the Croatian and Bosnian governments that Serb rights would be respected did little to propitiate Serb pockets in those regions. Clearly, it was not just fears of violence that underpinned Serb desires to remain part of Serbia. It was also a sense of ethnic solidarity. Many Serbs in both Croatia and Bosnia simply disliked the idea of being a minority in another country. A common saying at this time in the Balkans was: "Why should I be a minority in your country when you can be a minority in mine?" Slovenia, it would now appear, had the best chance of all the Yugoslav republics of being at peace because of its ethnic homogeneity.

The dream of a better life just over the border has fueled ethnic movements outside of Central Asia and the Balkans as well. Catholic insurgents in Northern Ireland have called for union with Ireland. Muslim rebels in Kashmir want either full independence or, at the least, affiliation with Pakistan.

Ethnic pockets are most destabilizing when the leaders of a neighboring state show a desire to rescue their stranded brethren. In the absence of a virulent Serb nationalism that championed the dream of a "greater Serbia," the Belgrade government would not have waged its relentless war against Croatia and Bosnia. More likely, it would have sought guarantees of Serb safety and warned of intervention if those guarantees were violated. At the same time, it might have allowed unlimited immigration of Serbs into Serbia proper. This is essentially the policy that Moscow has followed for ethnic Russians in the former Soviet republics.

The most destabilizing period of the Balkan crisis came when the leadership of Albania spoke openly about a "greater Albania," implying a potential willingness to aid repressed Albanians in Kosovo and also to incorporate the Albanian minority in Macedonia. Such a move could have triggered a major regional war. To their credit, U.S. officials paid enormous attention to this situation and sought to temper Albanian rhetoric. Likewise, there was great cause for alarm when Hungarian leaders began talking of their concern for the two million ethnic Hungarians in Romania and the 600,000 Hungarians in Slovakia. This situation, too, had the potential to escalate into serious interstate tensions with regional implications.

Over the past several decades, the stability of the situation in Kashmir has largely hinged on Pakistani attitudes toward the insurgency there. When Pakistan has proclaimed the right of the Muslims of Kashmir to join Pakistan and has actively supported the insurgency, relations with India have deteriorated and the crisis has heated up. For good reason, a key goal of U.S. preventive diplomacy in South Asia has been to convince Pakistan to deny any support for Kashmiri rebels. It goes without saying that the conflict in Northern Ireland would have been many times more serious if the Irish government had given active support to the IRA.

So far, the pockets of ethnic Russians in the former Soviet republics have not been cause for much conflict, even though Russian leaders have pronounced their willingness to use force to protect these populations if need be. There are several reasons for this relative quiescence. First, there is as yet no major movement in Russia to recapture former imperial holdings. Hypernationalists who issue calls of this kind remain a small minority. Second, ethnic Russians in the former republics have made no emphatic efforts to affiliate the territory in which they live with Russia. As discussed earlier, Russians in Ukraine have not felt persecuted and insecure, nor have they harbored ambitions of nationalist unity. Russians in the Baltic states have felt discriminated against in recent years, but there is little historical reason for thinking that this discrimination will escalate into violent repression. Third, ethnic Russians have a sense of security that other groups trapped in pockets do not: they know that mother Russia has more than enough power to rescue them if need be. Leaders in Moscow know that as well, whereas leaders of weaker states may worry that they will lose their chances to rescue ethnic pockets if they don't move quickly.

PREDICTION AND U.S. FOREIGN POLICY

Success and failure in prediction stem from several factors, including the perception of U.S. interests at stake in a potential conflict; knowledge of a given country and a history of political ties; the existence of distractions; the quality of diplomatic reporting; availability of information from media sources; and the quality of intelligence information.

Interests. It is little wonder that many ethnic conflicts have seemed to appear so suddenly on the radar screen of U.S. officials, given where these conflicts often occur. Throughout the postwar era, U.S. policy makers have tended to focus on a handful of regions. Central Europe was ground zero of the cold war rivalry and received the most attention. Asia was a close second, the scene of two major land wars that the United States was drawn into. Crises in the Middle East and Latin America demanded considerable U.S. energies, while Africa made sporadic appearances on the U.S. geopolitical agenda. The regions that are historically most prone to ethnic conflict—central Africa, Central Asia and the Caucasus, and South Asia—have not been home to many U.S. interests and have not been the focus of foreign policy considerations. The combination of indifference and unfamiliarity is a recipe for surprise when crises occur. In contrast, ethnic conflicts that have occurred in strategically important countries generally have been anticipated.

Burundi and Rwanda stand as quintessential backwaters in the grand scheme of U.S. global interests. They are landlocked states in one of the most strategically insignificant regions in the entire world. They are not sources of raw materials that the United States needs, nor are they lucrative trading markets. Neither country even borders states that are of vital interest to the United States and neither has significant military power with which to threaten its neighbors or destabilize its region. During the cold war, neither Rwanda nor Burundi was a major participant in the political-military proxy games of the superpowers, and the end of the cold war only increased the geopolitical marginality of sub-Saharan Africa. The disappearance of both countries would be of no consequence to the United States. A brief fluctuation in coffee prices would be the only sign of their passing.

Only recently has the United States paid much attention to Burundi and Rwanda. Before 1972, U.S. diplomats knew about the history of violence between Hutu and Tutsi, but there was no reason to monitor relations between these two groups closely. When Thomas Patrick Melady became ambassador to Burundi in 1969, he took over a small embassy. It was a sleepy diplomatic post of no importance. Melady had taken some time to delve through German and Belgian archives on Burundi's history and came to his post reasonably well informed. He knew that long-standing tensions between Hutu and Tutsi were rising, but there was no sense of urgency in official circles in Washington.

The horrific violence that consumed Burundi in 1972 did little to lessen U.S. apathy. Despite constituting an 85 percent majority, the Hutu were denied power in many parts of Burundian society throughout the 1970s and 1980s; indeed their situation actually worsened, with fewer Hutu in the army by the late 1980s than there had been in 1972.[15] After his stint in Burundi, Thomas Melady went on to become a prominent Republican foreign policy adviser. He played a role in the Reagan transition and warned of the inevitability of new violence in Burundi. Nobody cared. He was called to the State Department periodically to consult on central Africa, but on the topic of Burundi his advice never reached beyond the assistant secretary level. Burundi was a nonissue in U.S. foreign policy circles during the 1980s.

The violent repression of Hutu by the regime of Colonel Jean-Baptiste Bagaza during the mid-1980s caused the United States to cut back its aid to Burundi. Aid was increased, however, when the more moderate government of Pierre Buyoya took power in September 1987. American officials believed the internal situation was improving under Buyoya because he released Hutu political prisoners and pledged himself to a program of reform and ethnic reconciliation.[16] Had U.S. officials been paying closer attention they would have found that Buyoya remained unable to control hardline Tutsi extremists in his own government. These extremists, led by Major Bernard Cishahyo, chief of all internal military operations, perpetrated the massacres of August 1988, in which thousands of Hutu died.[17] After the violence, U.S. officials expressed shock and surprise.

The genocide in Rwanda in 1994 came as little surprise to low-level U.S. officials, but top policy makers had ignored warnings from the bureaucracy. During the early 1990s, the United States was involved in mediating the conflict there and supporting the role of the United Nations and the Organization of African Unity in bringing stability to the country.[18] By early 1994, as extremist Hutu leaders began arming their supporters and plotting a campaign of genocide, the U.S. embassy in Kigali was well aware of these ominous developments.[19] In February, Prudence Bushnell, deputy assistant secretary of state for African affairs, and Arlene Render, director of the Central Africa Office, visited Rwanda to learn more about the deteriorating situation. Back in Washington, officials at the Agency for International Development, along with Africa specialists at the State Department and the National Security Council, began to warn of an impending cataclysm in Rwanda.[20] Nobody at the highest levels of the Clinton administration was very interested in these warnings.

Following the deaths of more than half a million people in Rwanda in 1994, the U.S. government put significant effort into monitoring events in Burundi. None of its strategic or economic interests in that country had changed since the previous decade. Rather, Burundi became a priority because of its potential for another humanitarian disaster.

The Caucasus is another area to which U.S. officials have historically paid scant attention. For most of the twentieth century

this region was under the control of the Soviet Union and therefore had little interaction with the United States. (During the cold
war, however, U.S. intelligence agencies made efforts to cultivate
ties with anti-Communist dissidents in the Caucasus republics and
to exploit ethnic resentment against Moscow's rule; little came of
these initiatives, but they did lead to some U.S. knowledge about
the languages and culture of the Caucasus.) Although the region is
strategically located, bordering on several major powers, and has
significant oil deposits, there was not a strong sense, as the cold
war ended, that major U.S. interests were at stake there. There was
thus not a great effort to monitor and predict the trajectory of the
ethnic conflicts that began to emerge in Soviet republics like
Georgia and Azerbaijan, and once these republics seceded and violence in the region increased, the United States was quite slow
even to establish a significant diplomatic presence in the new states
Ultimately, the United States was only sporadically involved in
seeking to mediate the armed disputes in this area. Instead, it considered the Caucasus to be in Russia's sphere of interest and allowed Moscow a relatively free hand in trying to control events
there.

The history of U.S. monitoring of ethnic conflict in more important states shows how national interests often determine the
amount of attention paid to unstable countries. Even before major
fissures began appearing in Nigeria in 1966, the United States followed the situation closely. Nigeria is the most populous country
in Africa and it was considered in the 1960s to have more economic
and political promise than most of the newly independent states
on the continent. American officials believed that the success of
Nigeria would have implications for the overall stability of Africa.

As early as 1964, the U.S. envoy to Lagos, Joseph Palmer, expressed concern about the polarization of regions in Nigeria. Before leaving his post in 1965, Palmer talked to Prime Minister
Abubaker Tafaw Balewa about the future of Nigeria: "I told him
I was really fearful that this was polarizing more and more. Some
way had to be found for keeping the Nigerian system together."[21]
Palmer left Nigeria to serve as assistant secretary of state for Af-

rican affairs, and from that position he was able to ensure that developments in Nigeria were not ignored. When the first of the two 1966 coups occurred in mid-January, U.S. officials believed that it was not a standard coup. They saw it as further evidence of internal stresses that threatened the integrity of the country.[22] Bad diplomatic reporting from Nigeria led the United States to underestimate the gravity of the impending secessionist crisis, yet there was no neglect of the situation overall. It must be noted, however, that while the Johnson administration clearly appreciated the importance of Nigeria, its conception of U.S. interests there was circumscribed by the belief that the country lay in Great Britain's sphere of interest and that Great Britain was therefore responsible for dealing with the situation.[23]

Lebanon was not ignored either as it hurtled toward war in the mid-1970s. The United States had a long-standing interest in a stable pro-Western Lebanon. It had intervened in Lebanon in 1958 to ensure that goal, and through the 1960s and 1970s the United States cultivated good relations with Lebanon and granted it military and economic aid. Lebanon's neutrality in the Arab-Israeli wars was another reason for its strategic importance. The country was seen as a bridge between two worlds in the Middle East.

During the early 1970s, American officials watched with concern as the Palestinian presence in Lebanon grew and began to destabilize the country. Secretary of State Henry Kissinger commented on a 1973 visit to the country that "the danger while nascent was already visible. The Palestinians were beginning to be a disruptive element in Lebanon."[24] By early 1975, the declining effectiveness of Lebanon's central government and mounting antagonism between Muslims and Christians were widely noted in the U.S. foreign policy establishment and Lebanon was seen as teetering on the brink of collapse. "Lebanon is an extremely fragile, insecure state and it is sure to remain so at least until the Palestinians who live there . . . are given a homeland of their own," noted Senator Charles Percy after a January 1975 fact-finding trip. "The number of weapons per capita is said to be the highest in the world."[25] Two other senators visited Lebanon in the first half of 1975 and also pronounced the situation highly unstable.[26] When the civil war finally exploded, it was not a tremendous surprise. What did prove surprising were the duration and intensity of the war.

Two important countries that received significant attention as the cold war ended were Ukraine and Yugoslavia. As the Soviet Union broke up, U.S. policy makers considered developments in Ukraine to be pivotal. One of the most populous states in Europe, it had nuclear weapons, it was strategically located, and it had the potential to end up in a major rivalry with Russia. The large population of ethnic Russians in Ukraine was an obvious flash point. For these reasons, a major effort was made within the U.S. national-security establishment to scrutinize Ukraine's internal situation closely. U.S. diplomats maintained close contacts with Ukrainian leaders and used these contacts to understand Ukraine's situation better. The Central Intelligence Agency analyzed issues relating to Ukraine's nuclear arsenal and, in addition, undertook a study in 1991 on ethnic relations in the country. The agency's conclusions were highly pessimistic: it predicted that dissatisfaction on the part of ethnic Russians would lead to the disintegration of Ukraine.[27] This forecast turned out to be wrong: by 1995 Ukraine appeared to be politically stable, with no ethnic cataclysm imminent. Serious attempts at prediction do not always yield accurate results, for reasons discussed below. The significant point here, however, is that the stability of Ukraine was considered important enough for U.S. policy makers to devote much attention to internal developments there. Interests determine interest.

Much the same can be said in the case of Yugoslavia. Though never seen as a vital U.S. interest, during the cold war it was watched carefully and this attentiveness continued into the new era. The potential for a return to historic patterns of instability in the Balkans was an obvious danger. "I believe we, more than the West Europeans, understood how serious the risk was of having a terrible war," said David Gompert, an NSC staff member in 1990–91.[28] While many in the U.S. government were not prepared for the intensity and global repercussions of the Yugoslav war, they were

not shocked that the breakup of the country occurred or that it
was accompanied by violence. Slovenia had begun to push for secession in the late 1980s, and when Warren Zimmerman took over
the ambassadorship to Yugoslavia in early 1989, he did not take
Yugoslavia's unity for granted: "I pressed the talented and highly
professional political and economic officers in the American embassy in Belgrade and the consulate general in Zagreb, Croatia, to
consider worst-case scenarios for Yugoslavia. The worst case we
could think of was the breakup of the country. We reported to
Washington that no breakup of Yugoslavia could happen peacefully."[29]

The Central Intelligence Agency was also at work pondering the
future of Yugoslavia. By November 1990, the agency had completed an analysis that predicted that the breakup of Yugoslavia
would occur "most probably in the next 18 months"; a civil war,
it said, was "highly likely."[30] That forecast proved correct. Once
the civil war was under way, deeply alarming U.S. policy makers,
the CIA made efforts to plot its trajectory. In 1993, a CIA analysis
predicted that the war would result in a permanent redrawing of
Balkan borders, with Croatia and Serbia both absorbing parts of
Bosnia, and Albania ultimately gaining control of Kosovo. "I believe we are moving toward a greater Serbia, a greater Croatia and
a greater Albania as a result of this war," said David Kanin, the
CIA's chief analyst for Yugoslavia.[31]

Members of Congress were also worried about developments in
Yugoslavia well before the crisis escalated into a major war. During
the 1980s, many of them had taken an interest in the human-rights
situation in Kosovo, holding hearings and passing resolutions that
expressed concern for the fate of ethnic Albanians.[32] In July 1990,
Senate Minority Leader Bob Dole led a congressional delegation
to Yugoslavia, visiting a number of cities, including Pristina in Kosovo. Early in the crisis, in February 1991, the Senate Foreign
Relations Committee had held hearings to discuss U.S. policy toward the breakup of Yugoslavia.[33]

Another secessionist crisis that U.S. officials watched closely and predicted correctly was the breakaway bid of East Pakistan in 1971. The Nixon administration considered events on the subcontinent to be of considerable importance. It worried about renewed warfare between India and Pakistan as well as about tensions between India and China. It sought to cultivate closer ties with Pakistan in order to have a reliable channel to the Communist government in Beijing. Nixon and his aides were concerned also about India's growing influence among the nonaligned countries of the world. The crisis in East Pakistan had the potential to affect all these matters.

In his memoirs, Henry Kissinger comments that "in every administration some event occurs that dramatizes the limits of human foresight."[34] In this case, the unforeseen event was not the secession of East Pakistan but the internationalized conflict between Pakistan and India that followed. Kissinger and others foresaw East Pakistan's secession well before it occurred.

On November 12–13, 1970, a massive cyclone struck East Pakistan and killed some 200,000 people. Pakistan's incompetent handling of relief operations for one of the greatest natural disasters of all time exacerbated long-standing tensions with East Pakistan. On December 7, the Awami League—a political party dedicated to the autonomy of East Pakistan—won a major electoral victory. Zulfikar Ali Bhutto, a candidate fiercely opposed to autonomy, won major gains in the same election. With the Awami League pushing a sweeping program for autonomy, it was obvious that a major crisis was in the making. On February 16, 1971, Kissinger asked for an interagency study of U.S. policy alternatives should East Pakistan try to secede. On February 22, he sent his own analysis of the situation to Nixon, predicting that East Pakistani leaders would demand virtual autonomy and that if they didn't get their way (as was likely) they would declare East Pakistan independent.[35] On March 6, Kissinger convened the Senior Review Group to consider the situation. "Our consensus was that Pakistan would not be able to hold the East by force," he wrote later.[36] This prediction turned out to be correct: the state of Bangladesh was born out of one of the few successful secessionist efforts in the postwar period.

Knowledge and Historical Ties. National interests may determine how intently American officials monitor brewing ethnic crises overseas, but attentiveness alone is no guarantee of accurate prediction. If it were, the collapse of the Soviet Union—the most closely spied-on country in the history of espionage—would not stand as one of the great foreign policy surprises of all time. Various factors beyond national interests determine whether U.S. policy makers spot an emerging crisis. Officials sometimes have either a special knowledge about a country or an unusual ignorance that it is not necessarily related to that country's relative importance to the United States. Likewise, diplomatic ties may be either quite good or egregiously bad for reasons that are only partly related to national interests.

In the Balkans, the U.S. government was reasonably well equipped to analyze developments in the early 1990s. While it lacked adequate expertise on the new breakaway republics, it did have considerable knowledge about Belgrade and the Serbian leadership. An unusually large number of foreign service officers had served two stints in Yugoslavia.[37] One of these officers was Warren Zimmerman, the ambassador to Belgrade. Another was Deputy Secretary of State Lawrence Eagleburger, a leading expert on the Balkans who had spent seven years in Yugoslavia as an embassy attaché and ambassador. In addition, Brent Scowcroft, the national security adviser, had once served in Yugoslavia as a military liaison officer and had written his dissertation on the country.

Interest-group politics also played a role in familiarizing the U.S. government with the nature of Serb nationalism well before Yugoslavia's breakup. The significant Albanian community in the United States helped draw Congress's attention to human-rights abuses in Kosovo during the 1980s. Congress then passed resolutions to condemn the repression, and these resolutions, in turn, placed pressure on the executive branch to attend to the Kosovo situation earlier than it otherwise might have. Thus, well before Serb nationalism threatened the stability of the Balkans as a whole, U.S. officials were aware of the Serbs' twisted logic and hyperbolic claims as they pertained to Kosovo. It was there in the late 1980s that Slobodan Milosevic sharpened his chauvinist arguments and showcased his knack for perfidy. When the Yugoslav crisis began in the early 1990s, Kosovo was no longer an obscure region in the southern Balkans: it had become one of the most analyzed ethnic tinderboxes in Eastern Europe.

The great attention to Ukraine also had some basis in domestic politics. There are some 750,000 Ukrainian Americans in the United States and their interest groups have lobbied for a foreign policy that places more emphasis on promoting political and economic stability in Ukraine. The influence of these lobbying efforts is difficult to assess. Clearly, though, the presence of domestic ethnic constituencies has historically made it difficult for policy makers to ignore certain countries.[38] Israel is the most spectacular example of this. The policy debate over the Kurds would surely be different if there were six million Kurds living—and voting—in the United States. The Baltic states of Latvia, Lithuania, and Estonia are smaller and strategically less important than such states as Georgia, Tajikistan, and Azerbaijan, but they have received more attention from U.S. policy makers in part because of historic ties to immigration patterns earlier in this century.

Ethnic groups in the United States can also provide policy makers with information and contacts helpful for understanding a situation overseas. Americans who have trade links with their ancestral homeland or who frequently visit relatives there can be tapped for insights into the sources of ethnic tensions and the possible direction of an emerging conflict. Highly visible ethnic Americans (like Edward Said, of Palestinian ancestry) can play an important role in directing media and scholarly attention to a conflict. Ethnic interest groups in Washington often serve as clearinghouses for information, bombarding Congress with material and eagerly offering their services as experts. During the Lebanese civil war, for example, members of the Lebanese–American community were regularly asked by Congress to explain the puzzle of what appeared to be a national suicide attempt. Armenian Americans have been quick to unravel the complexities of Nagorno-Karabakh, while the Hungarian–American community has helped highlight the plight of ethnic Hungarians in Romania and Slovakia. There have been no comparable resources for U.S. government officials to draw on for insight into the Hutu-Tutsi conflict in Rwanda and Burundi. These groups have virtually no representatives in the United States. Likewise, there are very few Tamil Americans, Kashmiri Americans, or Moldovan Americans.

Distractions. Policymakers can focus only on a limited number of problems at one time. Even excellent information about a brewing ethnic conflict may never fully register. "Most high-level policy makers are swamped," Joseph S. Nye, Jr., observed while serving as chairman of the National Intelligence Council. "They spend their days drinking from a fire hose of information."[39] How much attention an ethnic crisis receives from U.S. officials has a lot to do with how busy their lives are with other crises. Because ethnic conflicts seldom involve vital U.S. interests and are often a secondary concern to begin with, they tend to be pushed even further to the sidelines of U.S. policy if something more important is happening elsewhere in the world. This is particularly true when such conflicts have not yet exploded into full-fledged warfare. Predictions of impending trouble that are accurately made at a lower level of government may be ignored at a higher level by officials who are absorbed in other issues.

American officials have often been busy with major crises while the fuse has been burning on ethnic powder kegs. Biafra's move to secession in early 1967 took place at the height of U.S. military escalation in Vietnam. The actual secession on May 30, 1967, occurred on the eve of the Six Day War between Israel and its Arab neighbors. In June, after Biafra had seceded but before its war with Nigeria had begun, the United States was focused on the aftermath of the Six Day War. Robert McNamara writes in his memoirs that the crush of events in the summer and fall of 1967—which included a historic summit meeting with Soviet leaders—made it difficult for U.S. officials to focus even on Vietnam.[40] Likewise, the Burundi crisis of May 1972 occurred while the U.S. national-security establishment was concentrating on a summit in Moscow aimed at bringing to culmination three years of arms-control negotiations and political détente with the Soviet Union.

In late 1990 and early 1991, U.S. diplomats and intelligence officers correctly predicted that Yugoslavia was sliding toward war. Yet this crisis received relatively little attention because the United States was engaged in its most ambitious military undertaking since Vietnam—Operation Desert Shield/Desert Storm. Numerous meetings related to Yugoslavia were held during this period by the interagency "deputies committee," and top-level officials were apprised of policy developments.[41] But their ability to focus on Yugoslavia was limited. Secretary of State James Baker did not undertake a diplomatic mission to the country until June 21, 1991. Warren Zimmerman wrote of that visit: "Baker's message was the right one, but it came too late. . . . By June 1991, Baker was making a last-ditch effort."[42] Follow-up efforts were not good either, as Baker and other top American officials were now concerned with the breakup of the Soviet Union. "Clearly our focus for months to come would be on managing the peaceful dissolution of the USSR," Baker would later write in explaining his inattention to the mounting Yugoslav crisis during the summer and fall of 1991.[43]

Given the focus on Iraq in early 1991, the Kurdish uprising and exodus should not have been the surprise that it was. At the same time, it is possible to see how this failure of prediction occurred. While the U.S. intelligence establishment did closely monitor developments inside Iraq during the Gulf War and immediately after the cease-fire, its resources were stretched to the limit by a number of demands. These included tracking Iraqi troop strength in and around the Kuwaiti theater of operations, assessing the damage done to Iraq's weapons of mass destruction by allied air attacks, analyzing the combined impact of economic sanctions and strategic bombing to predict overall Iraqi strength after the war, and scrutinizing the political situation in Baghdad for signs of vulnerability on the part of Saddam Hussein. Since the United States believed that the best hope for ousting Saddam was a coup by Sunni military officers, it was natural that this last task would receive greater priority than that of looking at what was happening in the Shiite and Kurdish regions of Iraq.

Diplomatic Reporting. Information about foreign countries comes to policy makers from a range of sources. The most important of these are diplomatic reports and the media. Intelligence information can be crucial in certain situations—in times of war, for example—but typically there are many more foreign service officers and journalists in a country than there are intelligence officers. Spies, in any case, have no monopoly on the best information. The likelihood that U.S. government analysts will see an ethnic conflict coming and that their predictions will be noticed by officials at the highest levels of government often depends on both the quality of diplomatic reports from the field and the quality and quantity of press coverage.

In some instances, for reasons already discussed, the U.S. diplomatic presence in a country or region is small and yields only limited information. The lack of a significant U.S. diplomatic presence in the Caucasus at the end of the cold war deprived policy makers of an important source of information. By the time the United States established well-staffed embassies in the former Soviet republics, the ethnic conflicts there were already under way. Diplomatic reporting from the republics on Russia's southern periphery has traditionally been hampered by limited familiarity with the languages and a general lack of professional interest. The end of the cold war found the State Department scrambling to find foreign service officers who could speak the main languages of a half dozen infant countries that had barely merited consulates in the past. Not since the height of decolonization had so many new states come into existence at once.

Following the breakup of the Soviet Union, there remained ethnic hot spots within the borders of Russia—Chechnya first and foremost. American diplomatic reporting on Chechnya during the several years following its attempted secession in 1991 was uneven for the same reasons that distant Soviet republics had been neglected during the late 1980s, that is, distance and unfamiliarity. "Most people who are so-called Russian experts, in fact, know nothing about the country beyond" Moscow, commented Paul Goble, a former NSC aide, during the Chechen crisis. "We have not developed a cadre of experts on Russia. We have a large number of people who are experts on Moscow and a couple of other cities."[44] More than a thousand miles from Moscow, Chechnya is way off the beaten trail for most diplomats stationed in Russia. The occasional visit or fact-finding trip is practical; sustained monitoring is less so. Goble observed that the United States would not have been surprised by the events in Chechnya if its diplomats had simply been reading the northern Caucasian press and paying attention to discussion of the Chechen issue in nearby regional capitals.

American diplomats are often either unable or unwilling to spend a lot of time in the remote regions where many conflicts begin. The 1988 massacres in Burundi grew out of rising tensions between repressive Tutsi government administrators and Hutu peasants in the north, a mountainous area that is difficult to traverse. The Kurdish areas of Turkey and Iraq are the most rugged parts of those countries. Occasionally, government restrictions make it difficult for U.S. diplomats to travel freely in regions where there is ethnic tension. At other times, rising strife makes such travel perilous. In all cases, remote regions are inconvenient places for U.S. diplomats to spend significant amounts of time, and their training may not equip them to collect information in these places.

In Nigeria, there was no shortage of U.S. diplomats in different parts of the country as the secessionist crisis began, yet there were major problems with their reporting of events. As recounted in Joseph Thompson's in-depth study of U.S. policy toward Nigeria before and during the Biafran war, the U.S. embassy in Lagos suffered from "clientele" tendencies—that is, it tended to see the situation from the perspective of the Nigerian government and to play down bad news. Thompson argues that in 1965 and 1966 embassy reports to Washington ignored evidence of Nigeria's drift and deterioration.[45] During this period, Robert Bernard, the consul general in Enugu, in the eastern region, had a different assessment; among other pessimistic judgments, he warned that Nigeria's military police force was losing its ability to control the country. The embassy in Lagos sought to suppress these reports. As a result, Bernard sent his assessments straight to Washington, and policy makers ended up with a confused picture. At the beginning of 1967, two views of Nigeria's future were being communicated to Washington: one from Lagos, which presented the unity of the country as safeguarded, and the other from Enugu, which depicted a country sinking into crisis. As secession came closer, the correctness of the Enugu view would become ever more apparent. Two weeks before the May 30 secession, for example, Bernard reported that the Biafrans were designing a national flag and composing a national anthem.

Clientele tendencies—or "clientitis"—can be a major obstacle to good reporting by diplomats in an ethnically riven country. Diplomats stationed abroad have a natural desire to ingratiate themselves with their hosts. As Henry Kissinger observes, "A Foreign Service Officer's job is always easier, or more pleasant, if he is able to produce good news for his client country."[46] Amicable relations with one's hosts can mean wide-ranging entrée into the local circles of power and a steady stream of inside information to report back to Washington. Bad relations can lead to isolation and irrelevance. To show excessive interest in the plight of an oppressed ethnic group is a sure way for diplomats to court this latter fate. Warren Zimmerman wasn't granted another meeting with Slobodan Milosevic for an entire year after he raised the issue of ethnic Albanians in Kosovo during his first talk with the Yugoslav leader.

Media. Media coverage of international affairs has always been an important source of information for U.S. policy makers, especially since the rise of CNN. Journalistic reports on ethnic tensions can be a crucial supplement to sparse diplomatic and intelligence analysis. Indeed, both the State and the Defense Departments have special offices that cull media reports from around the world and make important stories available to policy makers. At times, media reports have a better chance of reaching policy makers at the highest levels than paper produced by the foreign policy bureaucracy. A story on the front page of the *New York Times* or *Washington Post* about country X is sure to be seen by the president; an important cable or intelligence estimate about the same country may never get past the assistant secretary level.

Both the quality and quantity of media coverage of an emerging ethnic crisis can affect whether policy makers see the crisis coming and understand the dilemmas they may face. Media coverage is hampered, however, by some of the same factors that prevent good diplomatic reporting. Tiny backwater countries and remote regions of large countries receive little attention from major newspapers and television networks unless natural disasters or wars occur. If the death toll is large enough or the violence of sufficient intensity, media coverage is usually assured. But ethnic conflicts are often born out of quiet repression and slow-festering rebellions. Like diplomats, journalists tend to ignore these kinds of developments because they seem insignificant compared with other demands on their time. Under normal circumstances, no journalists from major American media outlets will be stationed in a tiny country such as Burundi or Rwanda. Instead, these places, along with a handful of other countries in the same region, will receive sporadic attention from a regional news bureau.

Like diplomats, journalists tend to be creatures of national capitals, staying close to the seats of government as well as to their offices and hotels. They may have neither the resources nor the inclination to travel frequently to out-of-the-way places. Government travel restrictions and physical dangers are other disincentives to visit areas of ethnic strife. A foreign journalist in Rangoon is more likely to stay in the national capital writing stories about prodemocracy activists than to take a long journey into the provinces to see whether the Karen separatist rebels are likely to mount a new offensive. Western news editors don't care about the Karen rebels. And even if they did, travel restrictions imposed by the Myanmar military regime might make such an expedition difficult.

All this means that policy makers are unlikely to receive much media warning of emerging ethnic conflicts in remote regions. Journalists failed to foresee the Kurdish uprising in northern Iraq after the Gulf War because they were focused on more important events that were also easier to report, and media coverage on the deterioration of ethnic relations in the Caucasus republics was nearly nonexistent until actual fighting broke out; even then it was sporadic. Rwanda received frequent mentions in the U.S. media during the 1980s and early 1990s as the country where Dian Fossey studied silver-backed gorillas. The tensions between Hutu and Tutsi, however, did not receive extensive attention until after the massacres of 1994.

Of course, many ethnic crises have been closely watched by the media, and the coverage has helped alert the policy-making world. As the most populous state in Africa, Nigeria received ample press coverage during the 1960s. The *New York Times* had a full-time reporter in Lagos and ran constant stories about the deterioration of the political situation in 1966. It reported on the two military coups and analyzed their significance for ethnic relations. It described the violence against the Ibo and the emergence of their demands for autonomy. It gave front-page coverage to the escalation of that violence in October and the mounting exodus of Ibo from northern Nigeria. Finally, it reported on the doomed efforts to negotiate an arrangement for keeping Nigeria intact. American policy makers didn't need to wade through conflicting reports from Lagos and Enugu to recognize as early as the summer of 1966 that Nigeria was careening in a very dangerous direction.

Lebanon was another crisis that received substantial attention even at a nascent stage. As the most cosmopolitan city in the Middle East, Beirut was a natural home for foreign journalists. And because most of the developments in Lebanon's slide toward civil war occurred within Beirut, it was easy for these journalists to cover the crisis. Any regular reader of the *New York Times* could see trouble coming well before Lebanon's national self-destruction began. The *Times* reported on the rise of an armed Palestinian state within Lebanon. In early 1975, it described tensions over Muslim representation in the Lebanese army and over the use of the army against Muslim fishermen. The political turbulence that directly preceded the civil war was also reported, as were the violent incidents that precipitated the war.

Intelligence. Intelligence capabilities consist of three main elements: electronic surveillance, human intelligence, and analysis. Each element has well-known limitations. Electronic surveillance in the form of overhead photography is superb for tracking military deployments but of scant use for monitoring political movements. Electronic eavesdropping is more useful in this regard, yet the problem here is often one of too much information: even with the help of powerful computers, sorting through myriad phone conversations and other communications can be a needle-in-the-haystack task that yields little of value. Human intelligence provides the best information, but it is also the hardest to get. Good spies in foreign countries are difficult to find and keep, while U.S. intelligence officers stationed abroad are often in no better a position than foreign service officers to gather information. Finally, the analysis produced by intelligence agencies can sometimes be first-rate; it can also be nearly useless. A common complaint of national-security officials has been that intelligence analysis is too often watered down and ambiguous.[47] In any case, such analysis is bound to reflect the limitations of the information that is available to analysts.

Nascent ethnic conflicts rarely attract a great deal of attention from the intelligence establishment. For the most part, intelligence agencies respond to the national-security agenda set out by the White House, the State Department, and the Pentagon. Political developments in many countries outside traditional core areas of U.S. concern are simply not at the top of that agenda. To be sure, intelligence agencies often take the initiative in providing warning of upcoming crises in obscure countries. But generally the distribution of resources in the intelligence world reflects the hierarchy of national interests. Priorities like monitoring political developments in Russia and the military activities of rogue states such as Iraq take precedence over keeping track of events in countries or regions that have little ability to threaten vital U.S. interests.

Good intelligence on ethnic tensions can be difficult to produce even with a major effort; indifference by policy makers in a given situation guarantees poor intelligence. U.S. intelligence may or may not have been able to predict the Kurdish and Shiite uprisings after the Gulf War had it committed major resources to this task. However, the insatiable demand of Washington policy makers for information about potential challenges to Saddam from within the military and Baghdad's ruling elite ensured that the attention of U.S. intelligence was focused elsewhere.

In Yugoslavia and Ukraine, the intelligence establishment made a sustained bid to predict the trajectory of ethnic tensions. In both places, U.S. interests were clearly at stake. In both places, as well, there were ample diplomatic, journalistic, and scholarly resources to draw on; these countries were by no means unfamiliar to the U.S. foreign policy establishment. As noted earlier, a national intelligence estimate correctly predicted the breakup of Yugoslavia in fall 1990.[48] In early 1992, the CIA also correctly predicted that recognition of Bosnia could trigger a wider war in the absence of efforts to stop Serb aggression.[49] Less accurate was its 1993 prediction that the Balkan war would lead inexorably to a greater Croatia, a greater Serbia, and a greater Albania. It may be, however, that such an outcome was prevented only by unforeseeable international efforts.

High-level U.S. intelligence estimated in late 1993 that Ukraine would fracture because of economic depression and conflict between Ukrainians and ethnic Russians. The eastern portion of Ukraine, heavily populated by Russians, would break away and join Russia, an unpopular move that would trigger a civil war.[50] In these predictions, the U.S. government was wrong, as were most of its allies. Ukraine's survival as a unified state was a major surprise.

DURING THE COLD WAR, U.S. policy makers paid attention to the Third World because they saw the competition with Communism as a global struggle in which every gain and loss mattered. They believed that too many setbacks on the periphery could lead to erosion of the Western position in core areas. As a result, U.S. internationalism had an activist agenda of trying to predict and head off instability in the Third World, with the United States undertaking major economic development initiatives and closely monitoring political events. That attentiveness has waned in recent years. Ethnic conflict in this or that obscure country is often seen as unconnected to U.S. policy in core areas of traditional concern. For the most part, as this chapter has shown, the United States has been surprised by ethnic conflicts not because it lacks the capacity to predict them but because either it hasn't devoted the resources to that goal or top policy makers haven't paid attention to the information that these efforts produced. Good prediction is the product of strong interest.

The case for an internationalism that puts more emphasis on the periphery rests partly on a modified version of the cumulative-threat argument of the cold war. If zones of instability expand or multiply, the well-being of the international system as a whole suffers. Regions that turn into battlefields often become dependent on aid from the developed world and cannot contribute to the growth of global prosperity. They become exporters of refugees, drugs, and terrorism. They require constant emergency attention from international organizations that should be working on long-term solutions to problems like economic inequity and environmental degradation. They become places to avoid, whatever their cultural riches or scenic beauty. More dangerously, a United States that fails to track and accurately predict the trajectory of nascent ethnic conflicts in the former Soviet Union, or India, or China may suddenly find itself facing crises that threaten vital interests.

Beyond this potential cumulative threat to the international system, there is now a lengthy record of secondary U.S. interests that have been affected by ethnic conflicts in peripheral areas and of failures of prediction that have led to missed opportunities for prevention efforts.

It has been said that an activist internationalist engagement on the periphery is out of the question, given the new isolationist mood in the United States. Because the end of the cold war has removed a global military threat to the industrial world, however, the United States should now be able to pay more attention to peripheral areas even as it downsizes its national-security establishment. Assuming a reasonable degree of high-level leadership, the main obstacle to better prediction of ethnic conflict is not a lack of resources or of public support but the need to retarget existing resources and learn to pay attention to an unfamiliar cacophony of warning signals.

CHAPTER THREE

Prevention

A CAPACITY TO PREDICT ethnic conflicts is of little use if it cannot be harnessed to policies of prevention. This is no easy task. Even when U.S. attention is fully engaged, which is rare, there is often not much hope of altering the trajectory of an escalating ethnic conflict. The United States may have more power than any other country in the world, but it is no miracle worker; in most situations its leverage ranges from limited to nonexistent. Because ethnic conflicts tend to erupt outside traditional spheres of U.S. interests, there are often few existing levers for influencing the actors involved. Typically, there are no large aid packages to suspend or major trading arrangements to reconsider. And frequently those levers of influence that do exist are inadequate, given the intensity of the passions on all sides. Ethnic groups in conflict tend to fear for their very survival; foreign threats to withhold aid or trade may matter little in the face of such stakes. Outside coercion, moreover, works best with state leaders; it is less likely to affect the calculations of substate extremists.

To acknowledge the limits of policies to prevent ethnic conflict is not to deny their virtues. The modest instruments available to the United States for preventing ethnic conflict have shown some worth in the past and could be used more systematically in the future. Crafting a systematic approach requires understanding the historical record of U.S. efforts at prevention. That record is mostly one of failures, for different reasons. The halfheartedness of U.S. policy has not infrequently compounded the difficulties inherent in attempting to influence the actors in ethnic conflicts. Often efforts to head off ethnic conflicts have come too late because of neglect and poor prediction, have lacked for political and financial resources, have been inconsistent or abortive, or have suffered from poor coordination with allies, international governmental organizations (IGOs), and nongovernmental organizations (NGOs). Occasionally, having sanctioned the use of violence—either implicitly or explicitly—by a state intent on resolving an ethnic dispute, the United States has seen the situation escalate out of control.

It is difficult to know when U.S. efforts might have been decisive had they simply been more sustained or better orchestrated. While some of Washington's missteps have clearly been idiotic, other bad decisions are harder to fault. In many cases it is impossible to imagine any actions that could have stopped a country's descent into communal warfare.

The U.S. record of success, sparser by far, is also not easy to assess. When an ethnically divided country pulls back from the brink of disaster, U.S. preventive efforts may be just one of many factors responsible. In Kosovo, Ukraine, and the Baltic states, U.S. policy makers devoted considerable energies to preventing violence. Yet there were other outside actors working toward the same goal, and many factors beyond international intervention affected the outcome of these situations.

Isolating the precise effects of U.S. policy is not a prerequisite for drawing broad conclusions about what works in the preventive realm. Past experience suggests the efficacy of a variety of measures. These can be roughly divided between long-range strategies and short-term actions. Long-range strategies use U.S. influence to foster an atmosphere of tolerance in countries that are at risk for ethnic conflict. These involve using both carrots and sticks to make clear to state leaders that repression of ethnic minorities is not in their interest. Economic and military aid, along with participation in global financial institutions and regional security arrangements, may be made contingent on meeting human-rights standards laid out in international covenants. The United States and its allies may press for custom-tailored goals, such as doing away with rigid citizenship requirements, increasing representation of an ethnic minority in a country's military or civil service, or eliminating discriminatory practices in education. Steps such as these are aimed at preventing the deterioration in ethnic relations that can lead to violence.

Short term actions are those taken when violence looks probable or even imminent. These include an escalation of threats and promises to state leaders regarding aid and trade. Partial penalties may be imposed, with assurances of more to come if extremist behavior goes unchanged; moderate behavior may be swiftly rewarded. Preventive diplomacy and mediation efforts, optimally in collaboration with NGOs and IGOs, are centrally important. Very occasionally, as in Kosovo, U.S. leaders may threaten military intervention.

As with prediction, the level of attention that policy makers give to prevention is largely determined by the national interests at stake in a crisis. The greater the wants, the greater the attention. Crises that threaten to destabilize a region, trigger a humanitarian calamity, and destroy a multiethnic democracy will receive the most attention and resources. Crises that promise more limited consequences will receive less. Policy makers may, however, give special attention to a situation regardless of the interests at stake if there is a good chance for easy and successful preventive actions or if the United States has strong historical ties with the country where a crisis is brewing.

The preventive instruments available are highly imperfect. Even when deployed with maximum resolve they cannot guarantee success. But an examination of the historical record of efforts to prevent ethnic conflict, now quite extensive, suggests how, when, and where different types of preventive actions are likely to yield results.

FAILURES

Convicting policy makers of incompetence is an easy task for retrospective jurors. The misdemeanors of shortsightedness and neglect seem as easy to identify as the felonies of official hubris and ideological excess. The trail of evidence in major foreign policy debacles can appear to support nothing but the most incriminating interpretation of events. But like failures to predict ethnic conflict, failures to prevent them often stem from a variety of causes and it can be difficult to pinpoint exactly where or why errors were made. Neglect may combine with a lack of quality information; shortsightedness may combine with distractions elsewhere in the policy arena; and realpolitik decisions to stay out of another country's business may seem justified at the time. The inherent intractability of a crisis, a lack of leverage, or an ill-conceived mediation strategy can all sabotage concerted efforts at prevention. Plain bad luck can be a factor as well.

Looking chronologically at the major ethnic conflicts that have confronted the United States over the past thirty years, one can readily see that there were some situations that the United States was essentially powerless to stop, despite efforts to do so, and some situations where better preventive efforts might have made a difference.

NIGERIA
Although U.S. policy makers watched Nigeria closely after independence, poor diplomatic reporting made them slow to recognize the gravity of Nigeria's internal crisis. Reports from the U.S. embassy ignored evidence of the country's drift and deterioration.[1] Had Washington been receiving a unified picture of impending

trouble, it might have moved forward earlier—in mid-1966, when the first anti-Ibo riots were occurring—with vigorous preventive efforts.

By August 1966, as large numbers of Ibo fled from the northern region, there was growing recognition in Washington of the country's instability. A coup in July by Lieutenant Colonel Yakub Gowan was widely seen as having destroyed the Nigerian army as a unifying force. Previously, Ibo had made up more than a third of its officers and a quarter of its troops, but after the coup they were purged from the army and numerous Ibo officers were slain.[2] Many diplomats in Lagos believed that the dissolution of Nigeria was possible in the near future; not since the Zaire crisis had there been such concern about a development in Africa.[3] In late October, the eastern region threatened to secede.

The United States did not engage in any high-level, high-visibility efforts to mediate the situation. In part, this was because the Johnson administration regarded Nigeria as outside the U.S. sphere of interest and felt that Great Britain should take the lead in dealing with its problems.[4] But it was also due to complacency in the State Department. Early in 1967, Assistant Secretary of State Joseph Palmer and Robert Smith, a top Africa official, continued to side with the optimistic view coming out of the Lagos embassy that Nigeria's crisis was manageable.

The United States did support the convening of a conference to discuss the constitutional future of Nigeria. Generally, as the crisis worsened and secession approached, the United States stepped up efforts to promote negotiation between the Nigerian government and leaders of the eastern region. But their success was limited. In April 1967, officials in the State Department held a brainstorming session but failed to come up with any ways to force negotiations between the government and the secessionists.[5]

Before secession was announced in May 1967, the United States explicitly warned the eastern leaders that it would not support an independent state or grant it diplomatic recognition. And when the Nigerian government imposed a travel ban on the eastern region in retaliation for its moves toward secession, the United States told the eastern leaders that it would abide by that ban unless they negotiated an end to the crisis with the Nigerian government. In effect, this meant a cutoff of U.S. aid.[6]

When the eastern region formally announced its secession from Nigeria on May 30, calling itself Biafra, the United States made good on its threats to withhold recognition and refused to say whether it planned ever to grant it. At the same time, however, the United States maintained counsular representation in Enugu.[7] The apparent U.S. strategy for preventing war in Nigeria was to give the Biafrans absolutely no encouragement and hope that their secessionist bid failed. This strategy reflected wide concerns about the future stability of Africa. As Assistant Secretary Joseph Palmer explained to a congressional committee in 1968, "There are great dangers if the principle of self-determination is carried to its logical conclusion. Instead of having 40 countries in Africa, that number could be greatly augmented beyond the 40. . . . You have to ask yourself where it is all going to end if anybody who wants to break away can do so on the basis of a perfectly free choice. . . . I think there are other countries where there are very severe tribal strains."[8]

Through the month of June 1967, a precarious peace prevailed in Nigeria as Lagos prepared for a military campaign to crush Biafra. Leaders of some African states sought to mediate the dispute, to no avail; the embassy in Lagos concentrated on the task of evacuating all U.S. dependents from Biafra. While the United States had, from the beginning, taken the position that Biafra's secession was a bad thing, it also stressed its neutrality in the conflict and gave little open support to Nigeria. After the war had begun, President Johnson would say that "the political dispute underlying this war is a Nigerian and an African problem—not an American one."[9] This mantra would be repeated by other U.S. officials. As Palmer told Congress, "I think it's primarily up to the countries in the area concerned to bring about the solution to this problem in an African and Nigerian context."[10] A State Department spokesman affirmed that the United States "regards the breakaway movement as an internal conflict which in the last analysis only the parties themselves can resolve."[11] On July 10, 1967, three days after the Nigerian government launched its invasion of Biafra, Secretary of State Dean Rusk announced that the United States would not honor past arms contracts with Lagos and would not ship arms to either combatant.[12] U.S. neutrality was not simply a matter of rhetoric.

The view that the Biafran crisis was an African problem or a problem within Britain's sphere of interest was a major reason for the paucity of U.S. preventive efforts during the half year preceding secession and during the opening phase of the war, when escalation might still have been contained. In addition, U.S. officials were deeply preoccupied with crises elsewhere in the world. Nevertheless, it is far from clear what more the United States could have done. Its leverage in both the Nigerian government and among the eastern secessionists was limited. American aid to Nigeria was not vast and the United States did not have deep historical ties to the Lagos government. Overall, there was a sense in Washington that the Biafran issue was both peripheral and unsolvable and that it shouldn't be a priority.

Had U.S. officials foreseen the full dimensions of the coming humanitarian disaster and the huge resultant pressures to alleviate it, they certainly would have made a greater effort. The Biafra calamity would produce the first televised images of famine in history. It would demonstrate, as never before, the power of the media to galvanize U.S. opinion on a humanitarian issue. In the 1990s, that power—the so-called CNN effect—would emerge as a central factor in U.S. foreign policy decision making. But in 1967 policy makers foresaw none of this.

EAST PAKISTAN

The East Pakistani grievances that led to secession were no great mystery to U.S. policy makers and other international observers during the 1960s. The Bengalis were economically and politically marginalized by the Punjabi-dominated government in West Pakistan. The separation of East and West Pakistan by a thousand miles of Indian territory made secession by the eastern sector eminently plausible. A farsighted U.S. policy might have experimented with making aid to Pakistan contingent on efforts to address the issues of exploitation and discrimination that fueled secessionist ambitions in East Pakistan. At the least, U.S. diplomats could have expressed concern about these issues. And, as the secessionist crisis began to escalate, the United States could have placed pressure on the Pakistani government to show restraint. American officials did none of these things, however—even in March 1971 as Pakistan was poised to make its fateful decision to try to hold on to East Pakistan by force.

President Nixon had a special fondness for Pakistan because he was received with respect there when he was out of office in the 1960s. He also felt he could communicate well with the military chiefs who ruled the country. Nixon and Kissinger cultivated Pakistan and its president, Yahya Khan, as a channel for communicating with Communist China.[13] They were profoundly grateful to Pakistan for playing a pivotal role in advancing one of their most important diplomatic objectives.[14] In the summer of 1970, Nixon rewarded Pakistan by approving an arms package worth $40 to $50 million. In October, Nixon assured Yahya Khan in Washington that "nobody has occupied the White House who is friendlier to Pakistan than me."[15]

In early 1971, as the crisis escalated, the Nixon administration clearly understood that a war was possible if not probable. Indeed, Kissinger himself predicted a secessionist bid. American policy makers also understood that an attempt by Pakistan to hold on to East Pakistan by force would be unsuccessful. At a meeting of the Senior Review Group of the National Security Council, convened on March 6, U. Alexis Johnson, an official in the State Department, expressed the prevailing view of his department that the United States should discourage Yahya from using force against the secessionist Awami League. But Kissinger, affirming Nixon's reluctance to jeopardize the United States' "special" relationship with Pakistan, went on to raise doubts that any warning from the U.S. ambassador in Islamabad, Joseph Farland, would have much impact.[16]

As it had with Biafra, the United States adopted an official position of neutrality. And as with Biafra, a stance that was neutral in theory tilted toward the central government in Islamabad in practice. In his memoirs Kissinger justifies this approach in three ways. First, both he and Nixon believed that the United States could not be seen as aiding the breakup of Pakistan: "If Pakistan broke up, it should be the result of its internal dynamics, not of American pressures. All agencies agreed that the United States should not get involved."[17] Second, the United States "had few means to affect the situation." And third, the United States had "every incentive to maintain Pakistan's goodwill. It was our crucial link to Peking; and Pakistan was one of China's closest allies."[18]

President Yahya's brutal crackdown on the Awami League in East Pakistan on March 25 resulted in hundreds of thousands of deaths and led to an internationalized war with India. It is impossible to say whether U.S. pressure on Yahya could have averted this disaster. What is clear is that the United States did not exert its full influence because of its realpolitik agenda of opening China and because of its desire to avoid giving any impression of supporting the breakup of an existing state. Kissinger would later say, "Nixon and I wanted to found American foreign policy on a sober perception of permanent national interest, rather than on fluctuating emotions that in the past had led us to excesses of both intervention and abdication."[19] This policy was a miscalculation, and it was one that would be repeated in the future.

BURUNDI: 1972 AND 1988

Because there have never been important U.S. interests at stake in Burundi, policy makers have tended largely to ignore both Burundi and Rwanda. It is no surprise that the United States failed to prevent the massacres that swept Burundi in 1972 and 1988 since it made no real effort to do so. Nevertheless, it would be wrong to see U.S. policy in Burundi as entirely a case of failure due to neglect—policy makers also made significant errors of judgment.

The central American errors prior to 1972 were to underestimate the extremist tendencies of President Micombero and not to

signal clearly to his regime that the United States would not tolerate repression of Burundi's Hutu population. Micombero made
his intentions evident from the first days of his rule. When he
seized power in 1965 there were widespread killings of Hutu. Occasional purges and anti-Hutu violence followed throughout the
rest of the decade. From 1969 to 1972, there was growing antagonism between Hutu and Tutsi.[20] The U.S. ambassador to Burundi, Thomas Patrick Melady, was a scholarly diplomat and
thoughtful student of Africa. He arrived in Burundi believing that
Micombero was "a moderate."[21] He recognized the growing alien-
ation of the Hutu population but wrote later that he "had under-
estimated how deeply rooted it was."[22]

One essential element of a preventive strategy is to put state
leaders on notice that they are being watched by the United States
and the international community and that repressive actions will
trigger punishment. A leader with Micombero's record of anti-
Hutu violence would have been a prime candidate to receive such
a warning. And while it is true that the United States historically
had limited influence with the Burundi government, it did have
potential leverage through its trading relationship. In 1972, U.S.
importers bought 80 percent of Burundi's coffee export, accounting for 65 percent of its foreign-exchange earnings.[23] When the
massacres began in Burundi, U.S. policy makers believed that punishing the government through a coffee boycott would do nothing
to change the situation.[24] This assessment was probably correct,
given the frenzied pace of the mass killing. The leverage from this
trading relationship might, however, have had some impact on Micombero if the United States had linked trade to human-rights
performance earlier in his regime and if he had therefore anticipated economic retaliation for new anti-Hutu violence in 1972.

To be effective, a strategy of deterrence must threaten negative
consequences that outweigh any positive gain an aggressor might
reap from an action. Inasmuch as many ethnic extremists already
see their very survival as at stake, it is frequently impossible for
outside actors to threaten consequences that are severe enough to
affect their calculations. Yet one thing is certain: a total absence of

effort to deter genocidal violence is guaranteed to have zero impact. Some effort is always better than none.

During the 1980s, the United States did attempt a preventive strategy toward Burundi that linked economic aid to human-rights performance. Policy makers failed in this instance because they overestimated the Burundi government's progress in ending anti-Hutu discrimination and failed to see the high potential for another wave of violence. In effect, poor prediction yielded lax prevention.

American aid to Burundi had fallen to $1.8 million a year by 1987, when strongman Jean-Baptiste Bagaza was overthrown by Pierre Buyoya.[25] To U.S. policy makers, the regime of President Buyoya seemed a major change for the better. After deposing Bagaza, Buyoya gave a speech in which he called for ethnic reconciliation and condemned violence. He released political prisoners and increased the number of Hutu in his government. Buyoya also cooperated with the World Bank and the International Monetary Fund to solve Burundi's significant economic problems.[26] "From the perspective of U.S. interests, particularly humanitarian, the Buyoya government has represented a distinct improvement over the previous regime and therefore has merited our support," commented Kenneth Brown, deputy assistant secretary of state for African affairs, in the wake of massacres in 1988.[27] Consistent with a carrot-and-stick preventive strategy, the United States rewarded Buyoya. In 1988, the Agency for International Development (AID) increased aid to $5.2 million.[28]

But U.S. officials were too optimistic about Buyoya's government. Despite his stated intentions, Buyoya made very little progress in addressing the structural discrimination against the Hutu population, discrimination that denied Hutu fair representation in all aspects of Burundian life. Buyoya also could not control the hard-line Tutsi extremists within his government led by Major Bernard Cishahyo. (It was Cishahyo's internal-security forces that were chiefly responsible for the massacres of August 1988.)

Had U.S. policy makers been more realistic about Buyoya's limitations and had they better understood the instability of Burundi's internal situation, they might have withheld aid. They might have pursued a more ambitious strategy of linkage, pushing Buyoya harder to address anti-Hutu discrimination and to remove hardline elements from his government. Again, there is no guarantee that this strategy would have prevented the mass bloodletting. Indeed, it could have backfired, undermining Buyoya's rule and allowing Tutsi extremists to take full control of Burundi's government and perpetrate even greater violence. Following the massacres, U.S. officials argued against any punishment of Buyoya's government. "We feel that this is a man who has the right intentions, is on the right track, and needs to be supported, needs to be strengthened," Deputy Assistant Secretary Brown told a congressional committee in September 1988.[29]

YUGOSLAVIA

Throughout the early 1990s, critics excoriated U.S. policy toward the former Yugoslavia, charging that better choices could have prevented the outbreak of a disastrous war and ended it quickly once it was under way. There is little question that, as the former Yugoslavia imploded, the United States pursued a preventive strategy that was an abysmal failure. Assessing blame is not as easy, however, as some commentators would suggest. Policy makers in the Bush administration clearly made mistakes, but it is far from clear that other choices would have yielded better results. The most commonly cited mistakes are relying on the Europeans to handle the crisis during its early phase, insisting on the unity of Yugoslavia and therefore perhaps giving tacit support to Serb aggression, and failing to use military force early on to demonstrate Western resolve. On each of these points, U.S. policy choices had a strong basis in logic even if they are questionable in hindsight.

The United States looked to its European allies to take the lead for several reasons. First, as the cold war ended, there was interest on both sides of the Atlantic in having Western Europe play a larger role in managing its own security affairs—as long as that role did not jeopardize America's fundamental leadership of the Western alliance or the perpetuation of NATO as the vehicle of that leadership. Attention was given to resuscitating the Western

European Union (WEU), the security arm of the European Community, and there was much discussion of having the Conference
for Security and Cooperation in Europe (CSCE)—later renamed
the Organization for Security and Cooperation in Europe
(OSCE)—play a larger role in continental security matters. Because it involved no threats to core U.S. security interests, the
Yugoslav crisis seemed a good opportunity to experiment with the
concept of a European Community that was more self-reliant in
the security realm. There was a sense in Washington, as Secretary
of State James Baker later recalled, that "it was time to make the
Europeans step up to the plate and show that they could act as a
unified power. Yugoslavia was as good a first step as any. . . . The
conflict seemed to be one the EC could manage."[30] Europe also
appeared to be both more invested in the outcome of the crisis
and more able to affect its outcome. "Why are we supporting the
EC's efforts, rather than taking the lead ourselves?" asked Deputy
Assistant Secretary of State Ralph Johnson in October 1991. "In
the first place, because we believe that Europe has the most at stake
in this crisis, and because European leverage—economic as well as
political—is, in general, greater than ours." Johnson cited Europe's
larger trade and investment ties with Yugoslavia as well as Yugoslavia's association agreement with the EC.[31]

    As the crisis began, European leaders professed a readiness to
handle it on their own. Beyond believing this role appropriate, U.S.
policy makers accepted European leadership in the Balkans because
the United States was in the middle of dealing with the Persian
Gulf crisis and had limited energy available for other matters. Later
in 1991, officials would be preoccupied with the disintegration of
the USSR.

    Policy makers who served in the Bush administration later ac-
knowledged that letting Europe take the lead was a mistake, though
an understandable one. "I agreed with the policy at the time; there
were a host of reasons," said Lawrence Eagleburger, who served
as deputy secretary of state. "I think the view was that it was a
European problem, so let's let the Europeans deal with it."[32] Brent
Scowcroft, Bush's national security adviser, made a similar point:

"The Europeans were saying, 'Hey, this is our problem, let us handle it,' and we were only too happy to let them do so. As Jim Baker said at the time, we didn't have a dog in this fight."[33]

The ideal of greater European self-reliance in security matters was and is an attractive concept, especially to those who believe that in the wake of the cold war the United States should shed its reflexive paternalistic tendencies and reduce its expensive military establishment. If the United States wants to escape the role of global policeman, it must eventually devolve some of the security responsibilities it now carries; the Yugoslav crisis was an early attempt at doing just that. The mistake was not in embracing this ideal but rather in taking it too far too fast. It was naive to imagine that the Europeans were ready to handle a major security challenge on their own after so many years of taking their cue from Washington. Moreover, the main institutional framework for Western Europe's security coordination, the WEU, was an amorphous organization of untested effectiveness in the early 1990s. The CSCE, with fifty-odd members and limited powers, was even less useful for addressing a crisis like the one in Yugoslavia. NATO was the only institution in Europe capable of organizing a decisive Western response, and the use of this body required the leadership, or at least the active participation, of the United States. "This was an eminently European affair, so Europe should have taken care of it; but Europe is immobilized psychologically and is dependent on the United States," commented the Bosnian foreign minister, Haris Silajdzic, in early 1993.[34]

Collective-security organizations and multilateral arrangements are vital instruments for preventing ethnic conflict, yet they can also be used as cover by Washington to escape direct involvement in a crisis and to pass the buck. In the Nigerian and Burundian crises, for example, policy makers emphasized at times that a lead role in resolving the situations properly lay with the Organization of African Unity (OAU). Yet as informed observers knew, the OAU was highly unlikely to have any impact on those situations. One moral of the Yugoslavia story is that in the absence of mature regional-security organizations with a proven track record, the United States must take the lead in engineering preventive policies.

As discussed earlier, the United States has occasionally exacerbated ethnic crises by sanctioning a state's use of military force to suppress a secessionist movement. This charge is made in regard to Yugoslavia by critics who claim that Washington's emphasis on a unified country gave the Serbs a green light to use military force against the seceding states. These claims are greatly exaggerated. The United States never embraced the vision of a Yugoslavia bound together by the toxic glue of Serb nationalism and military power. Policy makers did, however, prefer a democratic and reformist Yugoslavia that remained unified over a Yugoslavia that fractured along nationalist lines, with all the potentially negative ramifications that such an event might entail. A policy statement issued by the State Department in May 1991 presciently stated: "We believe that the ethnic heterogeneity of most Yugoslav republics means that any dissolution of Yugoslavia is likely to exacerbate rather than resolve ethnic tensions."[35] At the same time, policy makers emphasized that, if Yugoslavia did break up, such a process should occur in a democratic and peaceful manner.

When Baker visited Belgrade on June 21, 1991, he stressed these points to the Yugoslav leaders with whom he met. As Warren Zimmerman recalls, "Baker told Croatian President Franjo Tudjman and Slovene President Milan Kucan that the United States would not encourage or support unilateral secession; he hoped they would not secede, but if they had to leave, he urged them to leave by negotiated agreement. He argued that self-determination cannot be unilateral but must be pursued by dialogue and peaceful means. To Milosevic and (indirectly) the army, Baker made clear that the United States strongly opposed any use of force, intimidation, or incitement to violence that would block democratic change. Yugoslavia could not be held together by gunpoint."[36] Baker also criticized Milosevic for human-rights abuses in Kosovo and urged his acceptance of a looser constitutional arrangement in Yugoslavia. As Baker wrote later, "I warned that if force were used, it would lead to ostracism by the international community. . . . Serbia [would] become an international outcast within Europe for a generation or more."[37]

Baker would leave his marathon series of meetings in Belgrade believing that he had had no impact whatsoever. He would later describe this episode as one of the most frustrating during his years as secretary of state. After the meetings, Baker wrote to President Bush, "My gut feeling is that we won't produce a serious dialogue on the future of Yugoslavia until all parties have a greater sense of urgency and danger. We may not be able to impart that from the outside, but we and others should continue to push."[38] Baker did not suggest that the U.S. strategy should include encouraging the use of force to hold Yugoslavia together. As Zimmerman wrote of the secretary's trip to Belgrade: "Never was a green light given or implied to Milosevic or the army to invade the seceding republics."[39]

American policy makers may have been unrealistic to imagine, as late as mid-1991, that Yugoslavia could remain unified. Their desire for unity, however, was understandable, given the consensus among both diplomats and intelligence officials that any breakup would trigger violence. Seeking a democratic and loosely confederated Yugoslavia was probably the best preventive strategy available to the United States. The failure of U.S. policy was not, therefore, in its intent but rather in its halfhearted implementation. Baker's visit to Belgrade came too late, and through the rest of 1991 the United States did not use its full influence to discourage Serb violence and promote peaceful dialogue between the Yugoslav republics. Top Bush administration officials like Scowcroft and Eagleburger acknowledge in retrospect that a sustained diplomatic effort could have made a decisive difference during this period.[40]

The U.S. unwillingness to support the use of Western military power in the face of early Serb aggression may also have been a mistake, but again one that is far clearer now than it was then. If ever there was a time to send the Serbs a message that aggression would not be tolerated, it was when they began shelling the city of Vukovar in August 1991 and Dubrovnik in October. These indiscriminate attacks on civilian populations were blatant war crimes. NATO's supreme commander, General John Galvin, prepared contingency plans for using allied forces against the Serbs assaulting Dubrovnik. As Zimmerman recalled, "The JNA's artillery on the hills surrounding Dubrovnik and its small craft on the water would have been easy targets. Not only would damage to the city have been averted, but the Serbs would have been taught a lesson about Western resolve that might have deterred at least some of their aggression against Bosnia. As it was, the Serbs learned another lesson—that there was no Western resolve, and that they could push about as far as their power could take them."[41]

Zimmerman acknowledges, however, that he himself did not advocate the use of NATO military power in late 1991. Nor was there much other real discussion of this option in Western policy circles. Within the American military there was particular hesitancy about using limited force as part of a strategy of preventive action. The so-called Powell doctrine—based on the lessons of Vietnam and, more recently, Lebanon—held that force should be used only when it could be applied decisively with a near guarantee of success. This was not the situation in the Balkans in 1991 or in the four years of violence that followed. A central lesson from the Yugoslav episode is that the clear-cut standards of the Powell doctrine are incompatible with the demands of preventive action, at least as applied to ethnic conflicts.

TURKISH KURDISTAN

In March 1995, thirty-five thousand Turkish troops invaded northern Iraq to destroy Kurdish rebel forces that had been at war with the Turkish central government since 1984. The invasion was undertaken with the blessing of the Clinton administration yet was widely condemned by both the U.S. Congress and the fifteen-member European Union. While Turkish forces did destroy many Kurdish guerrillas, they also exacted a high death toll among Kurdish civilians and achieved no permanent solution to the eleven-year-old conflict.

In most ethnic conflicts, the U.S. government has found itself with minimal leverage over the warring parties. Turkey, however, is a country with which the United States has long had close diplomatic relations and to which it has supplied foreign aid. More than nearly any other ethnic conflict on the globe, the Turkish-Kurdish war has been one whose course the United States has had the potential—in theory, at least—to influence. Nevertheless, Washington did little as the war escalated over a decade. The failure of U.S. policy was characterized by a near-total lack of any strategy of prevention. Instead of applying pressure on Turkey to deal with its Kurdish problem after the civil war began in 1984, the United States adopted a stance of noninterference and did little as the situation worsened. By 1994, a debt-ridden Turkey was spending an estimated $7 billion a year on the war and compiling a human-rights record that horrified the European Community that Ankara sought to join.[42] Washington's policy of paying minimal attention to Turkey's war on the Kurds was motivated by a realpolitik agenda of seeking to maintain good ties with a key ally. Yet in the long run, U.S. interests would have been better served if Turkey had been pushed to come to terms with the Kurds and strive for a workable multiethnic democracy.

The Kurds account for some twelve million people out of a total Turkish population of sixty-five million. Historically, there has not been a mass movement among the Turkish Kurds to create their own state, and even after the brutal crackdown of the 1990s, surveys indicated that most Kurds wanted to remain part of Turkey.[43] In addition, during the mid-1980s, the main Kurdish insurgent organization, the Kurdish Workers Party (PKK), commanded minimal popular support. Indeed, the PKK alienated many Kurds by waging war against Kurdish moderates who opposed its agenda. Yet between 1984 and 1994, the PKK's ranks swelled to twenty thousand armed guerrillas as Turkey's Kurdish population became increasingly radicalized.[44]

This radicalization was the product of a campaign of repression subsidized by U.S. tax dollars. In response to the PKK's attacks in the 1980s, Ankara moved a quarter million troops into its southeastern region and used force indiscriminately against the Kurdish civilian population, destroying Kurdish towns, relocating hundreds of thousands of Kurds, and practicing torture on a wide scale. In 1991, the government enacted an antiterrorism law that made it a major crime to speak against the unity of the Turkish state. Kurdish newspapers were censored and closed, and many Kurdish intellectuals and writers jailed. The State Department's own human-rights reports documented in detail the horrendous treatment of the Kurds.[45]

A U.S. policy aimed at preventing an escalation of this war would have linked military aid—nearly a half billion dollars' worth annually during the late 1980s and early 1990s—to Turkey's human-rights performance, particularly to elimination of legal discrimination against the Kurdish population.[46] The United States should have told Ankara that it was free to wage a military campaign against the Kurdish guerrillas with U.S.-supplied arms but that this military effort could not involve indiscriminate attacks on civilians and, most important, that it had to be accompanied by a political strategy for addressing Kurdish grievances. Turkey should have been pressured to remove restrictions on the use of the Kurdish language and to grant cultural rights in regard to the education of Kurdish children. American diplomats should have been willing to play a mediating role, promoting dialogue between the Turkish government and Kurdish moderates and suggesting timetables for progress toward settling their disputes. The United States should have coordinated this effort with its European allies, making clear to Turkey that the Western democracies spoke with a unified voice and that Turkey's future participation in this community hinged in part on its treatment of the Kurds.

American policy makers generally resisted prodding Turkey on human rights as the Kurdish war escalated. The Bush administration said little and the Clinton administration only occasionally raised protests. Assistant Secretary of State Stephen Oxman commented in 1993, "We have told the Turks that there must be a political solution to the Kurdish problem, but we should remember that they face a real need to combat PKK terrorism."[47] Asked about reports that U.S.-made arms were being used against Kurdish ci-

vilians by Turkish forces, Oxman acknowledged that he didn't
know what was happening. The minimal expectation that U.S.
weapons not be used to kill innocent people was evidently never
one that Oxman had stressed to Turkish officials or instructed others to stress. Under questioning from members of Congress, Oxman didn't even know what the law stipulated about how U.S. arms
could be used in Turkey.[48] In a 1994 meeting with Senator Dennis
DeConcini, a Turkish foreign ministry official complained of getting mixed signals from the United States. He said that Clinton
administration officials didn't stress human-rights issues in their
meetings with the Turks, while members of Congress were always
linking aid to human-rights performance.[49] In late 1994, as Turkish
troops unleashed a reign of terror in Kurdish areas of the country,
Clinton officials finally stepped up their protests, warning Turkey
that its human-rights record was jeopardizing good ties with the
United States. John Shattuck, assistant secretary of state for human
rights, publicly voiced concern in December about Turkey's crackdown on rights, and the State Department's spokesman, Michael
McCurry, also made critical statements.[50]

It is difficult to know whether pressuring Turkey on the Kurdish
issue would have worked. If such a strategy had been pursued too
vigorously, Turkey's government might well have responded an-
tagonistically, producing a rift in relations between Ankara and
Washington. Yet such pressure might have been productive, allowing the more democratic elements in Turkey's government to justify liberalizing policies in the face of hard-line opposition. The
outcry of the European democracies and the threats by Congress
to withhold aid may account for the more conciliatory tone on
human rights that Prime Minister Tansu Ciller finally began to
take in mid-1995.

The United States always runs the risk of harming relations with
a state when it objects to repression of ethnic minorities. In the
long run, however, U.S. interests are better served by consistent
policies that hold all states to the same standards. For many countries, the only path toward lasting stability lies in the success of a
multiethnic democracy. The United States weakens its credibility

when it champions this ideal in some instances and dismisses it in others. Increasingly, one of the most important roles that the United States plays in world politics is that of mediator; no great power is more trusted to develop fair solutions to difficult conflicts. American officials must constantly watch that they do not tarnish this reputation for evenhandedness through preferential treatment of repressive nationalists.

CHECHNYA

Like many other of the international crises of the 1990s, Russia's disastrous war against Chechen secessionists caught Washington unprepared. Policy makers were not surprised by Russia's move against the Chechens in December 1994, but they were shocked —and then appalled—by the level of violence that accompanied it. Initially, the Russian operation in Chechnya was viewed by U.S. officials as a legitimate effort to maintain Russia's integrity. But soon the war had turned into a human-rights nightmare that damaged Russia's relationship with the West and prompted deep misgivings in the U.S. Congress over assistance for Russia.

Between November 1991, when Chechnya declared its independence, and December 1994, the United States had no active strategy for preventing a war between Russia and the secessionists. There were several reasons. First, the United States paid minimal attention to Russian actions in the Caucasus during the early 1990s and tended to view the area as a Russian sphere of interest. Second, to the degree that the United States did involve itself in the region, it focused on ongoing disputes in Georgia and Azerbaijan. Third, because the United States had no principled objection to the use of military force against Chechen secessionists, it made scant effort to halt it on the eve of the invasion or in the early phases of the war. American officials no doubt would have acted if they had understood the depth of resistance that Russian forces would encounter and grasped the tragedy that was about to unfold. The Chechen episode is another example of how a realpolitik policy of U.S. noninterference combined with inattentiveness to produce a disaster.

The willingness of the United States to allow Russia to play a dominant role in the Caucasus is understandable. In a region threatened by anarchy since the end of the cold war, Russia is a stabilizing influence—even if its motives and tactics are often questionable. It has the military power and economic clout to affect the course of conflicts in the former Soviet republics. As a reformist power under Boris Yeltsin, it has exerted a largely positive influence.[51] Russia is also the only power that is willing to play a stabilizing role in the Caucasus, an area that neither the United States nor the Western European countries regard as central to their worldview. In any case, the United States and its allies were busy with other crises in the early 1990s: Haiti, Bosnia, Somalia. With none of the three leading members of the Security Council interested in committing peacekeeping forces to the region, the United Nations played a minimal role. Overall, the message that Moscow received from the West was that it could deal with the region as it saw fit, so long as it avoided imperial excesses. On occasion the United States chastised Yeltsin's government, but generally its tone was supportive.

To be sure, the United States was willing to spend only limited diplomatic capital in the Caucasus. Policy makers focused some attention on Georgia, attempting to bolster the pro-Western government of President Eduard Shevardnadze, which was engaged in conflicts in Abkhazia and Southern Ossetia. They worried about the war in Tajikistan, which had killed thousands and had the potential to foster lasting instability beyond that country's borders. In addition, the United States played a role, in conjunction with the OSCE, in seeking to mediate the dispute between Armenia and Azerbaijan over Nagorno-Karabakh.

In comparison with these conflicts, the Chechnya problem seemed minor. Russia had imposed sanctions on the secessionist government of Major General Dzhokar Dudayev but had not attempted any military action to crush that regime. Instead, it pursued a dual-track policy of supporting Dudayev's armed opposition and seeking to negotiate an end to the crisis. Many Russians felt

that Russia should not get involved in the confused situation in
Chechnya.

While the Russian government pursued restrained policies
within Chechnya, it took steps in Moscow that aggravated the secessionist crisis. In October 1993, authorities undertook a repressive campaign against Caucasians living there, including many
Chechens. Thousands were expelled from the capital city or de-
tained. Chechens returned to their homeland with stories of doors
kicked in during the night and of manhandling by Russian police.
The Clinton administration's response was muted. Assistant Secretary of State John Shattuck raised the issue with the Russian
foreign ministry and there were other quiet expressions of U.S.
concern. But no high-level Clinton officials issued public protests.[52]
Their silence may have sent a dangerous signal, as Paul Goble, a
former National Security Council aide argues: "I believe that one
of the reasons that Chechnya was targeted was because there was
an assumption Moscow could get away with it on the basis of the
West's failure to do anything in October 1993."[53]

Still, through much of 1994 it was far from obvious that an
explosion was imminent. On August 11, 1994, President Yeltsin
himself told journalists: "Intervention by force is impermissible and
this must not be done. . . . This would rouse the whole Caucasus,
there would be such a commotion, and there would be so much
blood that nobody would ever forgive us."[54] Prophetic words indeed. In October, Deputy Prime Minister Sergey Shakhray said
that the Chechen conflict did not threaten the territorial integrity
of Russia and that Moscow had no current plans to intervene.

Through the rest of 1994, as the crisis escalated, the United
States came to see that military intervention was increasingly likely.
By late November and early December, the U.S. government was
receiving evidence of the military buildup around Chechnya.[55] According to James Collins, the special coordinator for policy toward
the New Independent States, the United States watched this
buildup closely and made known through diplomatic channels
"that this was a dangerous situation."[56]

The United States also made some public statements. Asked about Chechnya on November 30, a State Department spokesperson said that "we hope that in the efforts to pursue a solution to the problem that all of the sides will refrain from violence and be able to find a way to seek a peaceful outcome."[57] On December 3, Warren Christopher said on the *MacNeil–Lehrer Newshour* that the United States hoped for a guarantee of human rights and the pursuit of a peaceful settlement in Chechnya.[58] On December 9, two days before the invasion, Ambassador Thomas Pickering met with a high-level Russian official, Sergey Filatov, to discuss the situation.[59]

In January 1995 testimony to Congress, Collins acknowledged that efforts to head off the Chechen bloodbath had fallen short: "I probably in hindsight would have been more forceful and more open in saying that we were going to be very concerned about any denigration or derogation of human rights."[60] More generally, U.S. policy makers should have made clear to Yeltsin that any military action in Chechnya would exact a high political price in the West. With a Republican Congress coming to power, Clinton administration officials were well aware that economic assistance to Russia would face growing opposition among lawmakers and that missteps by Moscow on a range of issues—especially its behavior toward former Soviet republics in the "near abroad"—could exacerbate the situation; they should have stressed this reality to Russian leaders. Collins astutely observed, however, that there was no guarantee that more emphatic American warnings would have worked. After all, the Russian military officers planning the intervention did not foresee the nightmare that unfolded. They imagined a quick and successful operation to crush the Dudayev government.

Once the intervention was under way, the Clinton administration offered what could be interpreted as unconditional support for Yeltsin's action. On December 11, as hundreds of Russian tanks and thousands of troops rolled into Chechnya, President Clinton declined to criticize the move, saying that it was "an internal affair" and that he only hoped it could be resolved with "a minimum amount of bloodshed."[61] On a trip to Moscow a week later, Defense Secretary William Perry affirmed this view of the intervention: "Provided it is not destabilizing beyond the scope of that activity, I do not see it as affecting our desire to have a pragmatic partnership with Russia."[62] A spokesperson at the State Department likened the Chechen intervention to the U.S. Civil War.

Collins would say later that these statements, too, may have been misguided. "I have thought long and hard about, you know, whether it was a mistake to use the word 'internal.' Maybe it gave the wrong connotation. But I am persuaded the authorities and the people making decisions in the Russian leadership had no doubt of our views and our position. . . . It was not a green light."[63] The United States was walking a fine line. It was willing to accept Russia's use of force in Chechnya as long as the violence was restrained. Washington gave a green light to intervention while flashing a red light to human rights abuses. It is unclear whether U.S. intelligence agencies made assessments of the likelihood for a quick Russian success in Chechnya, but if U.S. officials had examined the situation more closely and understood the extremely high morale of the Chechen secessionist forces and their capacity to wage a protracted guerrilla war, they would have had cause to question the sanguine predictions of the Russian leadership and reason to doubt that any intervention would be painless.

The Chechen episode illustrated how unformed U.S. policy remained on self-determination issues and how little evolution there had been in U.S. thinking since the days of the Biafran war. As the United States apparently saw it, a country like Russia had the right to force unhappy ethnic groups to remain within its borders; efforts at enforced unity were often a good thing for the international system. "Russia is a multiethnic state [with] 100 different nationalities or ethnic groups," a policy maker told the *Washington Post* in late December. "Yeltsin is correct that allowing one group to secede would encourage others."[64]

At the same time, however, officials believed that there were limits to how vigorously state unity could be enforced. At some point, the costs of such enforcement would outrun the benefits. "Chechnya stands as a warning to Russia and to the rest of the world," said Deputy Secretary of State Strobe Talbott in April 1995. "If any government attempts to enforce unity with brute strength, if it insists on imposing its control on people who feel disenfranchised or oppressed, the result will likely be more disintegration, more violence, and more instability."[65] Talbott argued that fracturing states must create inclusive democracy and address legitimate grievances while also pursuing a political settlement. But nobody in the U.S. government could articulate clearly what would be permissible if these measures didn't work. What if secessionist groups remained determined to achieve independence no matter how well they were treated? Was there some maximum level of violence that a state could use in trying to preserve its unity? If the United States believed this to be so, if it believed, say, that violence against secessionists was justified as long as noncombatants were not harmed, how could policy makers predict when an intervention would be able to stay within those limits?

Such answers as officials had to these questions were utterly practical. A bad intervention against secessionists was one that didn't succeed. Too much violence was violence that made headlines. Enlightened policies that went awry were worse than despicable policies that succeeded. The Chechnya intervention would have been acceptable in Washington if the Russians had won quickly, even if Moscow hadn't exhausted all political avenues before using force. In this sense, U.S. policy here, as in Turkish Kurdistan, suffered from realist myopia. Washington's actions were strongly influenced by the long-range goal of strengthening its relationship with a strategic country and also by the goal of strengthening the country itself. Yet in Turkish Kurdistan and Chechnya military action against an internal adversary escalated beyond levels that the United States had envisioned, proved economically draining and politically divisive, and resulted in condemnation by the international community. In both areas, the United States could have played a larger role in helping key countries avoid traveling down a highly self-destructive path.

RWANDA

To many Western observers, the mass killings in Rwanda appeared to be a spontaneous event triggered by the plane crash that took the lives of the presidents of both Rwanda and Burundi on April 6, 1994. In reality, the genocide had been carefully planned for months by some of the most powerful people in Rwanda. This groundwork was being laid even as a U.N. peacekeeping force and monitors from the OAU sought to bring stability to Rwanda and as diplomatic efforts were under way to resolve the country's political divisions. In Washington, policy makers who paid attention to the Great Lakes of Africa region knew that a major crisis was brewing and they attempted to improve the situation. The sense of alarm in the Clinton administration was never great enough, however, that the United States developed a vigorous strategy to prevent what turned out to be the most rapid mass slaughter of human beings in history. The failure was one of prediction insofar as nobody anticipated just how great the bloodbath would be; had U.S. officials known that a true genocide was imminent, surely they would have done more. Still, the real failure was more one of will: the United States was simply not concerned enough about Rwanda to divert energies from other areas to prevent an ill-defined tragedy.

American policy toward Rwanda in the early 1990s was characterized by moderate attentiveness. Between October 1990 and February 1993, four outbreaks of violence took the lives of nearly two thousand people in Rwanda, mainly Tutsi. The government of President Juvenal Habyarimana was complicit in much of this violence, and the State Department noted these abuses in its annual human-rights reports. The United States was not moved to act against the Habyarimana government, however, until early 1993. In March 1993, the International Human Rights Commission published a report that implicated that government in systematic abuse.[66] The Clinton administration responded by reducing its aid to Rwanda and redirecting much of the remainder away from the government and into nongovernmental organizations.[67]

During 1993 the United States also had some involvement in

the peace negotiations aimed at addressing Rwanda's deep political divisions. From the late 1980s onward, the Habyarimana government had been at war with the Rwanda Patriotic Front (RPF), an organization that comprised mainly exiled Tutsi. In 1992, the United States joined other outside powers in pressuring Habyarimana's government to come to terms with the RPF. And it did more than exhort; it played an active mediation role in the Arusha peace process—the negotiations aimed at ending Rwanda's civil war. "In Rwanda, we have had facilitators in the field throughout the last ten months trying to keep the parties talking," Assistant Secretary of State Herman Cohen told Congress in March 1993. Cohen was encouraged by the recent success of U.S. mediation efforts elsewhere in Africa and believed that there was potential for a wider U.S. role across the continent: "U.S. involvement in conflict resolution is considered desirable by most Africans, and the United States is seen as impartial. American technical assistance is highly prized. Our involvement reassures the parties, and the presence of the only remaining superpower seems to serve as a moral guarantee that agreements will be implemented."[68]

Cohen believed that Africa needed a strong indigenous mediation and peacekeeping system and that the United States should make a major effort to transform the OAU in this direction. In Rwanda, U.S. policy makers experimented with efforts to give the OAU greater support. In response to a request by Cohen, the Bush administration had made the OAU legally eligible for security assistance. The United States then moved to give the OAU mission in Rwanda $1 million to improve its mediation and peacekeeping abilities. It also sent a military liaison to Addis Ababa to work with the OAU. During the Arusha talks, this liaison shuttled between Kigali, Kampala, and Arusha, providing technical advice to both parties. Other U.S. experts also played a role.[69] After an accord was signed on August 4, 1993, U.S. financing helped make possible the placement of OAU cease-fire monitors.[70] "The United States is pleased to support this effort, which we hope will be a model for future OAU involvement in conflict resolution," stated an optimistic State Department press release.[71]

The Arusha accord called for a twenty-two-month transitional period leading to free elections. The United States supported the deployment of a U.N. peacekeeping force, called U.N. Assistance Mission for Rwanda, to the capital of Kigali, where it would provide security and facilitate the process of implementing the accord. No Americans were part of this force of twenty-seven hundred lightly armed soldiers.

The Arusha accord and the deployment of U.N. troops to Rwanda did little to stop the country's slide toward greater violence. Habyarimana's government was dissatisfied with the agreement and began laying plans to unleash a new wave of anti-Tutsi violence. Radio broadcasts were filled with virulent propaganda, and large quantities of arms were passed out to Habyarimana's supporters. By early 1994, tensions were rapidly mounting in Rwanda. Foreign diplomats and nongovernmental organizations like Human Rights Watch were warned by Rwandans—including some highly placed government officials—that a major killing campaign was about to begin. Two State Department officials—Deputy Assistant Secretary Prudence Bushnell and Ambassador Arlene Render—traveled to Rwanda in February to see what could be done to get the peace process back on track. The State Department also sent Lieutenant Colonel Tony Marley, a military expert who had worked closely with the OAU on the technical details of the Arusha accord. It was during this time that Africa specialists in the State Department, AID, and the National Security Council began issuing warnings that Rwanda was moving toward an abyss of undefined dimensions.[72] Nothing was done about these warnings.

The United States had negligible influence over the government of Rwanda in early 1994 and there was little that it could do to stop the preparations for mass violence. As a member of the U.N. Security Council, however, the United States did have influence over U.N. military operations in Rwanda. As the situation deteriorated, it could have sought to bolster UNAMIR. The deployment of a larger U.N. force with heavier weapons and a less restrictive mandate on the use of force would have been an appropriate response to the ominous developments in Rwanda.

This option was never seriously debated in Washington. The Clinton administration had strong political incentives not to advocate a larger U.N. commitment to Rwanda. In early 1994 the administration was still reeling from criticisms of its handling of the Somalia mission. Much of this criticism centered on the role of the United Nations, with conservatives charging that the United States was being dragged into ill-considered U.N. operations. President Clinton himself had joined this attack in his September 1993 speech to the General Assembly in which he said that the United States must learn how to "say no" to the United Nations. Clinton promised more rigorous scrutiny of all future U.N. peacekeeping operations. In January 1994, Senator Bob Dole introduced legislation that would limit U.S. participation in U.N. operations.[73] As the Rwanda genocide approached, there had probably never been a worse time in U.S. politics to suggest sending more U.N. forces to a conflict zone.

Washington's unwillingness to bolster the U.N. forces in Rwanda persisted even after the genocide began, when there might still have been an opportunity to prevent the tragedy from escalating. The killing of ten Belgian peacekeepers at the onset of the violence led the Belgian government to withdraw its troops from UNAMIR and shattered efforts to sustain a strong U.N. presence. The resumption of war between the Rwandan government and the RPF also made it difficult to galvanize a U.N. response. On April 21, two weeks into the slaughter, General Romeo Dallaire, the Canadian commander of the U.N. force in Rwanda, stated that he could end the killing with five to eight thousand troops.[74] Instead, around this same time, the Security Council voted to reduce the U.N. force to 270. American officials supported the withdrawal of the U.N. force for its own safety. Over the next two months, the orchestrators of the Rwanda genocide would be able to carry out their work with no outside interference. In the wake of this disaster, as the United States led a hugely expensive international effort to aid the refugees who had fled Rwanda, Brian Atwood, an AID administrator, proclaimed the obvious: "We're now beginning to see the costs of ignoring crisis prevention."[75]

SUCCESSES

Over the past thirty years, U.S. leaders have typically been unwilling to commit national power to preventing ethnic conflicts. Although this unwillingness has stemmed mainly from a perception that vital interests are not at stake in ethnic crises, it has also, at times, reflected the view that greater U.S. involvement would not affect the trajectory of a conflict. Often these considerations have combined to produce inaction, with the United States staying out of conflicts that seemed both unimportant and intractable.

The United States' occasional successes in prevention have come when the nation has focused significant resources over a long period of time. Usually this effort is made because of the manifestly important national interests at stake. It can also be motivated by a sense of opportunity—a belief that an investment of U.S. effort in less important crises can yield results. As with preventive action in other foreign policy areas, the key to preventing ethnic conflict lies in devising policies that specify rewards and punishments, delineate what actions will trigger what responses, and then follow through on these promises. Artful bluffing, of course, can be useful as well.

KOSOVO

American efforts to prevent violence in Kosovo covered a wide gamut of approaches over the course of more than six years, from official condemnation of Serb repression and quiet diplomacy in Belgrade to the deployment of U.S. troops in neighboring Macedonia and open threats of force. Policy makers in both the Bush and the Clinton administrations were moved to act by a sense of compelling national interest and by the belief that they could make a decisive difference. The national interest was to prevent a wider war in the Balkans, one that could drag in U.S. allies and produce a humanitarian disaster. The opportunity was presented by the simple fact that Kosovo had, by late 1992, not yet been sucked into the maelstrom that raged in much of the rest of former Yugoslavia. It was the one piece of the Yugoslav crisis that the United States had a chance to handle right.

The fate of ethnic Albanians in Kosovo was an issue that concerned the United States as early as the mid-1980s. Escalating repression in Kosovo caught the attention of Congress, which held hearings and passed resolutions calling for Yugoslavia to change its policies.[76] In early 1989 Kosovo became the subject of U.S. concern when Slobodan Milosevic used it to showcase his agenda of Serb nationalism. Proclaiming Kosovo a sacred Serb homeland, Milosevic sought to take complete control of the republic's governing bodies and to deny the 90 percent Albanian majority any kind of autonomy from Belgrade. When Warren Zimmerman arrived in Belgrade in March 1989, he carried a message from the Bush administration that the United States was deeply concerned about Kosovo and that good relations with Washington depended on an improvement of the human-rights situation. Milosevic's response was to refuse to meet with Zimmerman for an entire year.[77]

The crisis over Kosovo deteriorated rapidly through 1990. Serb authorities arrested thousands of political opponents and dismissed tens of thousands of Albanians from their jobs. As Serb intimidation and repression escalated, Kosovo's Albanians increased their demands, insisting on the right to form a republic separate from Serbia or to affiliate with Albania. In August, the United States took the lead in invoking the human-rights mechanism of the CSCE process. In December 1990, Kosovo Albanians boycotted the national elections, despite advice from U.S. diplomats that they should seek to use a parliamentary minority to improve their situation. American diplomats in Belgrade also sought to alleviate the growing crisis by attempting to set up a meeting between Milosevic and the Kosovo Albanian leader Ibrahim Rugova. Rugova agreed but Milosevic refused.[78]

Through 1991, as the Kosovo crisis escalated, the United States continued to press the Serb leaders to moderate their behavior. A comprehensive statement of U.S. policy released in May 1991 strongly condemned Serb actions in Kosovo and announced that the United States would step up its efforts to address human-rights abuses in Yugoslavia through the CSCE.[79] When James Baker met with Milosevic in June 1991, Kosovo was high on his agenda and

he confronted the Serb leader about human-rights problems there.
The outbreak of fighting in Croatia and Bosnia confirmed the
worst about Milosevic's intentions and increased U.S. fears about
Kosovo. In August 1992, the United States conferred with other
Western democracies and advocated, among other measures, deploying CSCE monitors to Kosovo. Deputy Secretary Lawrence
Eagleburger said after the conference, "By moving the monitors
in, we are at least beginning a process, I hope, of assuring that, in
fact, outside forces will not be able to intervene in the Kosovo."
The United States and its allies, said Eagleburger, had delivered
clear warnings "to the government in Belgrade that they must be
very cautious in regard to the Kosovo."[80]

The failure of the United States to do anything to stop Serb
aggression in 1992—it wouldn't even enforce a "no-fly zone" over
Bosnia—and the resulting damage to U.S. credibility made it all
the more important to take a stand in Kosovo. The republic would
become the second "line in the sand" that George Bush drew during his presidency. In the fall of 1992, intelligence reports indicated
that the Serbs might unleash a reign of terror in Kosovo in late
1992 or early 1993. The paramilitary leader Zeljko Raznjatovic, a
notorious Serb war criminal known as Arkan, had established a
presence in Kosovo, and tensions were rising.[81] The Bush administration's response was to threaten military action if new Serb aggression occurred. In a letter delivered in late December to
Milosevic and the chief of the Yugoslav army, Zivota Panic, Bush
stated that "in the event of conflict in Kosovo caused by Serbian
action, the United States will be prepared to employ military force
against the Serbs in Kosovo and in Serbia proper."[82]

According to former Bush administration officials, the intention
was to employ air strikes against targets in Serbia. Pentagon plans
for such attacks had been in existence for some time, and despite
past bluffing and inaction, this threat was apparently real. "If in
fact anything had happened we were prepared to do what we had
said—that I promise you," Eagleburger would later remark.[83]

The Clinton administration came into office determined to continue the tough policy on Kosovo. President-elect Clinton had

been informed of Bush's December 1992 threat at the time and
supported it. The new administration reiterated Bush's threat
and made it clear to Belgrade that U.S. policy on Kosovo was
unchanged. During his first year in office, Clinton and his aides
would add two elements to that policy: the deployment of U.S.
troops to Macedonia and the pressuring of the Albanian government to tone down rhetoric that served to inflame the situation in
Kosovo.

The decision to send a small number of troops to Macedonia in
mid-1993 came on the heels of the administration's failure to win
European support for a new initiative to stop the war in Bosnia.
Like the Bush administration, the Clinton team focused on Kosovo
because the opportunity existed to do something effective and to
advance national interests without getting sucked into a shooting
war. Containing the Balkan war was the next-best thing to ending
it, and appearing to do something big about a horrendous tragedy
was the next-best thing to actually doing something big. Announcing on May 12 that the United States might send troops to Macedonia, Clinton said, "We want to try to confine that conflict so
it doesn't spread into other places, like Albania and Greece and
Turkey, which could have the impact of undermining the peace in
Europe and the growth and stability of democracy there."[84]

The deployment of 325 U.S. troops to Macedonia in July 1993
as part of a small U.N. force was a symbolic move. Nobody expected a Serb attack on Macedonia and the troops were not prepared to intervene in Kosovo. Their mission was to underscore
U.S. concern about Kosovo and Washington's willingness to project military force into the region if Serbia stepped up its provo-
cations. The hope was to shore up U.S. credibility, which had
fallen to an all-time low by summer 1993. The troop deployment
was preceded by new warnings from Secretary of State Warren
Christopher that the United States would not tolerate increased
Serb repression in Kosovo.[85] These warnings were reiterated a few
months later by Assistant Secretary of State Stephen Oxman. "We
have said before we would regard as a very serious matter any
conflict in Kosovo inspired by Serb actions and that we would

respond," Oxman said. "The stationing of U.S. troops in Macedonia, sent as part of the U.N. mission, was also to send an important message that the United States would view with great
seriousness any spillover of the conflict and we are determined to
do what we can to prevent that."[86] Beyond signaling Belgrade, the
deployment was intended to show the European powers that had
forces in Bosnia under U.N. command that the United States was
now ready to commit more of its own power to the Balkans.

Having amplified its message to Serbia, the Clinton administration began devising a message to Albania and a strategy for delivering it. During the early 1990s, the Albanian government had
helped stoke the flames of the Kosovo crisis by loudly supporting
the claims of the secessionists there. It had also contributed to
instability in Macedonia, whose population was 30 percent Albanian, by backing nationalist politicians. Macedonian government
officials accused Albania of going even further by providing arms
to Albanian extremists.[87] By late 1993, CIA intelligence reports
were predicting an unstoppable momentum in the region toward
a "greater Albania."[88] The death of Albanian citizens in minor
armed incidents on the Albanian-Serb border in January 1994 led
to acrimonious diplomatic exchanges between Serbia and Albania
and served to increase tensions.

The Clinton administration's goal in this volatile environment
was to induce Albania to temper its nationalist rhetoric and become
a proponent of moderate behavior among the ethnic Albanians in
Kosovo and Macedonia. This was no easy task. While Albanian
nationalism did not rival Serb nationalism in its ferocity, the dream
of creating a single state that included all six million Albanians
in the Balkan region was a powerful force in Albanian domestic
politics. In 1993 and 1994, there were strong incentives for Sali
Berisha, the Albanian president, to support Albanian militants in
Kosovo and Macedonia.

The United States sought to counter these incentives by offering
Berisha foreign aid and closer ties with Washington in exchange
for moderating his behavior. In early 1994, the United States established a military presence in Albania, using a base there to fly

spy missions over Serbia. Top U.S. military officials visited the country regularly, and the U.S. ambassador to Albania, William Reyerson, became an influential figure in government circles.

By spring 1994, President Berisha had significantly altered his position. Dropping his strong support for Kosovo's secession, Berisha began calling for talks between local Albanian leaders and the Serb government in Belgrade. He and Ibrahim Rugova, the Kosovo Albanian leader, issued a joint statement on May 27 announcing this new concession. Berisha also met with Kiro Gligorov, the Macedonian president, and promised to support the moderate, integrationist wing of the main Albanian party in Macedonia. Previously Berisha had backed a militant faction.[89]

In July 1994, Defense Secretary William Perry arrived in Tirana, Albania, to discuss U.S. military assistance and closer security cooperation with the West. While dangling these carrots, he reiterated the message that Washington opposed support for Albanian nationalists in Kosovo and Macedonia.[90] Through the remainder of 1994 and into 1995, U.S. officials continued to stress this point as they built closer ties to Albania. Tensions remained high in Macedonia and Kosovo, but the Albanian government was no longer actively fueling them.

THE BALTIC STATES

Shortly before Perry's trip to Albania, another patient effort at preventive action was reaching a climax elsewhere in Europe. On July 7, 1994, President Clinton visited the Baltic state of Latvia and was greeted by huge crowds. Clinton carried with him a two-pronged message: the United States would do everything in its power to ensure withdrawal of the last Russian troops in the Baltic states, but these states had to guarantee that they would respect the rights of the ethnic Russians who constituted a large percentage of their populations. "We will rejoice with you when the last of the foreign troops vanish from your homelands," Clinton told a crowd of fifty thousand Latvians. But, he said, "freedom without tolerance is freedom unfulfilled."[91]

Clinton's comments came after a year of careful work to find a

solution to a crisis that had the potential to derail U.S.-Russian
relations. The dissolution of the Soviet Union in 1991 had left
in its wake a tense standoff in the Baltic states. During the half
century that Moscow had controlled this region, hundreds of
thousands of Russians had settled in Latvia, Estonia, and Lithuania.
They had come, for the most part, to administer Soviet control of
the republics. When these states declared their independence, the
ethnic Russians stayed on, bitterly resented symbols of Soviet domination. In Latvia and Estonia, they made up more than 30 percent
of the population.[92] Tens of thousands of Russian troops also remained garrisoned in the newly independent states.

In April 1993, Latvia's foreign minister, Georgs Anrejevs, expressed the fears of many Latvians when he openly accused Russian
armed forces of attempting to subvert Latvian independence.[93]
That same month, Boris Yeltsin told President Clinton at a summit
in Vancouver that the withdrawal of twenty thousand Russian
troops in Latvia would be linked to that country's treatment of its
Russian minority. The clear inference of this statement and others
was that Russian troops might one day be called on to protect their
oppressed brethren in Latvia. Yeltsin's concerns were not without
foundation: in all the Baltic states, and especially in Latvia, efforts
were under way to deny Russians full rights in the new countries.
The pressure on the Clinton administration to resolve this impasse
was compounded by a congressional stipulation, dating from 1992,
that U.S. aid to Russia be withheld if Moscow did not set a time-
table for withdrawal by October 6, 1993.

In September, Clinton appointed a special envoy, James Collins,
to focus exclusively on issues related to Russian troops in the former Soviet republics. In conjunction with other U.S. officials, Collins worked through 1993 and into 1994 to refine and deliver the
administration's dual message. The administration argued to Russia's leaders that a failure to complete a timely withdrawal of their
troops would have profoundly negative ramifications, in terms of
relations both with the Baltic states and with the Western democracies. To the Baltic states, Collins and others stressed that anti-
Russian discriminatory measures were unacceptable to Washington

and would complicate Western efforts to help those states through trade and aid ties.[94]

Collins's efforts were supplemented by a relentless campaign by Nicholas Burns of the National Security Council staff. In March 1994, Burns engineered a visit to the White House by thirteen Latvian political leaders, including hard-line nationalists who opposed granting citizen rights to ethnic Russians. Vice President Albert Gore and Anthony Lake, the national security adviser, met with the Latvians in the situation room and successfully urged them to adopt a more conciliatory line so as to achieve a deal with Yeltsin over the timing of the troop withdrawal. Clinton also personally pressed Yeltsin on this issue and urged him to meet with President Lennart Mari of Estonia. Yeltsin agreed.[95]

By mid-1994, Estonia and Lithuania had established procedures that allowed for Russians to become citizens. Latvia remained divided, however, with its parliament considering legislation that would impose strict quotas on the number of Russians who could gain citizenship each year and that would deny noncitizens various rights. On the eve of Clinton's visit, the parliament passed a law allowing only two thousand Russians a year to become citizens. In late June, responding to American and Western pressure, President Guntis Ulmanis of Latvia asked the parliament to produce a more moderate version. U.S. officials hoped that Clinton's visit would help Latvia turn the corner on this issue. "The president's trip is not designed to put pressure on the president of Latvia," said the U.S. ambassador, Ints Silins, "but we think the country will most likely make the wise decision on citizenship."[96]

After Clinton's visit, the Latvian parliament passed a new citizenship law, which removed the restrictive quotas and allowed most of the country's ethnic Russians to attain citizenship over the next several years. The law was considered consistent with international norms by most human-rights experts in Western Europe and the United States.[97] American pressure on Russia to remove all its forces from the Baltic states also succeeded, with Moscow meeting the August 31, 1994, deadline.

BURUNDI

Following the mass killings in Burundi in 1988, U.S. policy makers became more attentive to the underlying causes of ethnic conflict in that country. They pressed Burundi's leaders to make greater progress in eliminating systematic discrimination against Hutu. Congress made economic aid contingent on such progress. With President Pierre Buyoya undertaking a sustained effort to promote ethnic conciliation, significant political reforms had taken place in Burundi by 1993. In June, the country held free elections and elected its first Hutu president, Melchior Ndadaye. The United States provided electoral assistance during this period and then gave its full support to Ndadaye, pledging to support his government with economic aid and encouraging him to continue the work of reform. Burundi was hailed as a showcase of African democratic transformation.

In October 1993, the Burundian army led an abortive coup that resulted in Ndadaye's assassination and touched off a wave of communal violence. Some fifty thousand Hutu and Tutsi died. Once again, the Tutsi-led army was responsible for massive atrocities. The United States condemned the killings and suspended economic and military aid. This stern response, along with aid cutoffs by other donors, helped undermine the prospects of the coup's leaders. After Burundi's elected government reconsolidated its control, aid was restored.[98] Still, the effect of the coup attempt was devastating, derailing all the progress that Burundi had been making. As René Lemarchand writes, it "destroyed a nascent interethnic consensus."[99]

The outbreak of violence in Rwanda in 1994 served to push Burundi back to the brink of disaster. The victory of the Rwanda Patriotic Front generated fears among Hutu in Burundi of Tutsi domination over both countries. Hutu extremists in Burundi, working in association with exiled Hutu from Rwanda, established an underground network to train and arm themselves for future battle.[100] Virulent propaganda was transmitted over the radio in Burundi, as it had been in Rwanda before the genocide.

American policy makers fully recognized the potential for a new bloodbath in Burundi, especially in the immediate aftermath of the Rwandan violence. As Assistant Secretary of State George Moose said in May 1994, "One of our greatest concerns and one of the highest motivations about trying to do something to calm the situation in Rwanda is to avoid that carnage and that tension spilling across the border into Burundi."[101] The massive humanitarian crisis triggered by the Rwandan violence, with its huge resultant demands for U.S. aid, made it impossible for the United States to ignore the potential for a repeat performance in Burundi. Through the second half of 1994, the U.S. government sought to defuse the rising tensions in Burundi. It urged the government there to reconcile with its internal opposition and seek to resolve their political differences. It supported the U.N. effort to promote reconciliation through the work of the secretary general's special representative in Burundi, Ahmedou Ould Abdallah. In September 1994, his work in facilitating multiparty talks produced a new power-sharing arrangement. The United States also supported the OAU's stationing of forty-six military observers in Burundi. Meanwhile, U.S. aid was reoriented to support programs aimed at promoting national reconciliation and strengthening the judicial system.[102]

Still, the situation continued to deteriorate through the last months of 1994. In mid-December, the different American intelligence agencies reached consensus on a National Intelligence Estimate that assessed the likelihood of conflict worldwide in 1995. The view regarding Burundi was unrelentingly bleak: "ethnic tensions . . . are approaching the levels witnessed in Rwanda" before the genocide. The "continued ethnic violence combined with the reaction of ethnic extremists to a final power-sharing agreement are likely to prompt an explosion in the next six months."[103]

To prevent this outcome, U.S. policy makers gave Burundi sustained attention. A steady stream of officials traveled to Burundi in late 1994 and the first months of 1995. Among them were National Security Adviser Tony Lake, Deputy Secretary of State Strobe Talbott, Undersecretary of State Tim Wirth, AID Administrator Brian Atwood, and three assistant secretaries of state. These visits were intended to reassure moderates there and, as Townsend Friedman, special coordinator for Rwanda, put it, to "warn everyone, including extremists, that the world is watching."[104] In mid-February, Clinton taped a Voice of America radio message urging the Burundian people to reject extremism. In March, the United States coauthored a Security Council statement that endorsed efforts by the Burundian government to investigate the massacres that followed the 1993 coup attempt and warned that perpetrators of any future acts of genocide would be pursued by international authorities.[105] (When the report was completed, however, the United States led an effort to delay its release, arguing that its conclusions were too incendiary and could trigger increased violence in Burundi.)

The most innovative aspect of policy during this period was the high degree of cooperation between U.S. officials and representatives from NGOs. American policy makers relied on these relationships both to gain information and to coordinate action. Organizations like International Alert and Human Rights Watch were often better informed than U.S. diplomats about developments in Burundi, and NGOs actively engaged in seeking to mediate the situation offered important insights. The Burundi Policy Forum was a focal point for unprecedented coordination between the U.S. government and both NGOs and IGOs.[106] Organized by several nonprofit groups in Washington and New York, the Burundi Forum held its inaugural meeting on January 13, 1995. Holding regular meetings through 1995, the Forum brought organizations concerned about Burundi together to exchange information and discuss policy initiatives. American policy makers from the State Department, the Defense Department, the NSC, the AID, and the USIA consistently took part in its meetings.

A year after the National Intelligence Estimate predicting an explosion within six months, none had occurred in Burundi; by 1996, however, the country seemed to be moving ever closer to civil war. Some observers called the situation "slow-motion genocide." In early January, the U.N. high commissioner for refugees made a two-day visit to Burundi and reported that massacres were

common and that the country was already in a "civil war situation."
He had traveled to Burundi as the personal envoy of Secretary
General Boutros Boutros-Ghali, who was urging the Security
Council to set up a standing U.N. force that could intervene if
Burundi began to descend into genocidal violence.[107]

The Clinton administration initially resisted pressure to create
a special U.N. force for Burundi. In late January, Madeleine Albright traveled to Burundi and issued a warning to Tutsi extremists
that any government brought to power by force would be isolated
by the United States.[108] But back in New York, Albright initially
opposed dramatic U.N. action to save a country that she described
as teetering on the "verge of national suicide."[109] The Clinton administration worried about sending U.N. peacekeeping troops into
a location like Somalia where they could be caught up in civil
warfare. It saw no evidence that the warring parties in Burundi
would cease fighting when U.N. forces arrived. There was neither
a clear exit strategy nor a reliable means of determining the size
or expense of the force that would be needed to take control of
the situation. Under the restrictive guidelines of PD-25, U.S. support for a deployment to Burundi was inadvisable. In a political
climate dominated by anti-U.N. Republican legislators, such a
deployment was unimaginable.

Boutros-Ghali's response to these concerns was that a peacekeeping force would be inadequate in Burundi and that the international community should be prepared to send a force with the
power to engage in combat. In a February 20 report to the Security
Council, the secretary general wrote, "The lessons drawn from the
United Nations experience in the former Yugoslavia, Somalia,
Haiti and Rwanda suggest that, in situations where there is no
consent and/or peace to keep, better results are likely to be
achieved through a multinational operation that can create the conditions for the subsequent deployment of a United Nations peacekeeping operation."[110]

After the release of Boutros-Ghali's report, Albright announced
that the United States was ready to support an international force

for possible intervention in Burundi. Boutros-Ghali had originally wanted such a force to be deployed in Zaire, but in recognition of political realities, his February 20 report suggested that member states earmark forces for Burundi that would be called on only when a deployment was authorized.[111] American policy makers were comfortable with this more modest vision. Albright said that such a force would serve two purposes: "one is as a deterrent, to show that the international community is there and is watching, and two, it speeds up the process of deployment."[112] The Clinton administration also made clear that such a force would not include U.S. troops. American participation would be limited to logistical planning assistance and airlifting troops to Burundi on short notice.

Even with the Clinton administration's reversal, movement toward decisive U.N. action in Burundi stalled. Some European diplomats, heeding the counsel of the Burundian government, worried that moves to create any kind of U.N. force would trigger a preemptive strike by extremists and touch off the cataclysm that everyone feared. By March, efforts to create a standby force had effectively been blocked in the Security Council and, in a compromise, the council passed a resolution stressing the need for diplomatic solutions.[113] As the situation continued to deteriorate, however, with new massacres occurring regularly, there was more discussion of an interventionary force. In early May, Boutros-Ghali sent a report to the Security Council again urging that a multilateral force with war powers be deployed to Burundi, with or without the consent of the government. Such a force was beyond the U.N.'s capabilities, he said, and therefore a member state should play a lead role in the operation. The Clinton administration made it clear that it would not be that member state and would not contribute any troops to Burundi, but it dispatched a team of State and Defense Department officials to New York to discuss other ways the United States could assist an intervention.[114] Later in the month, the outgoing ambassador to Burundi, Robert Krueger, reflected the rising concern of many observers when he said that

Burundi faced "a greater chance for major conflagration than [it had] at any time in the last two years."[115] Krueger believed estimates that up to a million people could die in a new wave of violence. Neither this warning nor others changed basic U.S. policy on participation in a U.N. force. Instead, in June, President Clinton appointed a new special envoy to Burundi, Howard Wolpe, who went there with an eleven-person team.

American inaction continued through late July, when Pierre Buyoya, the former Burundian president, regained power in a military coup. Western countries, including the United States, had issued stern warnings in the weeks leading up to the coup that a military takeover would be unacceptable. The emergence of Buyoya as the coup leader, however, undermined any Western determination to take action—if such determination ever existed in the first place, which is doubtful. While the United States allowed the ousted president, Sylvestre Ntibantunganya, to take refuge in its embassy in Bujumbura and declined to recognize the new military government, it did not seem highly perturbed by the coup. Buyoya, after all, had been the architect of Burundi's move toward democracy in the early 1990s and had played a pioneering role in seeking to foster ethnic peace. With no other leader able to stabilize Burundi's deteriorating situation, some U.S. officials believed that Buyoya was as good a bet as any for bringing peace to a tortured nation. "This coup could be a blocking movement to extremism," one unnamed White House official told the *New York Times*.[116]

Through the summer, U.N. efforts to assemble an interventionary force for Burundi went nowhere. In a report to the Security Council in late August, Boutros-Ghali reiterated his argument for intervention, recommending a force of fifty thousand troops. Once again his urgent pleas were essentially ignored. Of the fifty nations he approached either to lead such a force or to contribute troops, fewer than half even bothered to reply. Only seven agreed to make any material contributions, and only three offered to send soldiers to Burundi.[117] Meanwhile, the pace of the killing continued unabated. In late August 1996, Amnesty International estimated that six thousand Burundians had died since Buyoya took power.[118]

In 1994, the suddenness of the genocidal explosion in Rwanda had caught inattentive top officials of the Clinton administration by surprise. In 1996, officials were well aware of the highly ominous developments in Burundi and yet felt they had exhausted possible preventive actions. Even as the Clinton administration effectively doomed a successful mission to Burundi by declining to participate, its own officials openly declared that, in the words of Assistant Secretary of State John Shattuck, "Burundi today is standing on the brink of genocide."[119] It was a defining moment in post–cold war foreign policy, starker perhaps than any such moment during the Bosnian crisis: in spring and summer 1996, the U.S. government was openly acknowledging that it did not have the national wherewithal to prevent what had the potential to be one of the worst mass slaughters since World War II. Nearly fifty years after the Holocaust, top U.S. officials were suggesting that in some cases collective action to stop such horror shouldn't even be attempted. "If extremism is allowed to succeed, there is little or nothing the international community can do," said Anthony Lake, the national security adviser. "Only Burundians can solve the problems of Burundi."[120]

It is impossible to assess reliably the effect of American preventive efforts in Burundi. (As of this writing, the situation remains precarious.) Many factors have influenced the calculations of those in conflict and it is impossible to isolate the impact of a single variable. The United States did design a preventive strategy and made a sustained effort to stop violence. It did not, however, use all the preventive options available, most notably that of leading an international peacekeeping force, and the final historical record may well blame U.S. inaction for allowing another genocide to occur right before the eyes of an attentive international community. Nevertheless, the United States took many small steps and managed to give high-level attention to the problem for over two years. In terms of visits and pronouncements by top U.S. officials and of plans undertaken in conjunction with the United Nations, the effort made in Burundi is almost on par with U.S. actions to prevent an explosion in Kosovo.

IN RECENT YEARS, Republicans in Congress and their allies in the conservative policy community have mounted a sweeping attack on U.S. internationalist policies aimed at affecting developments on the periphery. They have targeted foreign aid for major cutbacks and sought to abolish the Agency for International Development. They have pointed to missteps in Somalia and Haiti to underscore pronouncements about how the U.S. military should stay out of the world's cesspools. And, in the most bitter attacks of all, they have blasted away at U.S. support for U.N. operations and depicted the international organization as a rogue elephant. Amid this on-slaught, the Clinton administration has managed to mount several impressive preventive policies, but its efforts have been restricted, most notably in Rwanda and Burundi. Of course, many factors influence the success of a preventive policy, and it would be wrong to blame rising isolationism for any single recent failure. Even at the height of U.S. internationalism, in 1967, the United States was wholly ineffective in preventing war in Biafra. And there is no guar-antee that a higher degree of U.S. internationalist wherewithal would have prevented the tragedy in Rwanda.

Nevertheless, it does seem clear that preventive policies can often have a major impact on ethnic conflict. Less obvious is how, politi-cally, to make the case for investing in such policies, given that most ethnic conflicts do not threaten vital U.S. interests. The U.S. inter-nationalist engagement in Western Europe, East Asia, and the Mid-dle East has proved sustainable in the current political climate for two reasons: one, the interests at stake are widely seen as vital and, two, the investment of U.S. resources is seen as effective—that is, U.S. spend-ing is seen as buying more security for the United States.

The case for preventive engagement on the periphery must rest on a slightly modified version of this argument. The specter of widening zones of instability should be invoked to illustrate, at the broadest level, how ethnic conflicts have the potential to disrupt the international system in which Americans live, travel, and trade. More concretely, the historical record must be used to show that the secondary interests affected by ethnic conflicts cannot be ignored and that the investment of U.S. resources in preventive policies on the periphery is money well spent. The country's secondary interest in humanitarian issues is especially apparent. For all the rancor that has surrounded U.S. policy toward ethnic conflicts over the past thirty years, there has generally been bipartisan agreement in favor of action to alleviate the human suffering caused by these conflicts. Most recently, Republicans and Democrats alike supported the humanitarian missions to help the Kurds in 1991, the Bosnians in 1993–94, and the Rwandan refugees in 1994. In principle, there should be agreement that policies aimed at preventing humanitarian tragedies are worth supporting. In practice, agreement has been elusive because preventive policies on the periphery seem expensive and prone to failure and because they often carry the possibility of deeper U.S. involvement.

Conservatives have argued with particular vehemence that foreign aid is wasteful and that the international affairs bureaucracy is too large. Advocates of preventive engagement must patiently explain again and again how small, well-targeted foreign-aid investments can forestall the need for future large-scale humanitarian assistance. They must show the ways that early intervention can help stop a growing spiral of rising antagonisms. They must point to examples like Burundi in showing how it is better to invest resources and focus high-level attention now than to deal with a horrendous refugee crisis later. They must stress that, while it is true that the U.S. interests at stake are modest, so, too, are the investments required—if those investments are made early. In addition, internationalist political leaders must be willing to spend more political capital defending preventive engagement on the periphery and educating the public about just how small the foreign-aid budget actually is and how far that money goes. They must stress that the logic behind the internationalist commitment in core areas and the logic behind a commitment in peripheral areas are the same, even if the means and ends differ in gravity and scope.

CHAPTER FOUR

Intervention

AMERICAN POWER IS AN INSTRUMENT of uncertain potential for affecting ethnic conflicts. While some conflicts are inevitable, others are avoidable. While Washington has leverage over some countries, it barely communicates with others. While some substate extremists will fight till the death, others will negotiate. Nevertheless, the central lesson of past preventive efforts is that when the United States harnesses its national power it can often stabilize a tense situation. The record of U.S. intervention (here defined as actions ranging from diplomacy to the use of force) to stop ongoing conflicts points to a similar conclusion. In recent years the United States has played a pivotal role in resolving stalemates in Bosnia, Israel, and Northern Ireland. It has also intervened to protect Iraq's Kurds by creating a safe haven in northern Iraq. Each of these episodes was characterized by a sustained effort and commitment at the highest levels of the U.S. government.

The failures of intervention in ethnic conflicts have been as spectacular as the successes. Among these failures one can count diplomacy to end the war in Biafra and efforts to supply humanitarian aid to its starving people, attempts to mediate the conflict in Lebanon and to use U.S. forces there, the early efforts to end the war in Bosnia, and efforts to restrain Russian forces in Chechnya and Turkish forces in Kurdistan. These episodes, too, were characterized by sustained commitment by high-level officials. Yet in each case, the United States made critical mistakes that hobbled its policy.

As with preventive efforts, intervention in ethnic conflicts has been driven largely by considerations of national interest. The United States has attempted to end ethnic warfare when the conflict threatened the stability of an important region of the world (Bosnia, Lebanon, Kashmir), when the conflict generated mass suffering and domestic pressures for action within the United States (Biafra, Iraqi Kurdistan, Bosnia), when the conflict threatened a multiethnic democracy (Bosnia), and when the conflict occurred in a country with historical links to the United States (Israel, Ireland). The United States has committed the greatest resources to intervention in those conflicts in which the first two factors have been present (Lebanon, Bosnia). In contrast, it has made little effort to intervene in conflicts where scant national interests were at stake (Burundi in 1972 and 1988, Rwanda in 1994, Sri Lanka in the 1980s and 1990s).

In seeking to stop ethnic conflicts, officials have used policy instruments that range across a wide spectrum, from those that require a minimum commitment of resources to those that require a major commitment.[1] These include diplomatic pressure and public condemnation, partial and full sanctions, war crime indictments, mediation, threats of military action, and actual military action. These instruments have been employed both unilaterally and multilaterally. Their effectiveness has varied greatly, and this chapter will draw on multiple examples to explore when and why different measures are likely to succeed.

DIPLOMATIC PRESSURE
AND CONDEMNATION

Diplomacy is a country's first line of defense. At its most effective, it can defuse threats to the national interest while they are still in their infancy. Diplomatic pressure can be applied to friends and foes alike. It may rely on simple persuasion and moral authority, coercive threats and intimidation, or some mix of these elements.

In most ethnic conflicts the United States has sought to influence the situation at an early stage, with diplomatic pressure or condemnation. These efforts have almost always failed and the reasons have varied. Often the United States has had no influence over a country where an ethnic conflict has been occurring. Sometimes the breakdown of a society has resulted in the disappearance of any real government with which the United States could communicate. At other times, diplomatic pressure and condemnation have not, in and of themselves, constituted a strong enough instrument to affect the course of an ethnic conflict in which groups believed they were fighting for their survival.

Washington's blundering, too, has limited the power of diplomacy. The United States has erred by failing to condemn violence early enough and at sufficiently high levels. It has sent mixed signals to governments engaged in ethnic warfare, ignoring or acquiescing in a state's military actions at first and issuing condemnations only after the actions have dragged on for too long or grown too violent. Sometimes this equivocation has been the product of genuine confusion, of not knowing how to view secessionist claims that might have had merit but have not represented the most desirable outcome. Also, in seeking to preserve important geopolitical relationships, the United States has often been hesitant to employ the full weight of its moral authority in urging an end to violence.

In the occasional instances in which diplomatic pressure has succeeded, U.S. concerns have been pursued at the highest levels, stressed in public as well as private forums, and sustained over time. A steady stream of condemnation by top U.S. officials can influence the thinking of many world leaders, especially when coupled with implicit or explicit threats of concrete punishment.

When the Biafran conflict began in July 1967, the United States issued no condemnations of either side but instead adopted a stance of public neutrality. Initial statements on the conflict criticized those states that continued to supply arms to the combatants, particularly the Soviet Union.[2] Throughout the conflict, the United States would invoke the moral high ground of neutrality and selectively use diplomatic pressure on third parties to maintain the arms embargo. Although officials knew about the light arms that Great Britain was secretly sending to Nigeria, they said nothing.[3]

The United States had communicated to Biafra's leaders its opposition to secession, but it did not publicly reiterate this position once independence had been declared. Nor did it openly back the Nigerian government in its effort to crush Biafra. Nevertheless, both public and private diplomacy during the Johnson administration was clearly directed toward the goal of a united Nigeria. Embassy officials in Lagos expressed their support for the assault on Biafra and were willing accomplices in the Nigerian government's effort to play down reports of starvation and human-rights abuses. In Washington, a State Department spokesman commented in February 1968, "The United States has in no way encouraged or otherwise supported the rebellion in Nigeria." The United States, he said, "regards the breakaway movement as an internal conflict which in the last analysis only the parties themselves can resolve."[4]

The official stance of neutrality was the easiest choice available. But in reality it was a way for U.S. officials to avoid backing either party in the conflict, and this led to problems. The policy gave false encouragement to the doomed Biafrans even as it bolstered the position of the Nigerian government. In September 1967, a top Biafran envoy commented in Britain, "I must pay tribute to America because they said from the start that they would not take sides and they have kept to this. America has done nothing for us and nothing against us and that's fair enough."[5] Later in the conflict, Biafra would turn to the United States with increasing optimism, naively hoping for more help than would ever be forthcoming. Because it received a smattering of support in the West and in Africa, the Biafran leadership had just enough hope to keep fighting long after its chances for victory had collapsed.

Once the Biafran war had begun, two potential outcomes were desirable: one, that Nigeria would rapidly crush the secessionist bid with a minimum loss of life; two, that Biafra would attract enough international support to resist Nigerian assaults and that Lagos would let it go without much of a fight. Neither outcome came to pass, and instead the worst-case scenario unfolded: Biafra was strong enough to fight on for several years but not strong enough to win, and the long brutal war left hundreds of thousands dead. The U.S. policy of official neutrality nurtured a dragged-out war and sharply limited the United States' ability to deal with the war's horrendous humanitarian consequences.

When Nixon came into office, an NSC study considered either recognizing Biafra or siding openly with Nigeria. Instead, it re-affirmed the policy of neutrality even while stating that the victory of a unified Nigeria was "in the long-term interests of the United States."[6]

An official position of neutrality also characterized U.S. policy toward East Pakistan. The United States was not intent on stopping the breakup of Pakistan, which it viewed as inevitable, given the distance separating that country's eastern and western regions. "We had no national interest to prevent self-determination for East Pakistan," Henry Kissinger would write later.[7] Yet the Nixon administration wanted to avoid any appearance of supporting the breakup and, more important, to maintain good ties with Pakistan. At a White House meeting on March 26, 1971, Kissinger told a group of national-security officials that Nixon "doesn't want to do anything. He doesn't want to be in the position where he can be accused of having encouraged the split-up of Pakistan. He does not favor a very active policy."[8] This outlook would lead the United States to remain virtually silent in the face of horrendous violence. Another factor that influenced the U.S. and international response was fear that public condemnation of Pakistani actions would jeopardize the safety of foreign nationals in East Pakistan.

During the first weeks and months of the crackdown in East Pakistan, Pakistani troops slaughtered hundreds of thousands of civilians and engaged in mass rape, torture, and mutilation. The State Department received detailed reports of the violence from its consul general in Dacca, which maintained a clandestine radio transmitter.[9] In early April, as hundreds of Americans were still being evacuated from the war zone, the State Department expressed its displeasure in very moderate language, commenting that the United States was concerned over the "reported loss of life, damage and hardship" in East Pakistan and hoped for a "peaceful settlement."[10] On April 6, Assistant Secretary of State Joseph Sisco paid a visit to the Pakistani ambassador in Washington and expressed concern about the use of U.S. arms in East Pakistan.[11] The next day, after five hundred Americans had been airlifted out of Dacca, the State Department slightly stepped up its public rhetoric, urging Pakistan to take "every feasible step" to achieve a peaceful accommodation in East Pakistan. It also expressed sympathy for the victims of the violence.[12]

Beyond these statements, the United States was silent. Officials in Washington explained to the press that there were conflicting reports about the scope of the violence and that, in any case, the war was an "internal matter" on which U.S. pronouncements would be unjustified.[13] This view was contested on both counts by U.S. diplomats in the field, who saw the evidence of systematic atrocities as overwhelming and the need for U.S. protest as self-evident. In April, twenty Americans in the consulate in Dacca sent a statement of dissent that was endorsed by nine officials in the State Department and AID; it called on the United States to denounce the atrocities and the suppression of democracy in East Pakistan "in order to salvage our nation's position as a moral leader of the Free World."[14] The ambassador to India, Kenneth Keating, also cabled Washington to urge the administration to "promptly, publicly and prominently deplore this brutality. . . . This is a time when principles make policies."[15] Still the United States made no strong statements, hewing to its realpolitik agenda. "We faced a dilemma," Kissinger writes in his memoirs. "The United States could not condone a brutal military repression in which thousands of civilians were killed and from which millions fled to India for safety. There was no doubt about the strong-arm tactics of the Pakistani military. But Pakistan was our sole channel to China; once it was closed it would take months to make alternative arrangements."[16]

It was not until August that President Nixon would make his first public comments on the mass killings in East Pakistan. He noted that the United States had donated $70 million to help those who had been victimized by the war. Beyond this, he had little to say. "We are not going to engage in public pressure on the Government of West Pakistan. That would be totally counterproductive. These are matters that we will only discuss in private channels."[17]

The U.S. response to the mass killings in Burundi in 1972 was also tepid. Shortly after the violence began, the ambassador to Burundi, Thomas Melady, met personally with Burundi's president, Michael Micombero, and implored him to restore order with minimal bloodshed. In Washington, the Burundian ambassador was quietly called into the State Department and told of U.S. displeasure. Beyond these measures, the United States still didn't take action to condemn the massacres. It tried to get African leaders and the OAU to take the lead in pressuring the Burundi government. When, instead, the OAU affirmed its support for Micombero, the United States still didn't initiate a public campaign to condemn what its own embassy was calling "selective genocide."[18] Asked in June why there had not yet been an official protest, a senior administration official said: "The State Department feels that it has no leverage. If it makes any public statement, its diplomatic missions there may be thrown out of the country."[19] The United Nations, worried about impediments to its relief operations, shared this concern about retaliation. It would not be until July that the U.N. issued a carefully worded statement on the massacres.[20]

The State Department also justified its silence by saying that the situation in Burundi remained murky. One month after the premier of Belgium said that "genocide" was occurring in Burundi, three weeks after reliable estimates had placed the death toll at over a hundred thousand and the "selective genocide" cable had already circulated widely in Washington, an African specialist in the State Department told a reporter that the United States was waiting for more information before it rendered judgment. "The early reports of genocide and mass slaughter in Biafra also proved unfounded. . . . The Burundi Government says that things are quieting down and our diplomats are now being given permission for the first time to leave the capital and move about the country."[21] Senator Edward Kennedy saw things differently: he released cables from the embassy in Burundi that showed that the government killing campaign was continuing and that the State Department was directly contradicting its own diplomats. "As in the case of Bangladesh, once again field reports to our government are being suppressed," Kennedy said.[22]

The United States felt constrained in Burundi by some of the same factors that underlay its declaration of neutrality in Nigeria. The late 1960s and early 1970s were a time of intense African nationalism, and U.S. officials feared making moves that could trigger an anti-Western backlash. In the aftermath of the coup attempt that preceded the violence, Micombero's government had railed against the "agents of imperialism" and described the attempt as aimed at installing a "pro-imperialist" government.[23] American policy makers were reluctant to provide more ammunition for this kind of propaganda. As Herman Cohen, director of the Office of Central African Affairs, commented in 1973, "Dramatic actions and public declarations from outside of Africa could only have served to influence African sensitivities to great power interference and rally African opinion in support of the Burundi government."[24] Ambassador Melady shared this assessment, writing later that "any direct action by the United States in the first few months would not, in my opinion, have changed the situation." Instead "it could have had negative, counterproductive results."[25] In the end, the State Department's only significant gesture of public chastisement of Micombero was to call its ambassador home for two months.

The lax U.S. response to the atrocities in Burundi, as well as to those in East Pakistan, must be viewed within the context of the times. In the early 1970s, the argument that the international community had a right to intervene in the internal affairs of countries to prevent human-rights abuses was just beginning to be made, and it faced stiff resistance from Third World states that had only recently emerged from colonialism. In U.S. politics, human rights was only just becoming a hot issue. Both policy thinking and the nonprofit advocacy groups designed to influence the human-rights records of foreign countries were still in their infancy. In this atmosphere, the Nixon administration could get away with its failure to condemn some of the worst outbreaks of ethnic violence in the twentieth century.

By the early 1990s things were very different. The war in the former Yugoslavia unfolded under intense scrutiny and there was exhaustive documentation of the human-rights abuses that accompanied it. The United States was under serious pressure from the beginning of the conflict to take a public stance against aggression and atrocities, especially when the war in Bosnia erupted in 1992. Various critics of U.S. policy toward Bosnia have claimed that the United States failed to condemn Serb actions between 1992 and 1994 and that it could have used diplomatic pressure more effectively during this period. In particular, critics have charged that the United States intentionally downplayed its condemnation of ethnic cleansing and Serb atrocities so as not to prompt demands for American military intervention.

These claims are exaggerated. Whatever faults one may find with the U.S. stances on humanitarian and military intervention, it is hard to blame either the Bush or the Clinton administration for forsaking the tools of public condemnation or private diplomatic pressure. Indeed, at times the United States may have gone too far in expressing its moral outrage and may thus have given the Bosnian government false hope that this rhetoric presaged eventual military action against Serbia.

With a few notable lapses, the United States compiled a consistent record of strong diplomatic protests regarding Bosnia between

1992 and 1994. Less than two weeks after Serb irregulars poured across the Drina River in April 1992 and began the war in eastern Bosnia, Secretary of State James Baker met with Haris Silajdzic, the Bosnian foreign minister, and affirmed U.S. support for Bosnia's territorial integrity. Afterward, a State Department spokesperson, Margaret Tutwiler, said that Baker unequivocally blamed Serb nationalists, especially Milosevic, for using force and intimidation to bring about the disintegration of Bosnia. Through Tutwiler, Baker warned that, if Serb leaders stayed "on their present course of destabilization, they will only ensure their international political and economic isolation."[26]

On May 4, the United States condemned Serb actions in shelling Sarajevo.[27] On May 6, the U.S. representative at a CSCE conference in Helsinki condemned Serb aggression and urged that Serbia be suspended from participation in the CSCE.[28] On May 12, Ambassador Warren Zimmerman was recalled from Belgrade after delivering strong warnings to Milosevic about the consequences of continued aggression. On May 14, a State Department spokesperson expressed concern about the Serb policy of ethnic cleansing. On May 22, Secretary Baker announced diplomatic sanctions against Serbia because of the "humanitarian nightmare."[29] On May 30, the United States helped push through a U.N. Security Council resolution imposing immediate sanctions against Serbia, and Edward J. Perkins, the U.S. permanent representative to the United Nations, condemned Serb aggression in the strongest terms. Perkins warned that the United States would not have normal relations with Belgrade until the Serbs ended their aggression.[30] On June 23, Secretary Baker again condemned the aggression and said the United States should not recognize Belgrade's ambassador and should suspend Serbia from international organizations.

This kind of U.S. condemnation of Serbia, along with an escalation of sanctions, continued through the summer and fall of 1992. As pressure built for U.S. intervention in the conflict, however, the Bush administration sought to downplay revelations about Serb atrocities and presented the conflict in more ambiguous terms. Amid increasing reports of mass killings at Serb detention camps

—including numerous eyewitness accounts considered reliable by mid-level State Department officials—the United States took the position that such atrocities could not be confirmed.[31] Several State Department officials would later say that the department had known of the existence of Serb detention centers as early as April and May of 1992 and that by the end of June department officials knew of large-scale concentration camps.[32] Nevertheless, Assistant Secretary of State Thomas Niles would testify to Congress as late as August 4 that the evidence regarding Serb concentration camps was inconclusive. On August 5, labeling reports of widespread atrocities at the camps "unconfirmed," the State Department called for a thorough investigation by international agencies.[33] In this fashion, it stalled on the issue through August and September, declining to make definitive statements or protests pending a complete investigation by international agencies.[34] Meanwhile, official rhetoric termed the conflict a civil war, implying disingenuously that clear-cut blame was hard to assign.[35] Given the Bush administration's unwillingness to intervene militarily, there was considerable logic to its strategy of public diplomacy. Bush officials recognized the dangers of allowing U.S. rhetoric to get too far ahead of policy. They did not make promises that they were not prepared to fulfill.

The Clinton administration was less successful on this score. As a candidate, Clinton had said, "We cannot afford to ignore what appears to be a deliberate and systematic extermination of human beings based on their ethnic origin," and had recommended air strikes against the Serbs.[36] His administration initially stepped up the intensity of diplomatic condemnation of Serbia, but when the administration failed to win European support for its "lift and strike" proposal—lifting the arms embargo on Bosnia and attacking the Serbs with air power—it toned down its rhetoric. Secretary of State Warren Christopher, who previously had portrayed the conflict as one fueled by Serb aggression, now said that abuses were committed on both sides and sought to spread the blame to all parties for refusing to end the fighting.[37] (Christopher's statement produced an angry memorandum from one of the State Department's own top analysts that disputed this assessment.)[38] Assistant Secretary Stephen Oxman said in June 1993, "Ultimately the killing will not stop until all parties are persuaded that it must stop."[39]

Despite these efforts to tone down U.S. statements, a chasm endured between the country's condemnatory rhetoric and its willingness to employ military force. This was especially true following official statements in August 1993 and February 1994 that the Serb siege of Sarajevo demanded a military response. American inaction following these declarations underscored the hollowness of its public diplomacy. The consequences of allowing rhetoric to get so far ahead of policy were disastrous in 1993 and 1994. American statements gave the Bosnians false hope while reducing the administration's credibility in Serb eyes. As Henry Kissinger accurately observes, "These commitments to higher moral principles unmatched by higher use of force led to a gradual emasculation of the people we were supposed to be protecting, by keeping the war going. . . . From the beginning, [Clinton] proposed objectives that were totally incompatible with the means proposed for achieving those objectives."[40]

Diplomatic pressure, both public and private, can in some circumstances yield results on its own. In Bosnia, however, it is hard to identify any impact that Washington's many protests had on Serb actions. Instead, the Bosnian conflict illustrates the limits of efforts to sway nationalist extremists with moral condemnation and threats of punishment. It illustrates as well the danger of overrelying on this instrument in the absence of a willingness to use military force. Without question, bluffing is an important part of any strategy of coercion, and sometimes it works. But two points must always be borne in mind: one, hypernationalist leaders can be expected to call bluffs and, two, bluffing tactics usually don't work with an adversary who has already called earlier bluffs.

Diplomatic condemnation was also a failure in Rwanda, yet this time the Clinton administration carefully sought to reduce expectations of any decisive U.S. action to end the crisis. Its public stance appeared cynical and callous as a result, yet the administration was right to take the approach that it did since it had no intention of intervening militarily in Rwanda.

When reports of the genocidal violence first emerged from Rwanda, the U.S. government initiated a diplomatic pressure campaign that combined frequent private appeals with protests by top officials. In early May, Assistant Secretary of State George Moose told a congressional committee: "I and other American officials have spoken directly to members of the Rwandan government, to the Rwandan military, and to the RPF in Washington via diplomatic channels and directly by telephone to Rwanda. . . . We have reinforced these private contacts with high-level public appeals and statements by the President and by other senior officials of the State Department."[41] In addition, the United States sought to coordinate its policy with the French and Belgian governments through extensive diplomatic contacts. It also asked Tanzania and the OAU to make an effort to achieve a cease-fire between the Rwandan government and the RPF.

The killing did not let up. The spectacle of officials in Washington calling long distance to urge restraint on the part of genocidal maniacs in Rwanda was almost comical. Predictably, it was of little use. Prudence Bushnell, deputy assistant secretary of state, spoke three times by phone with the chief of staff of the Rwandan military, who depicted the genocide as spontaneous civil violence beyond anybody's control. He said that the military was an overstretched organization that was simply trying to maintain order and that it could not contain the civil violence and fight the RPF at the same time.[42]

While public condemnations of the mass killing were strong and came from the highest levels, they did not contain any implicit promises of action to stop the violence. This restraint made sense, but it also resulted in some disingenuousness in U.S. policy. As with the Bush administration in Bosnia, the Clinton administration sought at points to play down the gravity of what was occurring in order to reduce demands for intervention. In June, the Clinton administration told its officials to avoid using the term *genocide* to describe the mass killing in Rwanda. Even as the systematic effort to exterminate Rwanda's Tutsi population continued, officials were instructed to say only that "acts of genocide may have occurred." Christine Shelly, a State Department spokesperson, explained this policy: "There are obligations which arise in connection with the use of the term."[43] She was referring to the 1949 Geneva Convention, which makes all participating nations, of which the United States is one, responsible for preventing genocide. If the violence in Rwanda was not genocide, the United States didn't have an obligation to act. Even as the reliable estimates of Tutsi deaths rose past a quarter million, David Rawson, the ambassador to Rwanda, said that the United States still didn't have enough information: "As a responsible government, you just don't go around hollering genocide. You say that acts of genocide may have occurred and they need to be investigated."[44]

The failure of U.S. diplomatic protests to end or mitigate the violence in Rwanda is not surprising. Like the Bosnian war, the Rwandan violence illustrates the limits of U.S. influence over ethnic extremists who believe they are engaged in a historic struggle for primacy. Words from Washington matter little, and even stiff punishments and credible threats of military force may have only a limited impact in such situations.

Diplomatic protests are more effective when lodged against a state that is waging a less nationalistically charged war on a secessionist group and that values good relations with the United States. These protests, however, must be sustained and consistent in tone. Belated complaints from Washington appear to have had little impact in restraining the Turkish operation in northern Iraq, mixed as they were with statements of sympathy. Meanwhile, U.S. protests and pressure may have had some impact on Russian behavior in Chechnya.

The United States originally supported the 1995 Turkish incursion into Iraq (Operation Steel) after receiving assurances from Ankara that the incursion would be of limited scope and duration.[45] When the operation dragged on and was accompanied by human-rights abuses and when it was roundly condemned by the countries of Western Europe, the Clinton administration was in the awkward position of having to criticize an ally for behavior it had first condoned. The administration began applying pressure on Turkey to withdraw from Iraq a week after the invasion. Secretary of State Christopher sent a message to Tansu Ciller, the Turkish prime minister, expressing concern about Turkey's human-rights violations and its apparent plans to remain in northern Iraq for a long stay. "We told them that we thought the support of the United States and the international community would be forthcoming only if troops were promptly withdrawn," Christopher said on March 27.[46]

At this point the U.S. message to Turkey was still accompanied by some signs of support. Even as the Clinton administration called for a troop withdrawal, it refrained from condemning the incursion as a violation of international law. "There is an administrative vacuum in that area," said a State Department spokesperson. "Countries have certain rights under international law to stop actions that may be taking place across international borders against them."[47] The administration also did not threaten to cut off aid or trade. (Congress took a harsher stance. In late March, legislation was introduced that would cut aid to Turkey unless it ended its offensive.) Overall, it appeared that the administration was criticizing Turkey in response to growing international and domestic pressure, not out of genuine concern on its own part.

With the Clinton administration's condemnation less than unequivocal, Turkey was in a position to resist the other international pressures that were brought to bear on it for the invasion. Instead of promptly withdrawing its troops, it kept them there into April and continued to use U.S. planes to strafe Kurdish villages and to wage a war that claimed many civilian lives.

The Clinton administration stepped up its criticism of Turkish actions during a visit by Prime Minister Ciller to Washington in April. Clinton urged Ciller to withdraw troops from Iraq, and U.S. officials repeated this message to the press. Yet again, the United States sent a mixed message. The simple act of granting Ciller a forty-five-minute audience with Clinton signaled a supportive stance. And even as Clinton criticized the invasion and raised human-rights concerns with Ciller, he repeated his view that the original Turkish move was justified. Clinton and his advisers also accepted Ciller's refusal to set a date for the pullout of Turkish troops. After the meeting, Assistant Secretary of State Richard Holbrooke expressed criticism of Turkey but also sympathy for its geopolitical position, saying that "no other country is surrounded by more problems."[48] There was nothing in U.S. statements to suggest that Turkey was jeopardizing its warm ties with the United States through its continued occupation of northern Iraq. Nor was there any indication that the Clinton administration was pressing Turkey to end repression against its Kurdish population and find a political solution to the civil war. On a visit to Turkey at the height of the Iraqi incursion, Deputy Secretary of State Strobe Talbott referred only obliquely to Turkey's need to find a political solution to the Kurdish problem. Generalizing from a discussion of the Chechnya situation, he said in a major policy speech, "The way to defeat outlaw groups is to deprive them of popular support by addressing legitimate needs and grievances. Inclusive democracy, in short, is the best antidote to extremism." He did not specifically urge Turkey to apply this thinking to its large Kurdish minority.[49]

The United States took a far more demanding line with the Russian government over the Chechnya issue. After an initial period of complacency in which it called the Chechen war an internal matter, the Clinton administration put Moscow on notice that high levels of violence against the civilian population of the breakaway republic were unacceptable and jeopardized good relations with the United States. It managed to sustain this message over time while still being supportive of Russia's overall aims in Chechnya. "Let me make clear that we support the territorial integrity of Russia, just as we support the territorial integrity of its neighbors," said Anthony Lake on January 1, 1995. "So the issue is not whether Chechnya should be part of Russia or not. The issue for us is what their military tactics are."[50]

In the last days of 1994 and the first weeks of 1995, as Russian artillery and air power razed the city of Grozny, the United States used multiple high-level contacts to pressure Moscow to show restraint. The first warning came in the form of a State Department protest on December 29. This, along with other international protests, led President Yeltsin to suspend aerial attacks on Grozny while continuing the use of rockets and artillery. Following Yeltsin's announcement, Secretary of State Christopher called Russia's foreign minister, Andrei Kozyrev, and received assurances that Russia was trying to limit civilian casualties.[51]

As the large-scale destruction of civilian areas in Grozny continued, U.S. officials stepped up their pressure. In January Clinton wrote to Yeltsin appealing for an end to attacks on civilians and urging him to find a political settlement to the war, starting with acceptance of mediation by the OSCE. Clinton's letter offered "friendly suggestions" but had a firm tone.[52] Before it was sent, Christopher pressed many of the same points in a telephone conversation with Kozyrev. Around this time, both Christopher and Defense Secretary William Perry made their first public criticisms of Russian operations in Chechnya. "That conflict should be resolved in a manner consistent with international norms," Perry said on January 6. "And we've been increasingly concerned by Russia's tactics, which have caused many civilian casualties."[53] The reference to civilian casualties would be repeated often by U.S. officials at all levels.

These initial expressions of concern were followed later in January by extensive personal contacts with Russian diplomats. Strobe Talbott flew to Brussels for an urgent meeting with a deputy foreign minister, Georgy Mamedov, while Christopher met in Geneva with Kozyrev. Talbott and Christopher expressed their support for good relations with Russia but stressed the negative consequences of allowing such horrific violence to continue in Chechnya. Christopher indicated that one such consequence might be cuts in aid.[54] On January 13, President Clinton voiced his first open criticism in a speech that otherwise expressed strong support for Yeltsin's government. The same day, Christopher criticized the "indiscriminate killing" in Chechnya while stating that the administration would push vigorously to get aid for Russia through Congress.[55] The United States also indicated the seriousness of its concern by charging that Russia had violated arms control agreements that required it to give notification of any large troop movements.[56]

The U.S. pressure campaign yielded pledges by Moscow that it would change its behavior. Following his somber Geneva meeting with Christopher, Foreign Minister Kozyrev said that Russia would allow humanitarian aid into Chechnya and that it would hold free elections there in an effort to achieve a political solution.[57]

Having made its position unambiguously clear in January, the Clinton administration promptly toned down its criticisms of Russian actions. It renewed them, however, as reports of civilian casualties continued and Moscow failed to make progress toward a political settlement. Again, the message was one of supportive but stern chastisement. In late March, Christopher described the Russian invasion as "foolhardy" and "tragically wrong" but said that the administration had not considered an aid cutoff.[58]

On April 11, after Russian forces had taken Grozny and extended their operations into other areas of Chechnya, the State Department unleashed a new broadside. "We continue to be very deeply disturbed by the reports of continued, large-scale bombing in the south of Chechnya," said Nicholas Burns of the State Department. "This conflict is having a corrosive effect on the development of Russian democratic institutions and Russian democracy and it's having a negative effect on American-Russian relations." Burns went on to say that the United States now believed that a military solution was not possible in Chechnya and that Moscow had to find a political solution.[59] Criticism of Russian operations in Chechnya continued during the weeks leading up to a U.S.-Russian summit in May and was sustained into June, when Yeltsin was urged at a meeting of the Group of Seven in Nova Scotia to settle the conflict by negotiation.

The overall impact of U.S. diplomatic pressure over the first six months of 1995 is difficult to gauge. The Russian offensive in Chechnya proceeded with enormous violence, leaving an estimated thirty thousand Chechen civilians dead. Nevertheless, things could have been worse. U.S. and international protests probably did save lives in Grozny by forcing Yeltsin to end aerial bombing of the city. These protests may also have made a difference in the human-rights situation by compelling Yeltsin to allow an OSCE human-rights mission into Chechnya in March. And U.S. pressure on Moscow to find a political solution to the war may have pushed the Russian leader to hold talks with the Chechen rebels earlier than he might otherwise have held them.

SANCTIONS

Economic and military sanctions are policy makers' most important coercive instruments short of armed action. They offer Washington a way to punish rogue states and isolate combatants without undertaking a commitment that places U.S. lives on the line. Sanctions are flexible instruments: they can entail anything from a partial cutoff of foreign aid or a denial of certain types of heavy weapons to full-scale isolation from the international system. Their aim can range from sending a strong signal to bringing a state to its knees.

Economic sanctions have been imposed on 120 countries during the twentieth century, but their effectiveness has proved mixed.[60] Partial sanctions have caused some states to change their behavior, while sustained and comprehensive sanctions have had only minimal impact in other situations. Putting such punishment into place has also often been difficult. Far-reaching sanctions require that many states agree to forsake trade earnings, and sanctioning coalitions can fracture easily. Lighter sanctions that target aid and arms are frequently opposed within the U.S. government by officials who fear such sanctions will generate a backlash and a loss of influence without yielding any gains.

Sanctions have proved to be an instrument of very modest effectiveness for stopping or mitigating ethnic warfare. They seem to be more effective as a tool for preventing conflict than as a means to stop conflicts that are already under way. Warring ethnic extremists who have ignored the protests of the international community have also not been easily swayed by punishment. Sanctions appear to have sometimes pushed states toward more conciliatory positions and limited the intensity of fighting. More often they have done nothing to stop carnage of hellish dimensions. There are multiple instances where the United States could have made greater use of the sanctions weapon. But again, it is difficult in hindsight to predict what the outcome of such efforts would have been.

In most crisis situations abroad, the reflexive preference of U.S. officials is to maintain maximum leverage over the parties involved. The continuation of aid and trade relationships is seen as desirable in all but the most exigent situations. These ties offer a way to sustain communication between the United States and a foreign government and thus some hope of influencing that government's behavior—if not through persuasion then through the threat, implicit or explicit, that the blessings of the United States will be withdrawn. This desire to retain influence is understandable. Yet if taken too far, it can have the opposite result, producing policies that are not tough enough and that coddle criminal governments.

During the Biafran war, the United States imposed an arms embargo on both groups of combatants and urged other countries to do the same. The arms embargo was the principal symbol of U.S. neutrality, but the sanctions policy illustrated that Washington had no wish to cripple the Nigerian government. American officials knew that Great Britain was continuing to supply Nigeria with light weapons and never publicly protested these transfers. The United States also did not impose economic sanctions on Nigeria, even as it became apparent that the government in Lagos was waging a brutal military campaign and using starvation as a means to win the war against Biafra.

In 1969, Undersecretary of State Elliot Richardson testified to Congress that "the United States has had to face the fact that we have no effective influence with either party" in the Biafra conflict.[61] This may well have been true, but it was also true that the United States was not experimenting with all the means of leverage at its disposal. A tougher sanctions policy would not have ended Nigeria's war against Biafra, but it might have been tied to efforts to pressure Lagos to take a more moderate position on the delivery of humanitarian aid to Biafra. As it was, the Nigerian government was allowed to pursue a policy of stunning inhumanity with virtually no punishment from the United States or the international community.

Sanctions were also resisted during the East Pakistan crisis. Under prodding by the Senate, the State Department—which knew nothing of the channel to China—insisted that the United States establish an arms embargo not long after Pakistan began its repression in East Pakistan. This embargo would prove porous in the extreme, since it prohibited only new licensing agreements and did not affect arms that were already in the pipeline—some $35 million worth of equipment.[62] Thus, even as Pakistani troops engaged in the wholesale slaughter of civilians, freighters loaded with weapons were leaving U.S. harbors and heading for Pakistan. Despite Senate votes calling for a cutoff of these arms as well, the Nixon administration refused to close down the arms pipeline.

The Nixon administration also refused to punish Pakistan by withholding economic aid. Even as most other Western countries suspended aid pending a political settlement in East Pakistan, the administration said that U.S. aid—nearly $100 million a year— would continue. In justifying this stance, U.S. officials said they disapproved of denying aid as an instrument of pressure. Christopher Van Hollen, a State Department aide, argued, moreover, that providing aid would give the United States leverage over Pakistani policies. How much leverage Van Hollen could not say.[63] The leverage argument would be repeated by President Nixon.[64]

Michael Micombero's government in Burundi was also not penalized for massive human-rights abuses. The U.S. government chose not to retaliate against Burundi by stopping the importation of its coffee, which accounted for most of its foreign-exchange earnings. To critics of American policy like Roger Morris, this trade relationship gave the United States leverage that should have been exploited during and immediately after the mass killings.[65] As one observer commented, "A country so poor as to execute people with hammer blows to the head in order to save bullets certainly couldn't resist any serious economic sanctions against it."[66] But to U.S. officials like Herman Cohen and Thomas Melady, trade with Burundi, along with a small amount of U.S. assistance, conferred little influence, especially in the light of the historically poor relationship between the two countries. At one point in the crisis, there was some sentiment in the State Department for at least threatening sanctions, but nothing came of this suggestion. As Cohen said in 1973, "We felt that a threatened boycott would not have influenced the immediate problems of ethnic violence, and if carried out, would have permanently deprived both Hutus and Tutsi of the foreign exchange to buy bread, medicine, clothing, oil products, and every other basic item to keep the country alive. In short, a coffee boycott would have been an inhumane response."[67]

Instead of opting for the most punishing option, the United States took far more modest steps against Burundi. It suspended its small economic aid package and reevaluated Burundi's role in the Peace Corps program. Even critics like Morris conceded that harsher actions would probably not have stopped the killing. These critics still believed, however, that the United States had a moral obligation to use every means possible to ameliorate a horrendous situation and to punish those responsible for the killing. That moral fervor was less intense in a State Department that believed that the United States could do more good in the long run by aiding Burundi's economic development.

Such reasoning also prevailed in the aftermath of the 1988 massacres in Burundi. American officials believed not only that the United States should continue to support President Pierre Buyoya because they saw him as a force for moderation but also that an aid cutoff would hurt those it was intended to help. In September 1988, Deputy Assistant Secretary of State Kenneth Brown said of American aid that it was "oriented toward assisting the individual citizens of Burundi not the government" and that it helped "those who have been disadvantaged by discrimination." He also argued that the U.S. military training program should not be suspended, because it was useful for instilling democratic values in the Burundi armed forces.[68] Compared with the benefits of continuing aid, a cutoff would yield little influence, given the intense emotions driving the conflict. "When it gets down to a question of survival, they don't really care about aid, whether it be international or national," said Brown.[69]

American officials made a correct judgment about Buyoya. In the wake of the massacres, his government accelerated its policies of ethnic conciliation, making a major effort to repatriate the fifty thousand Hutu who had fled the country and, in 1989, undertaking an extensive public-education campaign based on dialogue between Hutu and Tutsi.[70] In addition, Buyoya created a National Unity Commission of high-level representatives of both ethnic groups, named an ethnically balanced cabinet, and appointed a Hutu prime minister.[71] By 1992, Buyoya's reform efforts had yielded a new constitution, a reasonably free press, and plans for fair elections.[72]

Human-rights groups typically believe that the best way to change behavior is through swift punishment, regardless of the leverage that may be attained by continuing aid to an abusive regime. This may often be the case, especially when a regime is manifestly uninterested in changing its human-rights record. But as the Burundi example shows, there are some circumstances in which reformist leaders are engaged in a battle to control extremists within their governments, particularly within the military. Such leaders deserve U.S. support. Aid cutoffs and other sanctions should be threatened if such threats can be used by reformers to strengthen their position. Otherwise they can be counterproductive.

During the Lebanese conflict, too, the U.S. government believed that continued assistance could be used to advance its policy. The disintegration of Lebanon's central state in 1975 made it pointless to impose sanctions on the country, since there was no real government that could be expected to change its behavior in response to such coercion. As Lebanon's government began to revive, the goal of U.S. policy in the late 1970s and early 1980s was to build up state institutions so that they had the power to restore order. Thus, in 1977 the United States sent $77 million to Lebanon,

about a third of that in military aid, with the goal of rebuilding a
Lebanese army. American aid came with the stipulation that the
new army would have a balanced Muslim-Christian composition.[73]
This assistance was continued in 1978 with the goal of helping the
moderate government of President Ilyas Sarkis. As a State Department official explained to Congress: "The credit assistance
which the United States provides is a major political and psycho-
logical signal of American support for the unifying and stabilizing
policies of President Sarkis. With a rebuilt army, we hope that the
Lebanese government will be able to assert its authority throughout the country."[74]

In theory, the policy of maintaining neutrality by aiding rather
than punishing the Lebanese government made sense. In practice,
that policy gave the appearance that the United States favored the
Christian-dominated government. Also, since the unwillingness of
the Christians to concede greater powers to the Muslims was a
significant obstacle to achieving a negotiated peace, the United
States had to be careful that its backing did not simply strengthen
Christian obduracy. As a congressional report stated in October
1983, when U.S. marines were in Lebanon and efforts were being
stepped up to train the Lebanese army, "An open-ended commitment by the United States to the Lebanese central government
could relax the pressure that appears necessary to obtain the concessions by the various factions needed to achieve a stable government."[75]

American support for governments engaged in ethnic conflict
requires exceptional finesse. Encouragement and assistance from
Washington must be accompanied by the message that a lack of
progress toward addressing the causes of the conflict will trigger a
rapid withdrawal of such help. This kind of "tough love" diplomacy is awkward since open threats can make it hard to sustain
good working relationships. In addition, there is a natural tendency
among U.S. officials to grow overcommitted to states where the
United States has invested resources and prestige and to relax their
pressure for change. In Lebanon, the United States vacillated between taking a firm line with the central government and failing

to press it hard enough to make negotiating concessions. By fall 1983, when the marine barracks were bombed, Washington had become too closely identified with an inflexible Lebanese government.

The repression of ethnic minorities is an important indicator of a state's potential to pose threats to its neighbors and to the international community as a whole. Punishing governments that systematically violate minority rights can put aggressive state leaders on notice that they are being watched and that they will pay a price for any future disregard of international norms. Conversely, ignoring gross abuses may lead state leaders to believe that they can get away with greater transgressions.

The weak U.S. sanctions on Iraq for its genocidal war on the Kurds in the late 1980s resulted in a missed opportunity to issue a warning to a dictator with dangerous ambitions. Saddam Hussein's war on the Kurds—the infamous Anfal campaign—unfolded with unmitigated brutality. Arbitrary arrest, torture, and mass executions were standard operating procedure for Iraqi forces operating in Kurdistan, and nearly a half million Kurds were forcibly relocated from their ancestral villages, thousands of which were razed by Iraqi troops. On March 16, 1988, Iraqi warplanes dropped chemical weapons over the Kurdish city of Halabja, killing an estimated five thousand civilians.

The U.S. government was well aware of the massive violence against the Kurdish people, but the Reagan administration was disinclined to impose sanctions because it was engaged in aiding Iraq against Iran in an effort to contain the Islamic fundamentalism promoted by the ayatollahs in Tehran. Throughout the 1980s, trade between the United States and Iraq had increased steadily and included hundreds of millions of dollars' worth of technology with military uses. Iraq also was a recipient of agricultural loans under the Commodity Credit Corporation program. By 1987, the amount of that lending had reached $567 million and was still growing.[76] In addition, since 1984 the Central Intelligence Agency had been providing Iraq with satellite reconnaissance photos of Iranian positions. The end of the Iran-Iraq war in August 1988 did not change official thinking. On the contrary, U.S. officials saw an opportunity to cultivate Iraq as a strategic partner in the Persian Gulf and increased loans and trade

The Reagan administration's response to the human-rights disaster in Iraqi Kurdistan was to issue statements of protest and to hope that the issue went away. A statement by Secretary of State George Shultz on September 8, 1988, strongly condemned Iraq's use of chemical weapons but proposed no sanctions. Many members of Congress, however, were determined to see Iraq punished and legislation was introduced in 1988 to cut off U.S. loans to Iraq and impose trade sanctions. The Reagan administration fought this legislation vigorously, arguing that continued ties and quiet diplomacy were the best ways to affect Iraqi behavior. "We believe that enacting the sanctions now will inhibit our influence, will lessen our influence," said a State Department official, Peter Burleigh.[77] The United States ultimately meted out scant punishment against Iraq for one of the most barbaric war crimes of the decade. Administration officials were still fighting congressional attempts to impose sanctions against Iraq when it invaded Kuwait on August 2, 1990. It is no surprise that Saddam Hussein badly misjudged Washington's likely reaction and believed that it would allow the invasion to stand.

Realpolitik calculations underlay the U.S. decision to downplay the terrible fate of the Kurds and embrace Iraq. A more farsighted consideration of the national interest, however, would have dictated a harsh response to Saddam's pattern of internal aggression, much as it should have prompted punishment of Hitler when he began persecuting Germany's Jews several years before he set out to conquer Europe.

In nearly every ethnic conflict discussed so far, the United States availed itself of only some of the available sanctioning options. Historians are thus left to ponder counterfactual scenarios, wondering whether tougher U.S. policies might have changed the course of conflicts. Speculation of this sort produces very few solid conclusions. The Balkan crisis is illuminating because it is one of the few instances in which the United States has used comprehensive sanc-

tions to end an ethnic conflict. This punishment proved largely
unsuccessful in the short term, failing to stop the worst Serb aggression of 1992 and 1993, but was beneficial over the long term,
contributing to Belgrade's decision to seek a negotiated end to the
conflict in Bosnia.

The United States moved cautiously during 1991. It proposed
an international arms embargo on all of Yugoslavia on July 3,
shortly after fighting broke out in Slovenia, but well into the fall
it remained wary of stiffer punishment of Serbia. Even as Serb
forces began shelling the city of Dubrovnik in October, Bush administration officials argued that economic sanctions would reduce
U.S. influence in the crisis. Arguing on October 17 against a Senate
bill that would impose sanctions on Serbia, Deputy Assistant Secretary of State Ralph Johnson stated that the "current crisis is complicated and fluid, and the Administration must have the flexibility
to respond to changing circumstances and tailor its approach
accordingly."[78]

It took the extension of Serb aggression to Bosnia for the United
States to embrace the sanctions option. In late May 1992, the
United States initiated discussion at the United Nations on sanctioning Serbia under chapter 7 of the U.N. Charter. On May 30,
the Security Council adopted Resolution 757, cosponsored by the
United States, imposing immediate sanctions on Serbia that included a trade embargo, a freezing of assets abroad, and a range of
lesser measures. In public, some administration officials suggested
that sanctions would have an impact. "We believe that Serbia perhaps is a good example of a country that would be fairly vulnerable
to this sort of pressure," commented Assistant Secretary of State
Thomas Miles on June 23.[79] In private, there was skepticism that
anything short of a massive military intervention could alter the
course of the war. As James Baker acknowledges in his memoirs,
"I was under no illusion that these steps would be enough to
change fundamentally the behavior of the Bosnian Serbs and Belgrade."[80] Brent Scowcroft and Lawrence Eagleburger shared this
assessment.

Over the next two years, the United States would seek to tighten these sanctions, to participate actively in monitoring their enforcement, and to take measures to alleviate the negative economic impact that they had on Serbia's neighbors.[81] The imposition of comprehensive sanctions did nothing to alter the course of the Bosnian conflict in 1992 or 1993. Serb aggression continued on a systematic basis, with ethnic cleansing of one Muslim town after another and with the Serbs battering Sarajevo with a relentless artillery barrage. Initially, the sanctions may actually have served to strengthen Slobodan Milosevic's position within Serbia, where many Serbs believed that their country was being unfairly treated by the West.[82] At the end of 1993, a CIA assessment predicted that sanctions would not stop the redrawing of national boundaries in the Balkans and that the Serbs would hold on to gains won through aggression. The large-scale population shifts brought about by the war would be "difficult or impossible to undo," said the report.[83]

Yet by 1995, after three years of sanctions had reduced Serbia's economy to a shambles, it was evident that the Belgrade leadership had begun to question the economic costs of continuing to press its war aims. Milosevic clearly saw that the Serb economic position was untenable over the long run and that the price of readmission to the international economic order would be significant territorial concessions in Bosnia, where Serbs had captured 70 percent of the country. This turnaround in thinking helped make it possible for American negotiators to mediate a peace agreement in late 1995.[84]

WAR CRIME INDICTMENTS

Threatening the perpetrators of ethnic violence with international war crime indictments is a relatively new development. In the decades since the Nuremberg trials, U.S. leaders have almost never invoked the specter of criminal prosecution as part of a coercive strategy and, in general, have paid minimal heed to international law. There was no discussion within U.S. policy circles of bringing war crime indictments against the butchers of East Pakistan or the mass murderers of Burundi. Even Pol Pot was not pursued with this instrument. During the 1980s, the Reagan administration rejected a World Court ruling that condemned the U.S. covert war on Nicaragua. It was hard for the United States to stake out the moral high ground when it did not occupy that ground.

Iraq's invasion of Kuwait and the end of the cold war revived the United Nations and refocused U.S. attention on international law. Iraqi war crimes in occupied Kuwait produced serious discussion of indictments against Saddam Hussein and his henchmen. By the time war began in Yugoslavia, U.S. officials had given careful thought to how international legal restrictions on the use of military force could support U.S. policy objectives in regional conflicts. Organizations like Human Rights Watch were also giving this issue much attention, and governments and organizations alike believed that excessive wartime abuses of human rights might be curbed if the international community became serious about punishment. War crime indictments could serve notice to those responsible that their crimes would not be forgotten and that they would never again be able to circulate freely in international society without fear of arrest. In victory, war criminals would be confined to their own countries; in defeat, they would find themselves in prison or living as hunted fugitives.

American officials have been selective in threatening and pursuing indictments. Like the policy instruments of protest and sanctions, legal action has been pursued when it has been perceived as in the national interest. Several opportunities for such action have been passed up in recent years as the United States has deliberately ignored egregious abuses by friendly powers. When the United States has pursued war crime indictments it has often moved with extreme caution, concerned that indictments would only serve further to radicalize extremists who might fear arrest in the wake of any peace agreement. The effect of U.S. hesitation has been to undermine the power of legal action, or threats of it, to alter the course of conflicts. The United States has not always acted when it should have, and it has sometimes moved too slowly when it has acted.

The Serbs committed major war crimes in the former Yugoslavia when they began shelling the cities of Vukovar and Dubrovnik in the second half of 1991. These were the first indiscriminate attacks on civilians in Europe since World War II, and they were accompanied by a war of aggression elsewhere in Croatia. The United States protested the shellings, but it made no mention of using international law to punish those responsible. In retrospect, it would seem that threats were needed to put the Serbs on notice that barbarism would not be tolerated in Europe in the last decade of the twentieth century.

Reports of systematic Serb war crimes began surfacing shortly after the war began in Bosnia in April 1992. By the early summer there was a growing body of evidence that pointed to mass execution of civilians, systematic rape, illegal detention, and the widespread destruction of Muslim property. Yet it was not until August, at the height of the furor over Serb concentration camps, that the United States used the threat of war crime indictments. On August 4, the United States pressed for and obtained a statement from the U.N. Security Council that reminded those involved in running the camps that they might be held personally responsible for breaches of the Geneva Conventions.[85] The weakness of this threat was that it appeared to be limited in scope, focusing as it did on the detention camps rather than on all the war crimes that were occurring across Bosnia, often under the direction of top Serb leaders. On August 13, the U.N. Security Council passed a U.S.-sponsored resolution demanding immediate access to detention centers and establishing a process for investigating human-rights abuses. But neither the mandate of the investigation nor the time frame established for its completion allowed the inquiry to range far beyond the detention camps.

It was not until December 1992, during Bush's final weeks in office, that the United States took a hard line on war crimes. This turnaround came after Secretary of State Eagleburger met in Washington with Holocaust survivor Elie Wiesel. Previously, Eagleburger had believed that if the United States pushed too hard and named specific individuals it would hamper efforts to move toward peace because accused Serbs would be afraid of prosecution.

But after listening to an eloquent plea by Wiesel, Eagleburger decided that the time had come for firmer action. On December 16, Eagleburger gave a speech in Geneva in which he enumerated specific crimes and identified the individuals responsible for them. Eagleburger singled out several paramilitary leaders and detention camp commanders, and then he went further, saying that Slobodan Milosevic and Bosnian Serb leaders Radovan Karadzic and General Ratko Mladic would have to answer tough questions about command decisions that may have led to crimes against humanity.[86]

"I don't know that it's going to solve anything or change anything," Eagleburger said at a news conference after his speech, "but I think it's time, when we have the facts, . . . that we begin to name names; let them understand that, over the long run, they may be able to run but they can't hide; that we're going to pursue them."[87] Of course, the United States had had many of the facts needed for naming names months before Eagleburger made his speech. The evidence of direct complicity on the part of the top three Serb leaders was also far less ambiguous than Eagleburger suggested.

His speech attracted criticism both inside the U.S. government and in allied governments by officials who felt that he had hurt the chances for a negotiated peace. Many wondered how the West could bring the Serbs to the negotiating table when it seemed also to want to bring them before an international court. The Clinton administration, however, further elevated the war crime issue in 1993. In May, the United Nations established a war crimes tribunal with U.S. backing and financial support. Top administration officials regularly cited the work of the tribunal and pledged complete support. Madeleine Albright, the permanent representative to the United Nations, hinted in a speech at the Holocaust Memorial Museum in Washington that the tribunal's reach could extend to top Serbian leaders. "We oppose amnesty for the architects of ethnic cleansing," she said. "Today, there should be no question that political and military leaders may be held criminally accountable if they do not stop atrocities by their followers or do not punish those responsible. . . . If the architects of war and ethnic cleansing in Bosnia go unpunished, the lesson for would-be Milosevics around the globe will endanger us all, for today's world is a tinderbox of open and potential nationalist conflict." Albright also argued that even the threat of punishment for war crimes could save lives, citing Nazi behavior at the end of World War II and improved treatment of prisoners in Serb detention camps once the West began speaking of indictments.[88]

Yet despite such rhetoric the United States and the U.N. war crimes tribunal moved cautiously. Their concerns that indictments could impede peace negotiations were well-founded, for the Clinton administration's moral fervor did not extend to a willingness to use military force, and therefore the administration had few means to coerce the Serbs into making concessions at the negotiating table. Insisting on the prosecution of war criminals from this position of weakness was a risky proposition. As things turned out, however, the indictment of Karazdic and Mladic in 1995 did not stop peace negotiations from moving forward to completion. Indeed, targeting these top leaders may have made Milosevic worry that he would be indicted next if he did not move to end the war.

In Rwanda, the United States hinted at war crime indictments when the genocidal violence was at its height. In a statement issued on April 22, 1994, the White House urged four senior Rwandan army officers to end the violence. The United States was "letting them know that we knew who they were," a White House official explained.[89] In subsequent statements, U.S. officials spoke of the need to investigate and prosecute human-rights abuses. American threats never became more concrete, however.

The United States did not use the threat of war crime indictments in response to either Turkey's attacks on the Kurds or Russia's actions in Chechnya, though both cases involved aerial bombing and artillery assaults against civilian populations and military crackdowns accompanied by widespread torture and disappearances. In Turkish Kurdistan, security troops engaged in the forced relocation of hundreds of thousands of people and the destruction of Kurdish villages—actions not unlike ethnic cleansing. In Chechnya, the Russian assault on Grozny utterly leveled the city and was far more violent than the Serb siege of Sarajevo. Yet at no time during either of these conflicts did the United States even hint that war crimes might be occurring.

American officials wished, of course, to maintain good relations with Turkey and Russia, but they also justified these acts of extreme violence as quite different from Serb actions in Bosnia. The difference lay in intent. While the Serbs were waging a war of nationalist extremism, Turkey and Russia were defending legitimate security interests. There is a logic in this position if war crime indictments are viewed chiefly as a tool for punishing the architects of aggression and thus deterring future aggressors. Clearly this is how international law was interpreted in the aftermath of World War II, when Allied bombing of civilian populations went unpunished. If, however, international law is seen as a rigid code of conduct that applies to all nations and that is intended to curb violence against noncombatants in all wars, then there is a price to be paid for punishing some mass murderers but not others. Such inconsistency degrades the moral authority of the international legal system, just as bias in domestic judicial systems erodes faith in the state.

MEDIATION

The United States has sought to mediate nearly every major ethnic conflict in the past thirty years. Only on rare occasions have such efforts succeeded. More often, U.S. mediation attempts have failed or have produced mixed results. This discouraging record is not surprising. Ethnic conflicts tend to be exceptionally intractable, generating passions that are hard to put aside in reasoned negotiations.[90] Such conflicts are nearly always accompanied by heinous atrocities and mass attacks on civilian populations. Combatants typically include paramilitary groups and other irregular forces that are difficult for leaders to control. Invariably, one side in the conflict is not an internationally recognized entity, and this fact complicates the task of diplomacy. The simple act of getting negotiations under way can be difficult when state leaders view their opponents as terrorists or rebels with no legitimacy. The political aims of the parties in ethnic conflict are, more often than not, implacably at odds.

American diplomacy can have an impact in even the worst situations, but many obstacles stand in the way of decisive U.S. influence. The United States must have the trust of both parties and be acceptable as a mediator. It must have some leverage over at least one of the parties. It must be prepared to make a sustained effort, even as setbacks accumulate. It must coordinate its mediation strategy with the other elements of its policy, using sanctions and the threat of military force—along with promises of future aid and trade—to compel flexibility in negotiations. It must show that its highest-level leaders are fully committed to the effort and prepared to intervene personally to break stalemates. In short, if the United States wants results, it can't be content with occasional proposals and intermittent diplomatic jaunts. Instead, it must husband its resources, wait until the situation is ripe—that is, until there is an indication that mediation could make a difference—and then mount a carefully choreographed long-term intervention.[91]

Many U.S. failures to mediate ethnic conflicts have occurred when these dictates were ignored. The United States has dispatched to war zones special envoys who were not trusted by both parties, who had negligible power to either threaten punishment or promise rewards, and who represented administrations that had failed to devise a strong multifaceted policy. Some U.S. mediation efforts have been premature; others have not been adequately sustained. At times the United States has done everything right and still failed. Good policy is a prerequisite for success, but it does not guarantee it.

During the early stages of the Biafran conflict, the United States did not propose itself as a mediator. It believed that Great Britain and the OAU should take the lead since they had historic links to Nigeria. The first major mediation effort of the war came from Arnold Smith, a Canadian career diplomat who was secretary general of the Commonwealth secretariat. Smith began focusing on the war at its beginning and succeeded in starting talks between the Nigerians and the Biafrans in May 1968.[92] He would continue his efforts with little success as the war dragged on. The State Department played a role in this process by continually pressuring Smith to increase his efforts and by helping him shape his ideas.[93]

The United States began to focus more closely on the Biafran problem when mass starvation was predicted. In November 1968, Undersecretary of State Nicholas Katzenbach set up an emergency task force to study ways to respond to the mounting disaster within the secessionist enclave.[94] Much of this group's work centered on the problem of getting humanitarian relief to the Biafrans, but U.S. officials also looked at how a political solution could be found. In a December speech, Katzenbach said that a means had to be found to guarantee the unity of Nigeria while safeguarding the rights of the Ibo.[95] One of the conclusions of Katzenbach's task force was that the United States should pressure both sides to agree to a cease-fire. Members of the task force hoped that a new British diplomatic effort would produce results but believed that the United States had to be prepared for greater involvement if this did not occur.[96]

The British effort produced only a short-lived cease-fire, and Richard Nixon took power before the Johnson administration could attempt any other initiatives. Nixon came into office pledging to give the Biafran situation more attention. Beyond suggesting a greater relief effort, however, the NSC study undertaken in February 1969 proposed little new. For the first six months of 1969, the administration made no attempts at mediation. In July, with starvation in Biafra becoming ever more horrendous and with domestic pressures mounting, Nixon reacted to a full-page newspaper ad placed by a citizens' group appealing to him to stop the war. He dictated a memo to Kissinger that said: "I agree. Give me a plan."[97]

The NSC staff responded by preparing a detailed background paper on how the United States could bring about peace negotiations. Nixon then authorized the staff to undertake a secret diplomatic initiative to try to get the process moving. Roger Morris was instructed by Kissinger to hold talks with representatives of both the Biafran and Nigerian governments. He did so beginning in August 1969. The initiative, an utter failure, was kept secret from the State Department, which regarded high-level U.S. contacts with the Biafrans as having the potential to jeopardize relations with Nigeria. "It's a little difficult to do these things when you're working against your government," Morris would say later.[98] Morris was also operating with no clear instructions and no consistent high-level backing. Nixon's interest in the issue was intermittent, and he did not follow through on his desire to mediate the conflict.[99] The secret discussions with the Biafrans dragged into the fall before ending without success.

Around the same time, Undersecretary of State Elliot Richardson argued before Congress that U.S. diplomacy could not end the war. "To be precise, an American political initiative in the civil war must reckon immediately with several obdurate realities. At present, the two sides show no willingness to agree even on the context for political discussions, let alone the terms of a possible settlement. The FMG [Nigerian government] wants the principle of a unified Nigeria, Biafra wants their claim of independence. The FMG wants negotiations prior to cease-fire, Biafrans want a cease-fire first. . . . The United States has had to face the fact that we have no effective influence with either party to alter these realities."[100]

Roger Morris may well be correct in his later reflection that the State Department cared more about future U.S. influence with Nigeria than about ending the war.[101] Nevertheless, Richardson accurately depicted the stalemate that existed between the two parties and it is clear that this situation was not "ripe" for U.S. mediation. Secret White House diplomacy proved to be no magic wand, and even a larger public initiative would likely have failed.

AMERICAN DIPLOMATIC EFFORTS to end the Lebanese civil war unfolded over a thirteen-year period.[102] While these efforts had no decisive effect, the United States succeeded in promoting dialogue that otherwise might not have taken place. In part, the failure to achieve better results was due, initially, to U.S. unwillingness to make a major commitment of power to ending the war. And when the United States did make a major commitment, in 1982 and 1983, it pursued a flawed diplomatic strategy. That said, it is far from clear that any U.S. policy, however well constructed, could have ended one of the most ferocious communal conflicts of the twentieth century.

The first major mediation initiative came in spring 1976, when President Gerald Ford dispatched L. Dean Brown, president of the Middle East Institute, to Lebanon as a special envoy. As U.S. diplomats in Washington and the Middle East held discussions with the Jordanians, the Egyptians, and the Syrians in an attempt to galvanize an outside response to the war, Brown spent a month engaged in an intensive effort to get the factions in Lebanon to talk peace.[103] He shuttled between the strongholds of the different groups, floating proposals for conciliation. He talked not just to the warlords but also to educators, religious leaders, businessmen, and soldiers. What he found was a state where the institutions of civic life had collapsed, where basic services were scarce, where the economy no longer functioned, and where the national president commanded the loyalty of virtually no one. Lebanon was a quintessential "failed state" long before that term was coined. Brown believed that a U.N. or multinational force might have some hope of restoring order, but he could not use the prospect of such a deployment to push the peace process forward. Because the United States was not ready to send forces to Lebanon, Brown said, it "is therefore not in the position to create an outside force by others."[104]

Brown also argued that U.S. policy was doomed to fail because the United States was not making a serious effort to solve the Palestinian problem. The presence of Palestinian refugees and guerrilla fighters in Lebanon deeply destabilized the country. There would be no peace in Lebanon "until there is a Palestinian state," Brown said.[105] This was a commonly held belief, since the Palestinians could not easily leave Lebanon until they had somewhere to go. Yet solving the Palestinian problem would require a

major effort by the United States, including the exertion of enormous pressure on Israel. The United States was not prepared to
undertake such an effort in the late 1970s. American officials in
both the Ford and Carter administrations believed that they should
focus chiefly on defusing the conflict between Israel and Egypt,
which they rightly viewed as the most dangerous situation in the
Middle East. The Israel-Egypt peace process did seek to address
the Palestinian problem, but only tangentially.

Without a willingness either to commit military forces to Lebanon or to solve one of the root causes of the conflict, U.S. diplomatic efforts to end the war had a limited impact in the late
1970s. The United States played a key role in securing a cease-fire
in the Beirut area in the summer of 1978, though, and in September President Carter called for an internationally brokered peace.
The truce did not endure, however, and no agreement was ever
reached.[106] The administration's diplomatic energies were channeled instead into brokering peace between Israel and Egypt. During discussions at Camp David, President Anwar Sadat of Egypt
asked Carter whether he had paid much attention to Lebanon.
Carter would later write in his memoirs, "I had to admit that since
direct American interest was aroused primarily in moments of crisis, we had not mounted a concerted effort to find a permanent
solution to the continuing Lebanese tragedy."[107]

The United States engaged in a far more serious push to mediate
the war following Israel's 1982 invasion of Lebanon and the deployment of marines to Beirut. With the PLO driven out of Beirut,
U.S. officials believed that there was a historic opportunity to end
the country's crisis.[108] During late 1982, the United States focused
on providing aid and training to the Lebanese central government
and armed forces. In July 1983, with little progress toward a permanent end to the civil war, President Reagan appointed Robert
McFarlane, deputy national security adviser, as his special envoy to
Lebanon.

With U.S. forces in Lebanon and with a commitment to mediation coming from the highest levels of the government, the conditions were better than ever for a successful attempt to resolve the

civil war. Yet the Reagan administration's approach was badly mis-conceived, and by October U.S. policy had slid into an abyss.[109] The key to the United States' effectiveness as a mediator in the Lebanese conflict was its neutrality and its ability to inspire the trust of all parties. When the marines first arrived in Lebanon, the United States had the trust of not only the Christians but to some extent the Druse and the Shiite Moslems as well. As Scott Shuger points out, there were some Arabs in Lebanon who were sympathetic to the United States, some who were neutral, and a small minority who were hostile.[110] Within a year, a majority had moved into the hostile camp.

One cause of this erosion was the peace brokered by the United States between Israel and Lebanon on May 17, 1983. This accord, which heavily favored Israel, generated resentment in the Arab world and undermined the appearance of U.S. neutrality. But a bigger cause was Washington's overenthusiastic support of Amin Gemayel's government and U.S. training of the Lebanese army.[111] McFarlane rightly saw that his main challenge was to get Gemay-el's Christian government to acknowledge the "unfairness of Lebanon's existing distribution of power" and to make political concessions to the Muslims.[112] However, the United States never pushed the Christians hard enough toward these goals. Instead of giving impetus to the Gemayel government to negotiate in good faith, U.S. political support and the presence of U.S. troops were exploited by the Christians. During 1983, the Lebanese army un-dertook a huge crackdown. Through a wave of mass arrests, the dynamiting of homes, and many disappearances, Gemayel syste-matically alienated Lebanon's Muslims.[113] McFarlane found in Ge-mayel a leader who wanted the United States to solve Lebanon's problems yet showed no willingness to compromise.[114] But instead of clearly distancing the United States from Gemayel, McFarlane was widely perceived as embracing him, with negative results. As Scott Shuger writes, "The more McFarlane's fidelity to the Gemayel government increased, the more he turned previously neutral Arabs against us."[115]

American neutrality was further damaged when U.S. ships assisted the Lebanese army and fired on Druse-Syrian-Palestinian positions during a battle. The marine commander in Lebanon opposed this move, saying prophetically that if the United States began taking sides, "we'll get slaughtered."[116] America had gone into Lebanon as a savior; by the time it left the country after the marine bombing it had become, in Thomas Friedman's words, just another militia.

The United States continued sporadic peace efforts in Lebanon through the 1980s. The war finally came to a close at the end of the decade with the Taif accord. The United States was a quiet and important backer of the process that led to this agreement.

DURING THE 1990s, the United States played roles in seeking to mediate the conflicts in Rwanda, Kashmir, Nagorno-Karabakh, and Eritrea. But U.S. intervention during this period was most decisive in Europe—in Bosnia and Northern Ireland. In both places the United States won the trust of all parties; in both its efforts were sustained and received support at the highest levels of the U.S. government. In Northern Ireland, U.S. mediation took advantage of a situation that was ripe for outside intervention. In Bosnia, the United States helped create the conditions for a settlement through economic sanctions and the use of military force.

An entire book could be written about the tortuous diplomatic negotiations that took place over the three-year period of the Bosnian war. I will focus, therefore, on only those negotiations that were mediated by the United States. Two points will become clear: first, U.S. efforts succeeded only when the United States resigned itself to a solution that partitioned Bosnia and when it acquiesced to Serb gains won through aggression. Second, the United States' use of force, and threats to use force, did not always advance the peace process. Much like U.S. support for the Gemayel government in Lebanon, U.S. backing for the Bosnian government helped to harden Bosnia's position and reduced that country's flexibility in the peace process. This history suggests an unpalatable lesson for the future: unless the United States is ready to commit its full national power to righting an international wrong, it must be ready to put aside its moral preferences and mediate a less-than-optimal agreement. American diplomats might find it repugnant to preside over negotiations that reward aggression and confer legitimacy on war criminals, but sometimes this is a lesser evil than continued fighting.

The United States was not a central player in the first two peace initiatives in Bosnia, the plan that emerged from the EC-sponsored talks in Lisbon in early 1992 and the Vance-Owen plan that was discussed from late 1992 through May 1993. The Clinton administration was deeply unhappy with the Vance-Owen plan, which it believed rewarded Serb aggression. The administration felt, however, that it had little choice but to support this process. Clinton appointed Reginald Bartholomew as his special envoy to the talks, and administration officials made clear that the United States would be willing to participate in a NATO peacekeeping mission.[117] But the moralistic rhetoric of Bill Clinton and his top aides, both during the election campaign and afterward, had the effect of hardening the Bosnian government's negotiating position in the talks. The government harbored hope that the United States would eventually come to the rescue if the war continued. The final Vance-Owen plan thus had to concede greater territory to the Muslims to win their support and, not surprisingly, was rejected by the Bosnian Serbs in April 1993.

The United States played an important role in the next European-sponsored peace effort, which unfolded between July 1993 and January 1994. It again appointed a special envoy (Charles Redman) and stressed its willingness to participate in a NATO mission. This new peace effort envisioned a loose partition of Bosnia among the three warring parties, and the Clinton administration—having failed to win support for its lift-and-strike policy—seemed prepared to live with this outcome. By August, Croats, Muslims, and Bosnian Serbs had reached agreement on the division of Bosnia into three "constituent republics."[118]

This new plan crumbled when the Bosnian parliament overwhelmingly rejected it. And in the end, the United States may have done more to sink the peace agreement than to help it. American officials argued at the time that NATO's August 1993 pledge to use air power against Serb positions outside of Sarajevo aided the peace process.[119] But in fact, this decision—along with continuing U.S. statements that the arms embargo should be lifted and Redman's open sympathy with Muslim demands—served to renew the hopes of the Bosnian government that it might one day be able to win the war with U.S. help. To many observers, this was exactly the wrong message: the United States had to tell the Muslims bluntly that they had lost the war and press them to settle for the best deal possible, even one that rewarded aggression.

Clinton officials rejected this approach. They were ready to live with partition, but they weren't ready to advocate it. "We have not pressured the Bosnian government or the Bosnian Muslims into taking any particular position," said Assistant Secretary of State Oxman in September 1993.[120] Oxman said that the United States had made it clear that outside intervention was not going to save the Muslims, but the U.S. government would not actively counsel a negotiating stance that would ratify the results of ethnic cleansing. In February 1994, after the latest negotiating effort had collapsed, Walter Slocombe of the Defense Department reiterated this compromise approach, saying that the United States had tried as hard as "humanly possible to make clear to the Bosnian government that we are not going to intervene" but that "the administration will not join in a policy of putting pressure on the Muslims. . . . We think that the pressure needs to be put on the Serbs."[121]

Following the failure of the three European-sponsored peace plans, the United States came to play a direct mediating role in the negotiations that ultimately led to an agreement. While Oxman had said in 1993 that "we are not going to go in and try to take over the negotiation," his successor, Richard Holbrooke, would seek to do precisely that. And this time, President Clinton was much more personally engaged, participating closely in his advisers' deliberations and lobbying NATO leaders.[122] The first breakthrough came on March 1, 1994, when the United States brokered a framework agreement to end fighting between Muslims and Croats in Bosnia. That development was followed by nine days of intensive negotiations in Vienna, mediated by Redman, in which the two parties drafted a forty-nine-page constitution that created a Muslim-Croat federation in Bosnia.[123] The process was completed with a signing ceremony at the White House attended by Clinton and the presidents of Bosnia and Croatia. This so-called Washington agreement was made possible in part by the United States' quietly helping strengthen the military position of Croatia, mainly by turning a blind eye to that country's circumvention of the U.N. arms embargo.[124]

The ending of hostilities between Bosnia and Croatia led to Serb losses on the battlefield during 1994 and 1995. The United States stepped up its multilateral diplomacy, convening in April 1994 a "Contact Group" of British, French, American, German, and Russian representatives. Under U.S. leadership, the Contact Group developed a formula that would allot 49 percent of Bosnian territory to a Serb republic and 51 percent to the Muslim-Croat federation. More than ever, the United States was willing to accept the partition of Bosnia as the only outcome that would end the war.

The possibility, by mid-1995, that U.N. forces would have to stage a disastrous withdrawal from Bosnia increased the pressure on the United States to achieve a diplomatic solution. Such a solution was made more possible by the Croatian reconquest of the Serb-held Krajina region and the fall of Muslim enclaves in eastern Bosnia. With these developments, the distribution of territory in Bosnia further resembled the split envisioned under the Contact Group plan. Even without the use of air power by NATO against Serb targets, the Serbs were leaning toward accepting the Contact Group plan. This flexibility on the part of the Bosnian Serbs was due in large measure to pressure from Milosevic, who wanted the war in Bosnia ended so that the economic sanctions would be lifted. The sustained air strikes against Bosnian Serb targets in September, coming at the same time as a joint Muslim-Croat offensive in western Serbia, may have contributed to the Serbs' flexibility by making it clear that, over the long run, their military position was likely to continue deteriorating in Bosnia.

In the fall of 1995, a U.S. negotiating team led by Richard Holbrooke was able finally to capitalize on these conditions to forge a peace agreement. Holbrooke's mission had four attributes that distinguished it from past U.S. efforts. First, it was a higher-profile and more sustained undertaking than anything launched before—both Clinton and Warren Christopher would be actively involved in pressuring the parties during the final negotiations in Dayton, Ohio. Second, it was coupled with increased pressure on the Bosnian Serbs—including, eventually, military force—which Holbrooke saw as necessary to make them accept the Contact Group plan.[125] Third, Holbrooke started from the implicit premise that partition was the only solution and publicly accepted for the first time the possibility that a Bosnian Serb republic might wish to establish a "special relationship" with Serbia—that is, effectively secede from Bosnia and become part of Serbia. Finally, Holbrooke was more ready than any previous U.S. envoy to talk tough with the Bosnian Muslims, making it clear that they had to accept partition and that the United States would not abet their deluded dream of a reunited Bosnia ruled from Sarajevo. In effect, the United States was able to broker a deal in Bosnia when it put its moral fervor aside and simply behaved as the biggest snake in the snake pit.[126]

American efforts to mediate the conflict in Northern Ireland in 1994 and 1995 offer a classic example of what can be achieved by high-level pressure if the conditions are right. During his presidential campaign, Clinton had pledged to make a new bid to end the standoff in Northern Ireland. Nothing had come of that promise during 1993, but in the spring of 1994, as a new round of diplomatic maneuvering began among the combatants, the White House quietly used its influence to push for a breakthrough. At Clinton's direction, Tony Lake, his national security adviser, wrote to the Sinn Fein leader Gerry Adams and urged him to accept a secret offer by the British government to establish a dialogue on peace if the IRA ordered a cease-fire.

At the same time as it was cultivating Sinn Fein, the White House worked with the British to open a dialogue with Protestant Unionist politicians. In April, James Molyneaux, leader of the Ulster Unionist Party, visited the White House and met with Lake and Vice President Gore. This meeting helped assure the Unionists that the United States did not favor the IRA and that it was a neutral mediator that could be trusted to push a fair solution to Northern Ireland's problems.

The Clinton administration followed up these efforts by suggesting to John Major, the British prime minister, that he make a humanitarian gesture by moving some IRA prisoners from British jails to prisons in Northern Ireland, where they could more easily receive family visits. Lake continued to keep in close contact with Molyneaux, urging him to promote restraint among Protestants and assuring him that the United States would give its full backing to constitutional talks that followed a cease-fire.[127]

On August 31, 1994, the IRA announced that it would observe a cease-fire and participate in peace talks. At the beginning of October, the Clinton administration rewarded Gerry Adams by granting him a visa to travel to the United States. It also officially lifted its long-standing ban on contacts between U.S. leaders and members of Sinn Fein. Gore personally called Adams to deliver this news. On October 4, Adams arrived in Washington for talks with officials from the State Department and the NSC.[128] On November 1, the Clinton administration announced a package of initiatives aimed at revitalizing the economy of Northern Ireland. These included a spring 1995 White House conference on trade and investment in Ireland, high-level U.S. participation in a December 1994 economic conference in Belfast, increased foreign aid to Ireland, and several smaller actions. All these steps were implicitly linked to the continuation of the peace process.[129] Finally, on December 1, Clinton appointed Senator George Mitchell to be special adviser to the president and secretary of state for economic initiatives in Ireland.[130]

Before the Clinton administration's involvement, the British government had long held that Northern Ireland was an internal problem and that active U.S. mediation was unwelcome. Clinton's personal discussions with Major were instrumental in changing this position.[131] Through 1995, the administration continued to aid efforts to push the peace process forward. At the White House conference on trade and investment in Ireland in May, Clinton delivered a lengthy speech on the need to work for peace and prosperity.[132] At the end of the year, Clinton (already highly popular in Ireland) used a trip to Northern Ireland and Dublin to pressure British and Irish leaders to agree to make faster progress.

HUMANITARIAN AID

Ethnic conflicts have produced some of the most horrendous humanitarian disasters in recent history. During the Biafran war, millions of people were pushed to the brink of starvation and hundreds of thousands, possibly more, died. The 1991 Kurdish flight into Turkey and the massive exodus from Rwanda in 1994 were two of the most rapid and wrenching movements of human populations ever. Ethnic cleansing in Bosnia produced floods of refugees not seen in Europe since World War II.

The United States has repeatedly sought to alleviate the misery caused by ethnic conflict through humanitarian assistance. Its efforts have involved political and logistical issues of enormous complexity. American officials have worried about the implications of appearing to take sides by providing humanitarian assistance; they have worried that humanitarian missions would draw the United States into ongoing wars. Once authorized, U.S. humanitarian operations have proved extremely challenging and have required U.S. military forces to perform unfamiliar tasks. Not surprisingly, U.S. aid has often come too late and been of insufficient scope.

The United States has learned hard lessons in recent years about its role in providing humanitarian relief during ethnic conflicts. It has learned, first and foremost, that a primary U.S. role in dealing with any humanitarian disaster is almost impossible to avoid.

Whenever large numbers of human beings are at immediate risk and their plight is being spotlighted by the media, the government will be placed under intense pressure to take action. That pressure will come from domestic public opinion as Americans react in horror to what they are seeing on their television screens. It will come from elite liberal internationalist opinion, which holds that the United States has a responsibility to use its power to save lives. It will come from nongovernmental organizations that find their own relief capacities overwhelmed by the calamity. And it will come from international organizations and foreign powers that understand that only the United States has the military forces capable of mounting massive humanitarian operations. Given the inevitability of such pressures and the fast pace of humanitarian crises, U.S. policy makers will rarely have time for an extended debate over whether to respond; the question instead will be how to respond, and preexisting options for dealing with various scenarios will be invaluable.

HUMANITARIAN CRISES ALMOST always snowball into bigger disasters than are initially expected. As these crises unfold, American officials must therefore err on the side of pessimism in predicting the future course of events. It should not, for example, take a visit by the secretary of state for officials to realize that if a million or so Kurds are huddled on the sides of mountains in southeastern Turkey in harsh early-spring weather they will probably start to die at a rapid pace without massive international intervention. The moment huge shifts in human populations are reported, U.S. officials must understand a simple reality: when these refugee hordes arrive at their final destination, the United States will be saddled with much of the job of feeding and sheltering them. The United States will face similar responsibilities when wars generate famines or when civilian populations are denied food in the course of an extended siege.

A quarter century before the plight of the Bosnians of Sarajevo became a celebrated cause in the West, there was the even greater

drama of starvation within encircled Biafra. This was the first televised famine in history and it drew U.S. policy makers into an
imbroglio of extraordinary complexity. When images of Biafran
starvation first burst upon America in mid-1968, Lyndon Johnson
reacted decisively, at least in spirit. He called up Undersecretary
of State Katzenbach and reportedly said, "Get those nigger babies
off my T.V. set."[133] The Johnson administration preferred to do
nothing that would enmesh the United States in the Biafran crisis,
but it felt there was little choice but to act. As one scholar has
observed, Biafra "came to Johnson's attention primarily as an issue
of domestic public opinion, and his decision to send humanitarian
aid was in reaction to this sentiment rather than to foreign policy
goals."[134]

The aid decision came about after a long and anguished debate
within the government. The State Department did not want to do
anything that could be seen as helping Biafra. When the famine
first became a cause of concern, there was a growing belief among
most observers that Biafra would soon be defeated. Images of starving people in an encircled enclave served to strengthen this expectation. As Roger Morris writes, officials at State had a "reluctance
to offend victorious Nigeria as Biafra's collapse became imminent."[135]

Waiting out the situation did not prove to be an option. With
relief experts predicting that more than a million people could die
of starvation within the next few months, the State Department
formed a task force.[136] "While we have no intention of interfering
in Nigerian affairs, we do not believe that innocent persons should
be made the victims of political maneuvering," President Johnson
said.[137] Secretary of State Dean Rusk said that the U.S. government
had given $7.3 million to the International Red Cross and other
nonprofit organizations that were doing relief work in Biafra.[138]
Determined to avoid giving any aid directly to the Biafrans, the
United States channeled all assistance through third parties.

By the fall of 1968, starvation in Biafra had become a major
political issue in the United States. Richard Nixon, the Republican
presidential candidate, called for action, as did leading Democrats

in Congress. High-school students were skipping lunch and donating the money to Biafra, and ad hoc committees had been formed to alter American policy. The Johnson administration's policy of stalling and hoping for a Biafran defeat had become untenable. Many in the State Department still believed that humanitarian assistance would antagonize Lagos and prolong the war by helping the Biafrans meet basic needs while they fought on.[139] But in December, the United States announced a $20 million package of assistance to Biafra.[140] It also loaned private organizations eight military transport planes to help with aid deliveries. These moves brought condemnation from the Nigerian government.[141]

The Nixon administration took some measures to step up aid to Biafra. But U.S. and other outside assistance never approached the levels needed to prevent starvation on a massive level. While Nixon and Kissinger wanted to do more to rush relief supplies, they faced opposition from the State Department.[142] Because of this prohibition on bilateral aid, the United States had to funnel its aid contributions through an inadequate private relief network. When the Nigerians shot down a Red Cross plane in June 1969, that network virtually collapsed and aid slowed to a trickle. The Nixon administration did nothing.[143]

IF THE BUSH ADMINISTRATION had had its way it would have ignored the plight of the Kurds following the Persian Gulf War. For here, too, the dictates of geopolitics favored inaction. American military operations in Kurdistan had the potential to mar the record of a perfect war, forcing the United States into an extended relief operation and perhaps into the conflict between Iraq and the Kurds. Intervention on behalf of the Kurds also raised delicate issues in international law, as the United States and its allies established a safe haven in northern Iraq.

The Bush administration mounted one of the largest humanitarian operations in history because a policy of doing nothing was untenable, both domestically and internationally. The Kurdish exodus began in late March 1991, as Saddam Hussein's troops moved into northern Iraq to crush an armed uprising. By the first days of April, nearly two million Kurds were spilling over the borders with Turkey and Iran. Media images of the refugees were both ubiquitous and appalling. A huge outcry arose in the United States for action to rescue this pathetic mass of humanity, living in mud and walking barefoot in snow, dying by the hundreds every day. At the same time, the Bush administration came under pressure from abroad to spearhead relief efforts. The Turkish government appealed for U.S. and Western support on April 2. France and Britain pushed for action within the U.N. Security Council.[144]

The Bush administration was reluctant to heed these requests. Top American military officials were opposed to a humanitarian intervention that had no clear political objective and no obvious exit strategy. But under intense pressure, particularly from Prime Minister Major, the United States gave its support to Security Council Resolution 688, which called for international action to deal with the humanitarian crisis.[145] Shortly after this development, Secretary of State James Baker was deeply disturbed by a visit to Kurdish refugees in Turkey. By vigorously lobbying President Bush, he changed the tenor of discussion and advocated a major intervention using allied military forces. As political pressure on the Bush administration intensified, the president authorized U.S. forces to enter northern Iraq to deliver humanitarian aid and establish a safe haven for the Kurds.[146]

The decision to provide large-scale humanitarian aid to Bosnia was also made reluctantly by the Bush administration. By the summer of 1992, more than two million Bosnians had lost their homes in the war, creating a massive internal refugee crisis. Many of these Bosnians were trapped in cities besieged by Serb forces. The logistics of supplying this population with food and medicine were enormously difficult. Overland convoys were the only way to reach cities like Tuzla and Goradze, and these had been blocked by the Serbs since the spring. Meanwhile, convoys to Sarajevo were also blocked and the humanitarian airlift to the city was easy for the

Serbs to close down. The delivery of relief supplies to the trapped Bosnians could be guaranteed only through the use of military force.

As with Biafra and Kurdistan, images of acute human misery in Bosnia produced enormous amounts of pressure on the U.S. government. The Bush administration ruled out military intervention and initially sought to muddle through with diplomatic and political sanctions. It also contributed $9 million to assist refugees in Bosnia. Within a month, however, it was clear that the Serbs still had no intention of allowing a full-fledged relief effort and that existing U.S. and U.N. policy could do nothing to change their behavior.

Secretary of State Baker felt that the United States could not continue to resist pressures for action while a massive humanitarian disaster unfolded, but the top leadership at the Pentagon was opposed to using military force. Defense Secretary Richard Cheney and Colin Powell, the chairman of the Joint Chiefs of Staff, worried that more serious involvement would follow. Baker and the State Department argued that U.S. military involvement could be contained and that, in any case, there was no other sustainable course available.[147] Bush agreed with this view, and on June 30, 1992, Cheney announced that, if authorized by the U.N. Security Council, the United States was prepared to provide air and naval escort protection to a humanitarian relief convoy en route to Sarajevo. On August 6, Bush announced that the United States would push for a Security Council resolution authorizing the use of all necessary measures to ensure the delivery of humanitarian assistance to Bosnia.[148] The measure, Resolution 770, was passed a week later. U.S. military involvement in humanitarian operations in Bosnia would continue for the next three years.

By the start of 1994, U.S. national-security policy had undergone a transformation with regard to humanitarian operations. The missions in Kurdistan and Bosnia had produced a large reservoir of experience, both political and logistical, in handling situations in which millions of people were at risk. The U.S. response to the tragedy in Rwanda thus stands as a sobering reminder of how slow governments can be in operationalizing knowledge.

The U.S. response to the humanitarian crisis in Rwanda was disorganized from the start. There were two distinct debates during the crisis: First, how to protect Rwandans within the country at the height of the killing and, second, how to reestablish order in Rwanda and entice refugees in neighboring countries to return home. Within the Clinton administration, there was never any serious consideration of sending troops to Rwanda while the killing was under way. The administration was still feeling the aftershocks of the Somalia debacle, and anti-interventionary sentiments were powerful in Washington. Soon after the massacres began, Bob Dole and others pronounced that the United States did not have national interests in Rwanda and should not intervene in the conflict.[149] Administration officials agreed that Rwanda did not meet any of the criteria for direct U.S. military intervention. They saw Rwanda as the first test of the guidelines laid out in PD-25, the long-debated interagency paper on U.S. participation in U.N. operations, which was signed by President Clinton at the height of the Rwandan crisis.

After the killing began, the Clinton administration focused first on evacuating the 258 Americans in Rwanda. Meanwhile, a group convened at the National Security Council considered options for stopping the violence.[150] Attractive options were scarce, and there was great confusion in the government over exactly what was happening in Rwanda as RPF and government troops engaged in combat and militias carried out systematic massacres. Days after the killing began, the United States strongly supported a move to cut the U.N. peacekeeping force in Rwanda, UNAMIR, down to a token size—the logic being that there was no role for a peacekeeping force in the absence of peace.[151] The grisly torture and murder of ten Belgian peacekeepers at the onset of the crisis and the subsequent withdrawal of all 420 Belgian soldiers from UNAMIR were pivotal in reinforcing this outlook. As one State Department official told Holly Burkhalter of Human Rights

Watch, "You can't overstate the impact on our policy process of the Belgians leaving. People were saying, 'How can we get in if it is so bad the Belgians have to leave?' "[152]

Although the killing continued at a frenzied pace, top Clinton officials were cool toward proposals by Boutros Boutros-Ghali to take "forceful action" in Rwanda.[153] While officials in the State Department's Africa bureau, led by George Moose, pushed for an activist approach, including a strengthening of UNAMIR and new diplomatic measures, there was little consensus in the administration—or even among top officials in the State Department. Many in the administration believed that a principal lesson of Somalia was that the United Nations should not undertake operations that it did not have a very high chance of executing successfully. Pentagon officials forcefully opposed any commitment of U.N. forces to the conflict. To many administration officials, it was difficult to see a clear scenario for how a U.N. deployment would succeed, given the ongoing fighting between the Rwandan government and RPF forces and the absence of a commitment by the United States or other Western countries to supply troops for the operation. Some worried that U.S. troops would have to bail out a U.N. force that got bogged down in the Rwandan conflict. Nevertheless, after long consideration, the United States was willing to give guarded support to Boutros-Ghali's idea of creating an OAU force under U.N. auspices, a move that would fulfill the spirit of chapter VIII of the U.N. Charter, which called on regional organizations to take the lead in resolving disputes where possible. Clinton officials said at the beginning of May 1994 that the United States would be willing to provide financial support and logistical help to such a force.[154]

Through the first two weeks of May, however, U.S. and U.N. authorities fell into a tangled dispute. Boutros-Ghali wanted fifty-five hundred troops sent to the heart of the country; although unauthorized to use force, they would protect civilians and relief workers.[155] The Clinton administration felt that this concept was ill-conceived. It worried that the troops would be sucked into a long engagement, and it didn't see, in any case, where the troops would come from, since no African nations had volunteered men. Nonetheless, the United States voted in the Security Council to approve a U.N. force. With the specifics unresolved, however, the haggling continued.[156] To the dismay of some council members and human-rights groups who were urging immediate action, the United States insisted that the bulk of U.N. forces not enter the country until a cease-fire was in place and verified by observers.

A team of officials from the State and Defense Departments met in New York with U.N. officials and criticized the plans for the Rwandan operation. They reiterated earlier arguments and stressed that any outcome similar to Somalia would only undermine U.N. credibility. The team argued for an alternative plan whereby U.N. forces would enter overland from a neighboring country, set up a safe haven in a border area, and then gradually work farther into the country.[157] The U.S plan held out no promise for ending the massacres, yet Clinton officials saw it as the only prudent step available. Pronouncements by RPF leaders that they would attack U.N. forces that interfered with their operations only added weight to this perspective. "We want to be confident that when we do turn to the U.N., the U.N. will be able to do the job," Madeleine Albright told Congress.[158]

The caution of the Clinton administration was understandable, and it was shared by Western European governments.[159] Less defensible, given the overwhelming urgency of the situation, were the delays in the administration's reaction time during the U.N. deliberations. Boutros-Ghali's anger was in large part directed at the United States when he said, "More than 200,000 people have been killed and the international community is still discussing what ought to be done."[160]

The story of the armored vehicles offered by the Clinton administration to African troops underscores the disorganization that characterized its response. In late May, Ghana, Ethiopia, and Senegal volunteered troops, but since the Ghanian troops were not well equipped, the administration offered sixty armored vehicles.[161] Clinton had personally promised to "provide the armored support necessary if the African nations will provide the troops."[162] The

Pentagon began negotiations with U.N. authorities over the transfer of this equipment. Meanwhile, by the first week of June, Boutros-Ghali had found fifty-five hundred troops for the mission into Rwanda. The United States had abandoned its insistence that this force first establish safe havens in border areas, and the plan now was to fly the troops into Kigali. Two months after the killing campaign began, the international community was finally prepared to take action.

The armored vehicles, however, were far from ready. On June 8, the Pentagon said that it would take a month to provide the armored vehicles and train the Ghanians to use them.[163] This delay arose as a result of the difficulty in negotiating an agreement between the Defense Department and the United Nations. Although the United States was nearly $2 billion in arrears to the United Nations, Defense Department officials insisted that the United States be fully compensated for the vehicles. The dispute lasted for weeks and included disagreements over whether the vehicles should be tracked or wheeled, whether the United Nations would buy or lease them, and who should pay the costs of shipping. The Pentagon's demand that the United Nations carry these costs dramatically raised the overall price. Finally, although the negotiations were moving forward, the U.S. Army was not yet prepping the vehicles for rapid transport because Defense Department regulations held that this step could only be taken after contracts were signed. It was not until mid-June, following widespread criticism, that the White House intervened to expedite the process. The mystery, of course, is why top officials hadn't moved much earlier to cut through the red tape.[164]

The government was also slow to respond to the refugee crisis. The genocide in Rwanda began in early April. By the end of the month there were reports that up to 250,000 refugees were on the move and that this number was likely to increase.[165] Through May, the mass refugee movements into Tanzania and other countries swelled rapidly. By July, as many as two million Rwandans had fled and were packed into refugee camps in neighboring countries, where they died at the rate of nearly two thousand a day.[166] Clinton had ordered relief supplies flown to Tanzania, and by the beginning of May the United States had pledged up to $26 million in humanitarian aid.[167] But these steps were inadequate. Once again, U.S. officials did not anticipate the scope of the looming disaster. Even as the extent of the refugee exodus became clear, they failed to comprehend the vast quantities of outside assistance that would be needed to feed all the people and prevent the spread of disease. It would not be until July, two months after the flow of refugees began, that the United States would have a major humanitarian effort under way.[168]

On July 29, Clinton took this mission a big step further when he ordered U.S. troops to secure the airport in Kigali so that relief supplies could flow directly into Rwanda and thus induce the refugees to return to their country. At the same time, the administration continued to make available tens of millions of dollars in emergency assistance. High-level officials traveled to the region to ensure that the operation was going smoothly. Overall, once this response to the humanitarian crisis was under way it proved to be exemplary, much like the operation in Kurdistan in 1991. The tragedy is that thousands had to die while the United States initially dithered.

USE OF MILITARY FORCE

The United States has employed its military forces in ethnic war zones on four occasions: in Lebanon in 1982–83, in Kurdistan in 1991, in Bosnia from 1992 on, and in Rwanda in 1994. Only twice—in Lebanon and Bosnia—have U.S. forces engaged in combat aimed at affecting the outcome of an ethnic conflict. It is these episodes that are of principal concern here. While U.S. and U.N. peacekeeping operations have been exhaustively analyzed in recent years, there has been far less discussion of when military force should be used coercively in ethnic conflicts. The Lebanese and Bosnian experiences offer limited but still valuable insights.

Military intervention in ethnic conflicts is an intrinsically diffi-

cult proposition. Since the United States rarely will have vital interests at stake in an ethnic conflict, it will almost always be
inclined to use military force on a limited scale, if at all. It will
seek to keep casualties low and minimize the national prestige that
it lays on the line—goals that are notoriously hard to achieve. At
the same time, the United States and other outside powers face a
basic disadvantage in ethnic conflicts: because ethnic extremists often see themselves as fighting for survival, many will be willing to
pay almost any price and struggle for any length of time to prevail.[169] In a game of nerves with U.S. leaders worried about domestic support, nationalist leaders will invariably have the upper
hand.

Moreover, U.S. military power will usually be limited in its potential effectiveness. Ethnic conflicts typically involve a great deal
of guerrilla warfare or other types of low-intensity conflict. Insurgent or secessionist armies are likely to have decentralized and
low-tech command and control arrangements that are not easily
disrupted. Arms depots and supply lines will be dispersed and re-
dundant. Military forces will be intentionally stationed among civilian populations. The terrain in conflict zones may often be
inhospitable. Since combatants in ethnic conflicts are often substate
actors, the United States will usually not be able to target the high-
value assets of a state as part of a strategy of coercion.

None of this means that U.S. military force cannot have a decisive impact in some ethnic conflicts. But it does suggest that the
odds will never be good and that the United States must approach
the use of force with extreme circumspection. Any military action
must be tied to a clear-cut and near-term diplomatic strategy for
ending the war. There must, in other words, be a goal that U.S.
leaders think they can achieve through force and some way to
measure when that goal has been met. Within the context of limited interests and thus limited engagement, the United States must
be prepared to use force in a sustained and decisive manner once
it has opted for a military solution. Pinprick air strikes or other
symbolic actions are not likely to work. Finally, the United States
should never undertake military actions that it does not believe will

achieve its objectives, nor should it paralyze itself by insisting on a quick or certain success, since this criterion will be impossible to meet in most conflicts. A turkey shoot like Desert Storm does not happen often. Given this reality, U.S. leaders must carefully weigh the price of failure.

The United States did not send marines to Lebanon with the idea that they would engage in combat. Instead, U.S. forces were first deployed in late August 1982 as part of a multinational force to oversee the withdrawal of fourteen thousand PLO fighters following their encirclement by Israel. The marines stayed until the evacuation was completed, withdrawing on September 10. On September 14, Bashir Gemayel, the Christian president-elect, was assassinated, and a huge massacre of Palestinian civilians in the Sabra and Shatila refugee camps followed. This breakdown of order led the United States to send its forces back into Beirut. President Reagan declared that they were returning "with the mission of enabling the Lebanese government to restore full sovereignty over its capital, the essential precondition for extending its control over the entire country."[170] Explained in broader terms by other officials, their mission was to bring stability to Lebanon through support of the central government, training of the Lebanese army, and the creation of a climate conducive to a diplomatic settlement.[171]

This mission was flawed in multiple ways. First, the political strategy was not realistic. It overestimated the potential for achieving a peace agreement in Lebanon in the near term and misunderstood the role that U.S. forces should play. The withdrawal of the PLO did not solve all the country's problems or even most of them, as American leaders like Secretary of State Alexander Haig apparently believed it did. The fundamental dispute over power sharing between Christians and Muslims remained. No peace was possible unless both sides were committed to working through this dispute. In particular, a new spirit of compromise on the part of the Christians was absolutely essential. No such spirit existed in the wake of Bashir Gemayel's assassination and no effective framework for dialogue was in place when the marines returned to Beirut.

The use of the marines to build up the Lebanese army was misconceived. While U.S. officials cited statistics showing that the new Lebanese army had a fair mix of Muslims and Christians, it was still widely seen as a vehicle of the central government controlled by Amin Gemayel, Bashir's brother and his successor. By spring 1983, marine patrols reported that stones were being thrown at them. In March, four marines were injured in a grenade attack. On April 18, a bomb destroyed the U.S. embassy in Beirut, killing sixty people.

With little progress toward a diplomatic settlement and with hostility toward the United States mounting, doubts grew in Washington about the marine deployment. The report of a congressional delegation that visited Beirut in September stated, "It is undisputed that our military presence provides a necessary framework for the diplomatic efforts that would collapse if these military forces were withdrawn." At the same time, the report said, the "diplomatic and political process has placed the marines in Beirut in a highly exposed position."[172]

The use of U.S. battleship guns in September pulled the United States into a conflict for which it was unprepared. Colin Powell, then a special assistant to Defense Secretary Caspar Weinberger, would later reflect, "When the shells started falling on the Shiites, they assumed the American 'referee' had taken sides against them. And since they could not reach the battleship, they found a more vulnerable target, the exposed Marines at the airport."[173]

The October 1983 suicide bombing of the marine barracks and the increasing involvement of U.S. forces in the fighting in Lebanon underscored the central flaw of the whole operation: there was never a plan for what to do if Lebanon reverted to its natural state of chaos and U.S. forces were sucked into that vortex. A precipitous withdrawal from the conflict zone was not an attractive option, nor was it plausible that U.S. forces could decisively influence the situation unless the United States was prepared to escalate dramatically its use of military power, which it was not. The third course—reacting only defensively and trying to wait out the fighting—was a formula for incremental U.S. losses with no benefit in sight.

In the wake of the withdrawal from Lebanon, this mission became a celebrated example within the Pentagon of the perils of limited military engagement. Weinberger, who had opposed the operation from the beginning, drew on the experience to outline in 1984 a set of principles to guide future decisions. He argued that the United States should not deploy combat forces abroad unless vital interests were at stake, the United States had a clear plan for victory, a viable exit strategy existed, and the mission had the support of U.S. citizens and the Congress.

The specter of Lebanon hung heavily over U.S. deliberations about Bosnia. Colin Powell says that, whenever the Bosnian issue came up, "the shattered bodies of Marines at the Beirut airport were never far from my mind in arguing for caution."[174] Powell and others saw an essential similarity in the two situations: once the United States was involved in Bosnia, even in a very limited fashion, withdrawing without achieving its objectives would be undesirable. Yet it would be difficult, if not impossible, to achieve a decisive result without the massive application of force, an option hard to justify in terms of U.S. interests. Ever sensitive to the domestic component of foreign policy, Bush administration officials were convinced that intervention in Bosnia was politically untenable. "The necessary support by the American people for the degree of force that would have been required in Bosnia could never have been built or maintained," James Baker would later comment.[175]

As calls intensified in many quarters for the use of U.S. military power, Pentagon officials condemned what they saw as muddled suggestions for action. "We have learned to insist on clearly stated objectives for the use of military forces, objectives that are realistically attainable, with a clear understanding of who the enemy is and what constitutes success," Assistant Secretary of Defense Stephen Hadley told a congressional committee in August 1992. Depicting a scenario of U.S. forces bogged down in an endless guerrilla war, Hadley cited the precedent of Lebanon. A top aide to Colin Powell, Lieutenant General Barry McCaffrey, testified at the same hearing that 400,000 troops would be needed to end the war in Bosnia, and even they could not guarantee success. He observed that the Axis powers had kept eight to thirteen divisions in Yugoslavia during World War II and had still never been completely in control of the country. The "defense philosophy in the former Yugoslavia is borrowed from the guerrilla warfare of Giap and Mao," said McCaffrey. "And so the country has been laced with arms caches, munitions, bunkers, dispersed fighting areas." The Bosnian Serbs had enough equipment to fight on for some time even without outside supplies. In McCaffrey's view, holding open roads and lines of communication would be tougher in Bosnia than it had been in Vietnam.[176]

Of course, in attacking the idea of a massive ground intervention, Pentagon officials were toppling a straw man. Most advocates of U.S. military action were not calling for ground troops, suggesting instead that air power be used to support the Bosnian Muslims. But within the Pentagon there was no unanimity on the effectiveness of air strikes. Colin Powell personally led the opposition to the use of air power alone. "As soon as they tell me it's limited, it means they don't care whether you achieve a result or not," Powell told a reporter in September 1992. "As soon as they tell me 'surgical,' I head for the bunker."[177] During Powell's first meeting with the President-elect, Clinton asked whether there was some way to influence the situation in Bosnia with air power, as he had suggested on the campaign trail. "Not likely," Powell replied. But he said he would have his staff conduct further study of this option.[178]

Powell would not change his mind on this matter through the rest of his tenure as chairman of the Joint Chiefs of Staff. At an early National Security Council meeting with top Clinton officials, Powell outlined the full range of available air options, from bombing the artillery around Sarajevo to attacking both tactical and strategic targets throughout Bosnia and in Serbia as well. He stressed again that none of these actions was guaranteed to change Serb behavior and that only troops on the ground could do that. Powell argued at this meeting and future ones that the United States should not use military action until it had a clear and achievable political objective.[179]

Through 1993 and 1994, the debate over the use of air power had two dimensions. One argument was about whether air strikes could succeed in significantly diminishing Serb military capabilities; the other argument was about whether such attacks, even if effective, could alter Serb negotiating behavior. Army leaders like Powell reflected a long tradition of institutional skepticism over the ability of air power to change decisively conditions on the battlefield. Their position, articulated during the Gulf War as well, was that ground troops were always needed to ensure the complete destruction of enemy assets. Powell and his followers argued that the Serbs would be able to hide their tanks and artillery in the woods and fog of the Bosnian countryside and among civilian populations.[180] Air strikes would thus be unable to destroy enough Serb equipment to make a major difference in the war.

Air force leaders were predictably more optimistic. "Give us enough time, and we can drive across the top of every one of those artillery positions and put it out of business," said the air force chief of staff, Merrill McPeak, in April 1993. Air attacks could have an impact on supplies coming in from Serbia and on enemy morale, according to McPeak. In his view, these objectives could be realized with virtually no risk to U.S. aircraft, given the low quality of Serb antiaircraft equipment.[181]

To advocates of air power the possibility of degrading Bosnian Serb military capabilities without significant U.S. casualties made its use an option that Washington had a moral obligation to exercise. They suggested also that the bombing of high-value strategic targets in Serbia could well cause the leadership in Belgrade to cease or reduce its support for the Serbs in Bosnia. In pressing the "lift and strike" policy to the European allies, the Clinton administration held that air strikes against the Serbs and new arms supplies for the Bosnian government could level the playing field in Bosnia, producing a military stalemate that would lead to a diplomatic settlement.

But there was never a consensus within the U.S. government that this strategy would succeed, even if the allies went along. Powell expressed public skepticism: "The trouble is you do not know what will happen. Are we going to bomb people into an agreement that they otherwise would not wish to be part of? We did that in December 1972 [in Vietnam] and 3 years later they [the North Vietnamese] won anyway."[182] The otherwise optimistic McPeak commented: "I really do not know if destroying every gun position would have the desired effect in the long run as far as our political objectives go."[183]

Some observers believed that the policy could actually hurt U.S. political objectives, especially the preeminent goal of containing the conflict. Lifting the arms embargo on Bosnia would mean letting new arms into Croatia as well and could thus have the effect of generating further fighting between Croats and Serbs as Croatia tried to regain lost territory. Air strikes on Serbia could have the effect of strengthening Serb nationalism, leading to new pressures on Kosovo, where the United States wanted to prevent an outbreak of hostilities. As air strikes commenced in Bosnia, Serb forces could respond with massive infantry offensives to overrun besieged Muslim cities. They could also take U.N. peacekeepers hostage and threaten to kill them if the strikes did not end. Finally, the use of air power to support the Bosnian Muslims could reduce their flexibility in negotiations and encourage them to believe themselves capable of achieving a military victory. At the same time, Bosnian Serbs could hunker down and become more extremist in the face of Western military action—not an uncommon response among a people subjected to bombing. The net effect could be a larger, longer war in Bosnia.

Advocates of air strikes argued that the United States had to act to preserve its credibility and the credibility of NATO. But they had no good response to the argument that this credibility could be further damaged if air power was used and did not work, as was quite possible.

The actual record of NATO military action and threats of action in Bosnia between 1993 and 1995 lent support at various times to both the opponents and the advocates of air strikes. The August 1993 threats of air strikes apparently produced Serb flexibility in negotiations. But they also may have hardened the Bosnian position and they had no net benefit on the diplomatic process. The success in February 1994 of a NATO ultimatum demanding that the Serbs withdraw their heavy weapons from around Sarajevo suggested that the Serbs believed that air strikes could indeed be effective. Warren Christopher and Anthony Lake followed up this development by seeking ways to apply the threat to other parts of Bosnia.

Top leaders in the Pentagon believed, however, that it was hard to conclude from the Sarajevo ultimatum that air power could affect the course of the war throughout Bosnia. "There were very specific conditions around Sarajevo that lent themselves to the application of air power that don't exist in any other places in Bosnia today," said John M. Shalikashvili, chairman of the Joint Chiefs of Staff, in early March 1994.[184] Defense Secretary William Perry argued around the same time that, since the other besieged Muslim enclaves were under attack by small arms and infantry, air power would be of little use in defending them. "We cannot enforce safe havens with air power alone," he told Congress.[185] Perry said that any new and wider attempt to apply air power had to meet several criteria: it had to assist the diplomatic process, result in significant reductions in civilian casualties, and be achievable with NATO air power and existing U.N. Protection Force (UNPROFOR) ground troops.[186]

Meanwhile, European and U.N. leaders continued to argue that air power could not be used effectively in Bosnia so long as U.N. forces on the ground were vulnerable to hostage taking and retaliation. Events later in 1994 would bear out these claims, as Serbs did take U.N. hostages and even placed some of them at important military sites to deter NATO bombing. After the fall of Bihac, a U.N. safe haven, in November 1994, Clinton administration officials believed that the effectiveness of air power had reached its limit. "Bihac's fall has exposed the inherent contradictions in trying to use NATO air power coercively against the Bosnian Serbs when our allies have troops on the ground attempting to maintain impartiality," Lake reportedly wrote in a memo to Clinton.[187] Lake and other officials believed that the decisive use of air power was impossible under the circumstances and that more had to be done on the diplomatic front, including making concessions to the Serbs.

The sustained use of NATO air power in late August and September 1995 was made possible by the fall of various safe havens and a reduction in the number of U.N. personnel stationed in these pockets, vulnerable to Serb retaliation. The attacks were unlike anything that NATO had ever tried before, hitting a wide range of Serb assets, including command facilities, air defenses, and munitions depots. Their effect was to weaken the Serb military position just as a joint Muslim-Croat offensive was taking place in central and western Bosnia. To those closely involved in the diplomatic process, the air strikes were crucial. Richard Holbrooke strongly supported the bombing campaign as he pursued his diplomatic initiative.[188] Robert Owen, a member of Holbrooke's team, commented, "There is no question in my mind that we bombed the Serbs to the bargaining table."[189] Adroit U.S. diplomacy reduced the chances that the bombing would render the Bosnian government less flexible. When Bosnia's president, Alija Izetbegovic, hesitated about agreeing to a cease-fire, Holbrooke made it clear that the support of NATO air power was not guaranteed. He also bullied both the Bosnian and the Croatian leaders into not taking excessive advantage of the changing situation by overrunning the Serb city of Banja Luka.[190]

The U.S. experience in Bosnia highlights the enormous complexities and risks associated with the limited use of force. The lessons of this episode would not seem to lend much support to the proposition that the United States can rely on military force to affect the outcome of ethnic conflicts. But many circumstances in the Bosnian conflict were unusual. If U.N. peacekeepers had not been deployed in such vulnerable positions throughout much of the war, the debate surrounding the use of air power would have been dramatically different: the NATO nations would have been more unified and would have had a freer hand to act. The kind of bombing launched in the last days of the war could have been used earlier and sustained longer, slowly but systematically destroying Serb heavy weapons and arms depots. The deployment of a small number of NATO or U.N. special forces to direct air strikes might also have made possible the effective use of air power against Serb infantry operations and changed the course of the war in areas outside of Sarajevo. Close air support of a Bosnian army that was allowed access to new arms and received training from the West could have had a decisive impact. All these measures, moreover, could have been undertaken with minimal U.S. casualties and thus could well have been sustainable on the domestic front. Whether they would have changed the ultimate outcome of the war is impossible to say.

THE RECORD OF U.S. INTERVENTION in ethnic conflicts over the past thirty years looks largely as one might expect: U.S. policy makers have responded to limited threats to U.S. interests with limited commitments of power. Except in Lebanon, where things went badly awry, the expenditure of diplomatic energy, financial resources, and human life has generally matched the degree of secondary U.S. interests. To the extent that the efforts of the United States have been disproportionate, the most common mistake has been an undercommitment of resources, especially at the early stages of a conflict.

This record suggests that fears that limited intervention will lead to excessive commitments tend to be exaggerated. American policy makers have proved quite capable of establishing, and abiding by, limits on the use of U.S. power even amid intense global pressure. This is not surprising. Political leaders with even a modicum of caution will always favor limited participation in messy, internal wars in nonvital regions of the world. They will prefer solutions that give the appearance of U.S. compassion and leadership while carrying minimal risk of open-ended commitment, excessive expenditures, or loss of American life. The dictates of political prudence will, as well, tend to favor delayed action, since the reflexive hope of policy makers is that problems from hell will simply disappear or shrivel to the point that they no longer require U.S. attention. As the record shows, procrastination has been the rule rather than the exception.

All this suggests that the new isolationist attack on U.S. engagement in peripheral areas has been misguided. Such engagement does not have a natural expansionary momentum that inevitably exceeds U.S. interests. On the contrary, the historical record, while certainly not conclusive, points to a need to counteract tendencies toward inertia. It suggests that the United States must act with greater speed and decisiveness, not less, to project its power into ethnic crises that affect widely recognized secondary interests and have the potential to destabilize the international system by widening zones of instability. The price of delay can be missed opportunities to limit the scope of a conflict. The consequences of caution can be harder choices and higher expenses in the future.

Given that the United States often has limited leverage over warring ethnic parties, more vigilant policies of intervention carry no guarantee of succeeding. Even as the historical record counsels the need for more active engagement, it also underscores the enormous obstacles to success. No matter how well constructed U.S. policies are, policy makers must be prepared for failures. The most carefully orchestrated campaigns of private and public diplomatic protest will at times go unheeded. Airtight economic sanctions may send a nation spiraling into poverty without altering the extremist agendas of its leaders. Mediation efforts may achieve nothing in an atmosphere of bitter distrust. War crime indictments may be scoffed at or, worse, may harden the determination of those indicted to resist peace agreements that would leave them on the run from international authorities. Ambitious humanitarian efforts may still only scratch the surface of human suffering and may even inadvertently prolong wars. Finally, military intervention is always unpredictable, no matter how well conceived and executed.

Uncertainty and frustration are permanent features of post–cold war internationalism. They are most acute in policies aimed at the periphery, but they exist as well in policies aimed at traditional core areas of concern where U.S. goals are no longer clear-cut and the Western community is no longer cohesive. It is tempting, as the internationalist road becomes harder to travel, to look for an exit and concoct excuses for taking it. Unfortunately, there is no exit that can lead the United States into an international society that is free of depraved extremists. And as long as violence can be prevented or lessened, many Americans will feel a powerful desire to have their government take steps toward that end. The responsibility of the policy world is thus to devise better strategies for action, not better rationales for retreat.

CHAPTER FIVE

Toward the Future

THE UNITED STATES came of age on a steady diet of success. Pragmatism and a belief in the solvability of problems are deeply ingrained in U.S. culture. Forged at a time when much of the industrial world lay in rubble, postwar internationalism tapped into this can-do spirit, and it was popular in large part because it worked: it rebuilt Western Europe and East Asia, it held the Communists at bay, and it kept oil flowing from the Persian Gulf. Support for this crusade was strong enough to endure even after the searing debacle in Vietnam. Key elements of the crusade have, in modified form, also survived the end of the cold war.

Today's internationalism is not the same kind the public supported during the cold war. American engagement on the periphery is easy to attack because the problems are frequently intractable and genuine success comes only sporadically. There is no noble crusade here, no inexorable march toward victory—only a constant stream of nasty dilemmas that the public usually can't understand and that policy makers would prefer to avoid. While skepticism has been most vocally expressed by isolationists, some internationalists also harbor doubts, and understandably so. The limitless supply of problems and the secondary nature of U.S. interests on the periphery are reasons cited for focusing scarce resources on the core. Moreover, the internationalist project as a whole may be threatened if its agenda is too expansive, too global, and if it includes goals so ambitious that disappointment is guaranteed. Because the liberal international order created in the mid-1940s is now at risk of decaying, it has been argued that the dominant task of foreign policy officials must be to shore up what has been called "internationalism on stilts."[1] Adventures on the periphery are seen as a distraction from this central mission.

In principle, this perspective has compelling elements. Sustaining and revitalizing the international order built over the past fifty years should be the chief goal of U.S. foreign policy. Failures on the periphery can have an overflow effect, souring the public on international engagement generally. Busy policy makers do have to establish priorities, and problems in core areas should top their lists.

In practice, the argument has two weaknesses. First, the core areas of U.S. concern do not exist in a bubble; rather they have myriad interconnections with less developed parts of the world. The liberal international order will prosper best within a global system that is gradually becoming more stable and peaceful. This goal, in turn, requires containing zones of instability. For example, if India disintegrates into ethnic turmoil, one of the most economically dynamic countries in the world will no longer be a market for Western investment and high-tech exports; instead, it will demand emergency attention and foreign assistance from the rich countries. If ethnic conflict spreads in Russia, that country could be diverted from the path of economic and political reform, a development that would slow its integration into the international economic system and potentially produce an isolated nationalistic government once again in conflict with the West. The war in Chechnya, contained though it was, provided a glimpse of this. The war not only weakened Yeltsin's government but also caused a major rift with the West that extended into all areas of political-economic cooperation.

Domestically, Americans are all too familiar with the consequences of allowing certain places to sink into despair and squalor. Most Americans have no regular contact with inner cities, and the central pillars of the U.S. economy are barely affected by happenings there. The ghettos are largely isolated from the mainstream of U.S. life. But still, their cost to the public at large is enormous in both economic and social terms. Instead of contributing to national prosperity, these areas require steady infusions of emergency assistance. While most of the violence of inner-city residents is targeted at one another, some of it is perpetrated against citizens in the wider society, creating enormous fear and division. The ghettos are symbols of inequality and failure, forbidden places that mock the idea of national harmony and degrade the quality of life for all American citizens.

Global ghettos like Burundi or Kurdistan have similar effects. The horrors that take place within them do not directly affect people living in the industrial core or impinge much on the global economy. To be sure, though, the misery and chaos within these isolated backwaters degrade the quality of life for all people on the planet. Like the ghettos in the United States, these places require steady assistance and impede collective prosperity. The violence within them regularly overflows in the form of terrorism or drug and arms exports. Refugees flee from these trouble spots in vast numbers and place strains on the countries where they end up. The global ghettos are disaster zones where travelers cannot visit, where businesspeople cannot go to trade, where deadly diseases are incubated and exported, where journalists and aid workers frequently die, where diplomats feel unsafe. These places of desperation make a shrinking world that much smaller.

A second pitfall of overfocusing on the core is the tendency to mistakenly imagine that humanitarian catastrophes can simply be ignored. Sometimes, of course, they are. The brutal war in Angola, the continuing anguish of Sudan, and the descent into chaos of Afghanistan are all examples of nightmares that have been kept off the list of U.S. foreign policy priorities in recent years. But the historical record going back to Biafra is equally replete with episodes that have galvanized U.S. attention for month after month and have been impossible for policy makers to turn a blind eye to. Just as presidents always discover that things like nomination fights and petty scandals regularly distract them from their big policy goals, so too do national security managers inevitably find that crises in peripheral regions demand their attention. Whatever the musings of grand strategists and the edicts crafted by interagency planners, policy makers often have little choice but to focus on less important priorities.

The key to minimizing the time and resources spent on ethnic conflicts on the periphery is not to ignore or downplay these problems. It is to give them enough salience in policy planning that they are worked on constantly, at their earliest stages, not left to grow to the point that a full scale effort is needed to handle them. This emphasis requires several adjustments in current policy. First, the United States must build on the recent progress it has made in cooperating with international and nongovernmental organizations to manage crises in peripheral regions. Second, U.S. strategic planners must play a leading role in conceptualizing stable political orders in regions plagued by ethnic conflict, and U.S. diplomats must help bring these orders into existence. Third, the national-security establishment must implement organizational changes that will ensure that ethnic conflicts receive the attention they require.

COLLECTIVE RESPONSES

Throughout the twentieth century, isolationists have seen international organizations and treaty commitments of all kinds as threats to U.S. sovereignty and freedom of action. To many of those who now feel that the end of the cold war means that the United States can radically reduce its engagement on the periphery, the United Nations is seen as the most powerful force pulling in the opposite direction. As a result of domestic criticism, U.S.

efforts to further empower the United Nations have virtually come
to a halt. Meanwhile, with its fiscal situation more perilous than
ever, the United Nations has barely been able to carry out the
missions it has under way. Hopes that sprang up in the early 1990s
for a United Nations that could function as its founders envisioned
now seem like a distant dream.

These hopes must be revived if U.S. foreign policy is to grapple
successfully with the problem of ethnic conflict and other kinds of
crises on the periphery. The isolationist critique is precisely back-
ward. The worst-case scenario is not a United Nations that pulls
an unwilling United States into imbroglios on the periphery—for
this is difficult given the existence of the U.S. veto. Instead, it is a
United Nations that is incapable of heading off nascent conflicts
and so weak that it cannot galvanize collective action, thus leaving
the United States to bear a disproportionate burden for managing
crises on the periphery or, worse, allowing these crises to multiply
unchecked.

That is essentially the situation today. In 1992, the Bush administration chose to ignore Boutros Boutros-Ghali's call for a
strengthening of U.N. capabilities for preventive diplomacy and
the creation of a standing rapid-reaction force. The Clinton administration came to power with a more sympathetic view of the
United Nations, but in the wake of Somalia and in the face of a
rising isolationism, it often ended up joining the critics instead of
fighting them. In the current political climate, it has become difficult enough simply to keep the United States from falling much
further behind on its U.N. dues. Plans for giving the organization
new powers are rarely even discussed in official Washington.

And yet two lessons of recent history suggest the wisdom of
empowering the United Nations to play a more effective role in
managing internal conflicts. First there is the evidence that U.S.
policy makers are acutely limited in the number of problems they
can pay attention to at once. Even were the national-security bureaucracy to track and analyze all the brewing crises in the world,
higher-level policymakers would simply never have the time to
concentrate on more than a handful. Some crises inevitably get

short shrift, including ones that the United States has a significant interest in defusing at the earliest possible stage.

Boosting U.N. capacities for preventive diplomacy is the best way to compensate for these limitations. The U.N. secretary general should have the resources to dispatch observer teams, investigators, and conflict-resolution specialists to wherever he or she believes they are needed. Resources should also be available for staffing regional U.N. offices and supporting more extensive liaison work with regional organizations. An expanded U.N. capacity for human-rights work should be closely coordinated with preventive diplomacy.[2] The result of these steps would be a secretary general with greater global influence, a result the U.S. government has traditionally resisted. Inevitably, the secretary general will choose to invest preventive diplomacy resources in conflicts that do not affect even secondary U.S. interests, and, inevitably as well, he or she will occasionally act in ways that U.S. policy makers deem counterproductive. The specter of a powerful secretary general criticizing U.S. friends like Turkey and attempting high-profile intervention in crises that Washington believes should be handled quietly is not a pleasant one for U.S. officials to consider. It is, however, a basic fact of life that delegating power of any kind means losing control. A central adjustment in post–cold war foreign policy must be for the United States to accept new limitations on its influence over the management of international problems. In those situations in which Washington is not prepared to lead, it must be ready to support the leadership of others, even if the results are sometimes mixed. Crises that are managed imperfectly are better than crises that are not managed at all.

A second lesson from the historical record is that the United Nations needs a greater capacity for using force. The decisive use of force by an outside party might have altered the course of several recent ethnic conflicts and contained the scope of fighting. But no outside parties—least of all the United States—felt that their interests justified putting lives and national prestige at stake. As things now stand, U.N. forces have only as much wherewithal as their members contribute and there is no reason to believe that

U.N. members will show a greater determination than they have in the past to undertake risky interventions in unimportant wars. Thus no reliable mechanism exists within the international-security system for responding to genocidal thugs and the various lesser villains who operate in geopolitical backwaters. Unless this changes, we can expect more distressing instances in which the United Nations is forced to stand by impotently as acts of barbarism are perpetrated.

One commonly suggested remedy is to create a standing U.N. force made up of professional volunteers. A U.N. military corps of five to fifteen thousand experienced, battle-hardened troops could be deployed by the Security Council into crisis situations without member states anguishing over casualties in their national contingents. Obviously, such a small force could do only so much, but a highly trained and well-equipped one could prove more than a match for many of the ragtag militias and free-lance killers who often spearhead the worst excesses of ethnic violence. A U.N. military corps could also multiply its effectiveness through military training and assistance programs, which currently only national militaries are able to undertake. According to one detailed proposal by the Project on Defense Alternatives, the cost of developing a fifteen-thousand-person force equipped with light tanks, air defense and artillery batteries, and armed helicopters would be $2.6 billion over the first thirty months.[3] A larger force with heavier equipment would obviously cost more, but even expenditures of $3-6 billion annually should not be beyond the realm of imagination, given what U.N. member states spend collectively on their national militaries.

Had such a force been in existence during the attempted genocide in Rwanda, the Security Council would have had a more attractive set of options for halting the killing. Instead of having to assemble an ad hoc force, it could have called on a corps that was ready to move. Instead of begging for troop contributions, it could have simply given orders to professional soldiers on the U.N. payroll. Instead of worrying about whether the members of an ad hoc force could fight well together, it could have had confidence

in a group that had long been training together and had already
been through previous combat.

A United Nations with military capacity would have to concern
itself with maintaining its credibility and prestige, just as states do.
It would want to avoid sending forces into situations where they
might fail and to avoid threatening military actions that it was not
prepared to carry out. It would want to make sure its forces had
achievable goals and an exit strategy. These criteria would prevent
deployments in many situations—indeed, they might have fore-
closed a military option in Rwanda. U.N. military action would
still be far more feasible than it is now, however, because one par-
alyzing test would be eliminated: member states would no longer
need to have individual interests powerful enough to warrant their
sending their soldiers to fight and die. Security Council deliberations could focus more clearly on humanitarian considerations and
the collective interests of the international system.

It is hard to imagine in the present political climate that the
United States would support the creation of a U.N. military corps.
U.S. officials have a low regard for the institutional capacity of the
United Nations and in recent years have doubted its ability to handle new responsibilities. In part, the Clinton administration pulled
back from its enthusiasm for the United Nations because of dis-
illusionment about the basic competence of the organization. "We
developed a better understanding of the political and structural
reforms that need to take place in the institution for it to be able
to fulfill the role that we wish it would," commented Douglas J.
Bennet, assistant secretary of state, in 1994.[4] Arguably the more
important obstacle to greater U.S. support for the United Nations
has been the hostility of conservative lawmakers in Washington.
In a major misstep, the Clinton administration sought to avoid
political damage by joining in the criticism of the United Nations—often with unfair accusations, especially over Somalia. The
result has been a vicious cycle: the less support the United Nations
receives from the United States, the less capable it is of enhancing
its institutional capacities and performing its missions effectively.
A report sponsored by the Council on Foreign Relations concluded

in August 1996 that Washington's hostility toward the United
Nations not only damaged the organization but also hurt the national interests of the United States.[5] In earlier congressional testimony, Madeleine Albright made essentially the same point. She
stressed that the United States could not lead efforts to reform the
United Nations if it didn't pay all its dues.[6]

In U.S. domestic politics, attacks on the United Nations have
tended to ebb and flow in recent decades, and there is no reason
to believe that the current wave will last indefinitely—especially
given the consistent public support for an activist U.S. role in the
United Nations. In time, it should be possible to move forward
again with efforts to further empower the United Nations. That
process may already be under way. In July 1996, the Security
Council took a modest but important step toward enhancing the
organization's military capacity when it began to create a mobile
military headquarters that could rapidly field command teams. The
purpose of these teams would be to enter areas of civil strife or
humanitarian calamity and quickly set up rudimentary missions
that would lay the groundwork for the deployment of peacekeeping
forces. Under the previous arrangement, just establishing the command team for a new U.N. mission was a process that could take
weeks or months. Creating the mobile headquarters did not solve
the problem of finding troops on short notice to serve under U.N.
command, but it represented a move in that direction. While the
United States supported this new initiative, put forth by twenty-
four countries, it did not volunteer to share the costs of implementing it.[7]

To pay for a stronger U.N. capacity for preventive diplomacy
and military intervention, a new system is needed for financing the
United Nations and other international organizations. The current arrangement of member contributions neither raises enough
money nor functions reliably. The most promising exit from this
trap lies in proposals for international taxation. Even a minuscule
tax on international currency exchanges could raise several hundred
billion dollars annually. Taxes on international airline tickets, in-

ternational telephone calls, and the like could also raise significant revenue without imposing a noticeable burden on individuals.

Empowering the United Nations is the most important of a series of steps needed to make international organizations more effective in dealing with ethnic conflict. Already, U.S. policy makers have sought to strengthen other organizations, and this work should be given an even higher priority in the future. As discussed in previous chapters, the United States began working closely with the OAU during the early 1990s to bolster its capacity for preventive diplomacy and peacekeeping. It changed the laws on foreign assistance so that aid could be channeled directly to the OAU at a time when the organization was trying to play an innovative new role in the Rwandan peace process. Besides providing financial assistance, American officials gave technical and political advice to the OAU as it grew more involved in Rwanda. The United States has also played a major role in supporting the West African peacekeeping force in Liberia. This 8,500-strong force received millions of dollars in support from the United States, which saw it—despite its many flaws—as a hopeful example of indigenous African peacekeeping efforts.

But both the OAU and the West African experiments have proved difficult to sustain because of a lack of adequate funding mechanisms. As the poorest continent in the world, Africa has difficulty finding the funds needed to underwrite prolonged peacekeeping operations or extensive preventive diplomacy activities. The near collapse of the West African peacekeeping force in early 1996 provided a case in point. Poorly equipped and trained, and wracked by corruption, this force was unable to prevent a resurgence of fighting in Liberia that drew in the United States to evacuate Americans from the country. The Clinton administration announced a willingness in April 1996 to provide $30 million in new assistance to the force. The larger problem, however, is that there exists no system for tapping other contributions from the West and, especially, using the resources of global international organizations to support regional organizations. "There is no mechanism at the United Nations, indeed no precedent at the U.N. for these kinds of regional initiatives," complained Assistant Secretary of State George Moose during the Liberian crisis.[8]

In principle, the United Nations is supposed to work in tandem with regional organizations to maintain international security. In the Bosnian crisis it has done so, coordinating with NATO and the Organization for Security and Cooperation in Europe (OSCE) on a range of issues. Ideally, the United Nations would go beyond coordination and provide a forum to raise badly needed funds for impoverished indigenous organizations. In practice, however, the process of soliciting money has been ad hoc, and the United Nations is too weak and underfinanced itself to create a formalized process for such fund-raising. The consequence of a hobbled United Nations is once again that either Washington takes action or nothing happens. In the case of Liberia, it fell to the United States to lead an effort to raise money in the West to support the West African peacekeeping force. These efforts were laudable, but in a sense the United States was reaping what it helped to sow.

In Europe, the United States has taken some steps to help strengthen the OSCE's role in managing ethnic conflicts. The Bush and Clinton administrations strongly supported an active role for the OSCE in Kosovo, where OSCE monitors tracked Serb abuses of ethnic Albanians and sought to prevent further deterioration in conditions. These monitors, which included Americans, had little influence and ultimately were ordered by Belgrade to leave in summer 1993. Nevertheless, their deployment marked the first time that the OSCE human-rights mechanisms had been fully implemented, and U.S. officials paid close attention to the lessons of this episode. During fighting in Chechnya in early 1995, the United States again supported the deployment of OSCE monitors and placed pressure on the Russian government to accept a visit by such a team. The OSCE's high commissioner on national minorities, Max van der Stoel, has also played an important role in addressing the plight of ethnic Russians in the Baltic states, the Hungarian minority in Romania and Slovakia, and the Slovak minority in Hungary.[9] The high commissioner's work has been especially significant in the southern Balkans, where he has been involved in trying to defuse the tensions in Macedonia.

Despite these innovations in the work of the OSCE, what has been most notable in many of the ethnic conflicts in Europe and Eurasia is the limited role of regional organizations. In the Caucasus, Russian military power and political authority have had a dominant influence over the outcome of secessionist efforts. In the Balkans, the Baltic states, and Northern Ireland, U.S. power has been decisive in mediating peaceful outcomes. In all these places, spheres of influence continue to prevail. American and Russian policy makers have similar explanations for intervening in ethnic conflicts: nobody else is capable of doing it. The United States entered the Balkans imbroglio only after Western European efforts to end the fighting had failed. It mediated in Northern Ireland and the Baltics because there was no other state or institution that could play such a role. The Russian interventions in the Caucasus have been less altruistic, but Western officials readily acknowledge that the Western capitals and the United Nations lack the wherewithal to become involved and that Russia has been left to manage as it sees fit.

This is not an optimal state of affairs. American efforts are too inconsistent and Russian power is too controversial for either to be relied on exclusively. Even though Europe has the most mature regional organizations in the world, there remains a pressing need to develop their potential further, and the United States must be a leader in that effort. It must put aside its historical ambivalence toward indigenous European collective-security mechanisms. Traditionally, U.S. policy makers have worried about moves that might undermine the leadership that the United States enjoys in European security affairs through its dominance of NATO. In the early 1990s, Washington opposed efforts to develop the Western European Union (WEU) into a fully operational security arm of the EU. Likewise, it has been ambivalent about various proposals to turn the OSCE into a more robust collective-security organization capable of raising and deploying peacekeeping or peacemaking forces.

American officials have made strong arguments for why both the OSCE and the WEU are poorly suited to an expanded collective-security role. But they have failed to be equally frank about the limitations of NATO. These are obvious: the alliance does not have continentwide membership, it is dependent on U.S. leadership, and the Russians distrust it. In its current incarnation, NATO does not offer an escape from a situation in which conflict resolution hinges on the wherewithal of either Russia or the United States. None of the plans for expanding NATO, moreover, promises to remedy its central limitations. Instead, as many observers have argued persuasively, the expansion of NATO could create a new division in Europe.[10] The war in Bosnia graphically underscored the shortcomings of Europe's collective-security mechanisms, yet in the wake of that appalling failure of the West, no new security structures have been proposed. Clearly the United States needs to revisit issues of Europe's security architecture.

Strengthening the OSCE is one option that U.S. policy makers must consider. More than any other organization, the OSCE has demonstrated an ability to play a constructive role in highly volatile ethnic conflicts in the former Communist bloc. By 1995 the OSCE had undertaken missions in Estonia, Latvia, Macedonia, Ukraine, Georgia, Moldova, Tajikistan, and Sarajevo. These involved either preventive diplomacy or crisis management, with the preventive work yielding more success than its attempts at mediation.[11] The OSCE is an institution that Russian leaders have shown a willingness to trust, and Russia has worked with the OSCE on conflicts in Moldova, Georgia, Nagorno-Karabakh, and Chechnya. As one study notes, "The OSCE may be the only international institution that is able to engage Russia and provide an alternative to Russian-dominated peacekeeping and purely Russian influence in its 'near abroad.' "[12]

Strengthening the OSCE requires both the diplomatic and the financial support of the United States. In the past, the United States has helped block efforts to further institutionalize the OSCE and provide it with coercive instruments. Beyond their traditional fears about a collective-security organization in Europe that would erode NATO's centrality, U.S. policy makers have feared the rise of a new bureaucracy that would unnecessarily duplicate the role of other institutions and would therefore have problems sustaining financial and political support. At a time when the United Nations is perpetually underfunded, the WEU is searching for a purpose, and NATO's Partnership for Peace is becoming more institutionalized, there is some basis for these fears. Nevertheless, the strong track record of the OSCE suggests that it has unique attributes, and it has done a lot of good with a budget of less than $50 million a year in the mid-1990s. An expanded OSCE would not only be able to step up its current activities but also have the institutional capacity and resources to play a major role in safeguarding peace in the Caucasus once permanent settlements are reached.

Beyond making a new commitment to empowering the United Nations and strengthening regional organizations, the United States needs to undertake multilateral efforts to control the conventional-arms trade. The ready availability of weaponry is not a cause of ethnic conflicts, but it can exacerbate tensions in a pre-war situation and increase the level of violence of ethnic wars once they have begun. Lebanon was a sea of weapons on the eve of its self-destruction, and once the war was under way, the rise of numerous heavily armed militias vastly complicated the task of forging an enduring cease-fire and rebuilding a central army with enough of a military edge to impose order. The wide dispersal of arms in the Caucasus may also have contributed to the intensity of the fighting and the difficulty of securing peace agreements. In the peace talks in Northern Ireland, disarmament has proved to be among the hardest and most time-consuming problems for negotiators. In contrast, prospects for political stability have probably been aided by the relative lack of weaponry among civilians in the Baltic states, ethnic Hungarians in Romania, Muslims in Kashmir, ethnic Albanians in Kosovo and Macedonia, Palestinians in the Occupied Territories, and several minorities in India.

Most ethnic conflicts are fought with light weapons like assault rifles, mortars, grenade launchers, and land mines. Vast quantities of these arms are readily available at cheap prices in many areas, and regulating them through international agreements is difficult. Nevertheless, several proposals have been made in recent years for reining in the global trade in light weapons.[13] The United States has not been supportive of such suggestions. Historically, the United States has been ambivalent about restrictions on conventional-weapons sales, and in recent years the Clinton administration has actively promoted the sale of U.S. weapons. American policy makers have seen arms transfers as a way to aid U.S. industry, bolster friendly regimes, and strengthen diplomatic ties.

Over the long term, there are many good reasons for the United States to change fundamentally its policies on arms exports and lead multilateral efforts to curtail the global arms trade. Legions of experts have recited these reasons for two decades, and this is not the place to repeat them. Instead, a more modest point bears reiteration: efforts to reduce the flow of light weapons into ethnically volatile regions can be undertaken without jeopardizing the bulk of U.S. arms sales. The United States should support U.N. efforts to monitor and regulate the light-arms trade and to restrict the activity of the black market. It should support similar work by regional organizations. And, of course, the United States should closely scrutinize its exports of light weapons and prohibit transfers to volatile regions. In situations of ongoing conflict, the United States should play a leading role in embargoing arms to combatants and contribute resources to ensure that these prohibitions can be enforced. The international effort to stem the flow of arms into Burundi and Rwanda following the 1994 genocide is an example of the importance of this kind of work.

A new commitment to multilateralism in its varied forms must be supplemented by new ties with nongovernmental organizations in the areas of human rights, humanitarian relief, and conflict resolution. A central lesson of the recent past is that these organizations often have the best understanding of both the causes of, and the potential solutions to, ethnic conflict. Human Rights Watch, for example, has repeatedly distinguished itself for providing first-rate analysis of deteriorating ethnic situations and identifying those who are to blame. Organizations like Human Rights Watch and International Alert maintain multiple contacts among local NGOs and activists and are less likely than U.S. personnel to be inhibited by a desire to maintain good relations with a host government. Nongovernmental organizations like Search for Common Ground have unique advantages as well. They have specialization that is not widely available in the U.S. diplomatic corps and can sponsor dialogue that is informal and ongoing.

For these reasons it makes sense for the U.S. government to cultivate extensive contacts in the NGO world, as awkward as this can sometimes be. NGOs are often harsh critics of U.S. policy, attacking Washington for its lax human-rights policies, its irresponsible arms sales, and its slow responses to refugee crises. Cooperating with one's critics is not easy for anybody, and it can be especially difficult for policy makers, who always worry that what they confide in others might be turned against them or cause embarrassment. Nevertheless, the gains of maintaining paths of communication outweigh the risks, since in many ethnic conflicts U.S. officials will not be adequately served by the sources of information available to them within the government or the media.

The Burundian crisis illustrates the usefulness of U.S. ties to NGOs. From 1994 through 1996, dozens of NGOs worked on different aspects of the crisis, monitoring massacres in the countryside, seeking to prevent the delivery of new arms, promoting peaceful dialogue between Hutu and Tutsi, addressing discrimination in work and education, trying to counter hate radio, dealing with nutritional and medical needs, attempting to strengthen government organs like the judiciary, aiding efforts to bring war criminals from the 1993 massacres to justice, and so on. These groups had access to a wide array of information and could provide insights and advice unavailable within the U.S. government. In Washington, the Burundi Policy Forum provided a crucial vehicle for the exchange of information between NGOs and policy makers.

Closer relations between the U.S. government and nongovernmental organizations will stem mainly from an evolution in attitude. Policy changes, however, can also affect these relations.

Clinton administration officials have attempted in recent years to channel more foreign assistance in the areas of development and family planning through local and international NGOs. The logic of bypassing the state in providing assistance has long been recognized by development experts, but forging such formal ties with NGOs also lays the groundwork for more effective efforts to prevent future ethnic conflicts.

NEGOTIATING STABILITY

Building a global collective-security order would do much more than enhance capacities to manage ethnic conflicts. Stronger international and regional organizations would also help stabilize relations among the great powers and provide better mechanisms for responding to major aggression by rogue states. Investing U.S. resources and energies into strengthening collective security would thus yield dividends that would go well beyond the country's traditional concerns about secondary interests on the periphery.

The task of crafting new political orders in regions of ethnic strife has fewer overflow benefits but is crucially important nevertheless. Creative U.S. diplomacy could help prevent new waves of violence in the Balkans, the Caucasus, the Great Lakes region of Africa, and Kurdistan. While some of these regions are comparatively quiet now, all could become volatile in the future. As the world's lone superpower and its most trusted mediator, only the United States has the influence to forge lasting frameworks for peace in these regions.

In the Balkans, the current peace is exceedingly fragile. The Dayton accord of December 1995 may have ended the fighting in the former Yugoslavia, but it has not settled the conflicts. While many factors will influence the future of Bosnia following the withdrawal of the international peacekeeping force, the country will probably divide permanently along ethnic lines. New fighting is likely. According to a draft analysis of a National Intelligence Estimate circulated within the U.S. government in spring 1996, the chances are poor that Bosnia will be transformed into a democratic multiethnic state as envisioned in the Dayton agreement.[14] The leaders of all three ethnic groups fear a loss of power within a multiethnic state and none is strongly committed to real power sharing. The Bosnian Serbs want either to have their own state or to join Serbia. There is good reason to expect that the cease-fire line—or "interentity boundary line," in Dayton parlance—separating the Serbs and Muslims will become permanent, much like the line dividing Cyprus or the Korean Peninsula, and that the two groups will never truly cooperate in a common government.

The primary danger of a new war, however, lies not in renewed military conflict between the Serbs and Muslims but rather in the violent dissolution of the Muslim-Croat federation that controls roughly half of Bosnia. Between April 1993 and February 1994, the Croats and Muslims fought a brutal war, and this conflict could well reignite. The Croats of Bosnia are a minority in the federation, and recent history would seem to indicate that they will eventually renew their quest to affiliate with Croatia proper. The May 1996 national intelligence estimate suggested that the federation was largely a figment of the U.S. imagination and cast doubt on its survivability, despite U.S. pressure on the Muslims and Croats to integrate their militaries and economic institutions.[15] A brief outbreak of fighting in Mostar between Muslims and Croats in early 1997 was a reminder of the distrust that endures between these groups.

In a less-poisoned atmosphere the proper goal of U.S. policy would be to continue efforts to make the Muslim-Croat federation work, for such arrangements may offer the best hope for resolving various ethnic conflicts. Regrettably, however, the most realistic strategy for preventing a new war is probably for U.S. officials to mediate the further partition of Bosnia, dissolving the federation peacefully while there is still a chance to do so. The ultimate goal of U.S. diplomacy, unpalatable though it may be, should be the creation of a far smaller and homogeneous Muslim Bosnian state.

Sustained diplomatic efforts are also needed to deal with the explosive situation caused by the Albanian diaspora. The Dayton agreement did nothing to resolve permanently the situation in Kosovo, and in Macedonia the demands of ethnic Albanians remain a source of conflict. In 1994 and 1995, the Clinton administration persuaded the Albanian government to temper its support for Albanian nationalists in Kosovo and Macedonia. The stationing of U.S. troops in Macedonia probably also had a calming effect. These were great successes, but they are only temporary fixes. In the long run, an arrangement is needed that allows Albanians who live outside Albania to express their cultural identity, to feel free from repression, and to associate freely across national borders.

This situation is a prime instance where arrangements of semisovereignty should be explored. The goal of U.S. diplomacy should be to encourage the creation of a "historical homeland" for Albanians that encompasses Kosovo, Macedonia, and Albania. All sides would compromise. The Albanians of Kosovo would formally relinquish their quest to secede from Serbia (and those in Macedonia would end their own nationalistic agitation) in exchange for governing autonomy and some rights to participate in the national life of Albania. There would be "soft" borders in the region and freedom of transit and cultural and political expression. There might be some kind of transnational Albanian assembly or congress.

This kind of arrangement is not impossible. While powerful nationalistic claims exist among Serbs, Albanians, and Macedonians, there is no history in this region—not yet, anyway—of violence so horrific that it fatally poisons all prospects for political compromise. There are also signs that tensions in Kosovo are on the wane: Serbs have been leaving the region in large numbers and President Slobodan Milosevic of Serbia is no longer focusing on Kosovo as a symbol of Serb nationalism.[16] For Milosevic, it appears that making peace with the West is beginning to take precedence over pressing the Serb cause in Kosovo. Milosevic has shown a keen desire to integrate his country into the global economy and get rid of the "outer wall" of sanctions that has remained in place since the Dayton accord. (These sanctions include denying Serbia admission to international financial institutions and blocking its access to international credit.) In turn, Albania's president, Sali Berisha, has already counseled Kosovo Albanians to abandon their bid for independence and seek a political solution based on autonomy. The U.S. strategy should be to keep up the pressure on Serbia to ease tensions in the region. U.S. goals should include establishing an international presence in Kosovo, compelling Serbia to end elements of its repressive rule in Kosovo, getting border restrictions eased, and eventually mediating talks among the parties. On July 20, 1996, the United States opened an information center in Pristina, Kosovo, at a ceremony attended by Assistant Secretary of State John Kornblum. The Clinton administration has said that it will not send an ambassador to Belgrade as long as Serb police continue to engage in repression in Kosovo.

American policy toward Albania and Macedonia should continue the preventive strategy that has been established over recent years. Once the situation in Albania stabilizes, Washington should continue to offer it closer ties, along with military and economic aid, on the understanding that it will use its influence with Albanians in Kosovo and Macedonia to promote moderation and nonviolence. In addition, the United States should encourage the Albanian leadership to continue talking with the leaders of Serbia and Macedonia. Meanwhile, U.S. participation in the U.N. Preventive Deployment in Macedonia (UNPREDEP) remains important for its calming effect on the region. The United States should also take other steps to stabilize Macedonia, including support for internal political and social reforms and continuation of its involvement in NATO's Partnership for Peace initiative.[17]

American policy in the Balkans will not succeed through sporadic efforts by mid-level officials. It will require a sustained undertaking that involves a special envoy and the secretary of state and, on occasion, the president.

IN THE CAUCASUS, the United States has pursued a strategy of limited involvement in recent years. For the most part it has been content to let the Russians play a leading role, flexing their political, economic, and military muscle in ways that have often been dubious. Russian power can play a constructive role, but meddling by Moscow has characteristically been partly driven by neoimperialist or other self-serving objectives, such as protecting ethnic Russians. Russia's credibility as a neutral mediator in the region is low, not least because of the butchery in Chechnya.

Given the historically limited nature of U.S. interests in the Caucasus, along with the myriad other problems that confront U.S. policy makers, it is unrealistic to imagine that the United States will become a central player in settling the conflicts in this region. Nevertheless, there are several ways in which the United States can become a more important participant. First, as the Clinton administration has recognized, new opportunities have arisen for constructive diplomatic efforts in the Caucasus. As of mid-1997, cease-fires were in place in the three principal conflict zones: Nagorno-Karabakh, Abkhazia, and South Ossetia. At the same time, peace processes involving the United Nations and the OSCE were under way. The Clinton administration has been wise to exploit this moment with sustained high-level efforts. President Clinton and Vice President Gore have met many times with the presidents of Georgia, Azerbaijan, and Armenia. In March 1996, senior U.S. officials traveled to Azerbaijan to meet with leaders there and support a new Russian peace initiative.[18] In July 1996, Undersecretary of State Lynn Davis traveled to the capitals of all three countries to discuss security issues. At a lower level, these conflicts received sustained attention from the State Department's coordinator for the New Independent States, James Collins; his deputy, John E. Herbst; and a special negotiator, Joseph Presel, whose mandate was to focus exclusively on the three conflicts.[19]

Given its good bilateral relations with Georgia, Armenia, and Azerbaijan, the United States is well positioned to continue playing a more active role in the Caucasus. Its large assistance program to Armenia, combined with improved ties to Azerbaijan—where U.S. oil companies are deeply involved in developing the country's petroleum reserves—gives it some influence over the direction of talks on the Nagorno-Karabakh dispute, and the Clinton administration has taken important steps to use this leverage. The United States also has a close relationship with the Georgian government headed by Eduard Shevardnadze. It would be unfortunate if U.S. officials did not energetically exploit these propitious circumstances.

In an ideal world, the disputes within the Caucasus would be handled through a full range of multilateral mechanisms to create a political order based on neutral conflict resolution rather than Russian power, with all its capriciousness and controversy. American policy has helped build the framework for such an order by supporting mediating efforts by the OSCE and the United Nations and by nurturing the membership of Caucasian countries in NATO's Partnership for Peace. But U.S. resistance to playing a larger role in the Caucasus—most notably its unwillingness to contribute troops to U.N. peacekeeping missions—and donor fatigue among other major powers have kept truly multilateral solutions out of reach. Russian power will inevitably be the dominant factor governing the settlement of the wars in this region. An important intermediate goal of the United States, therefore, should be to ensure greater accountability for Russian operations. As analysts Jarat Chopra and Thomas G. Weiss argue, the Caucasus could be a laboratory for refining a model in which the United Nations subcontracts peacekeeping operations: "Russia as the regional power would be the main troop-contributing nation rather than a 'partner' in a coalition, while the United Nations would provide an overall political framework. . . . UN observers deployed throughout the command structure of the operation would ensure international accountability."[20] This arrangement would not be an optimal one, but it is probably the best that can be hoped for under the present circumstances.

FOLLOWING THE 1988 MASSACRES in Burundi, Thomas Melady, the former ambassor to that country, suggested that the only long-term solution to the Hutu-Tutsi dispute was to partition the country permanently.[21] To be sure, with as many as one million people

dead in ethnic conflict in Rwanda and Burundi over the past quarter of a century, there is an intrinsic appeal to partition as a solution
in both countries. This is especially true given the ominous future
facing the Great Lakes region of Africa. Mounting demographic
pressures in what is already some of the most densely populated
terrain in the world may create the basis for even greater ethnic
tensions. In countries where most people farm minuscule plots of
land, property will be subdivided even further. Resource competition and environmental degradation are causes of conflict
throughout the world; these will become ever more salient in
Rwanda and Burundi in the early twenty-first century.

If partitions could be effected in Rwanda and Burundi, they
might eliminate the fear of new campaigns of extermination. Under
present circumstances, however, it is hard to imagine such a massive resettling of people (although the India-Pakistan population
transfers after independence involved some sixteen million people).
A radical reconstruction of the political order governing the lives
of Hutu and Tutsi is thus not an option available to U.S. and other
international policy makers. Even more modest transnational,
semisovereignty arrangements are probably not workable either.
While some of the violence in Burundi over the past twenty-five
years has been related to Tutsi repression of Hutu peasants in particular parts of the country, the conflicts in Burundi and Rwanda
have never been driven by secessionist or irredentist claims in any
subregion of either country. There exists no historical homeland
for either Hutu or Tutsi. There is no obvious negotiating track
that involves the granting of more cultural independence or greater
political autonomy—strategies of de facto segregation. Instead,
these two groups are bound forever to live in a densely intermingled state, sharing power within political structures that are currently dysfunctional in the extreme.

For these reasons, solutions to the conflicts in Burundi and
Rwanda must be akin to those employed to save "failed states."
Despite much discussion on this subject in recent years, there is
little consensus on how the international community can actually
rescue states in which political, social, and economic institutions

have ceased to function well enough to provide basic order.[22] The United States helped rebuild several states in the aftermath of World War II, feeling that it had a vital interest in both preventing a recurrence of global war and ensuring the prosperity of central players in the international economic system. It has no such compelling interests in regard to Burundi and Rwanda or countries like them. Occasionally, as in Haiti and Somalia, the United States may intervene on a major scale in a failed state where it has no vital interests, but such a use of force is likely to be the exception rather than the rule. Strategies for saving failed states that hinge on the commitment of U.S. power are not currently viable. Certainly the United States is not going to spearhead any large-scale effort to offer salvation to Burundi and Rwanda in the near future.

The United Nations, along with regional organizations, must bear principal responsibility for the task of saving failed states. The United Nations must have the resources and international support to intervene deeply in the internal affairs of countries for years at a time. Depending on the severity of the societal breakdown, its role may take the form of governing assistance, assumption of a large degree of governmental authority, or full trusteeship.[23] Each role involves complex political problems and requires major commitments of both financial funds and military forces. Each also carries the risk of failure. Success in state building can never be guaranteed. The U.N. experience in Cambodia offers some grounds for optimism, while its experience in Somalia suggests reasons for pessimism.[24]

As argued throughout this book, it is a basic fact of post–cold war life that interventions on the periphery will produce mixed outcomes. This reality cannot be allowed to deter such interventions, as the situation in Burundi and Rwanda makes abundantly clear. A large and prolonged U.N. commitment to stabilizing these countries could be difficult to mount under current circumstances and could prove a failure in the end, but there may be no alternative if conditions deteriorate further. Nowhere in the world are more people at immediate risk of losing their lives in mass violence. Nowhere do long-term trends carry more ominous potential to exacerbate ethnic tensions. The international community faces a clear choice between paying less now or more later. Washington should be an energetic partner in organizing and sustaining a long-term U.N. intervention in Rwanda and Burundi. In addition, it should maintain the tempo of its recent bilateral diplomatic and aid efforts in the region.

THE CONTINUING PLIGHT of the Kurds presents a daunting challenge to U.S. policy makers. Neither Iraq nor Turkey has shown a real willingness to end the wars in Kurdistan with lasting political solutions like the granting of cultural autonomy to Kurdish regions, the protection of Kurdish human rights, and guarantees of political participation by Kurdish leaders and political parties. In the long run, though, the creation of a transnational historical Kurdish homeland with some degree of self-governance stands as an attractive goal, since the creation of a Kurdish state is probably impossible and, indeed, most Kurds in both Iraq and Turkey do not insist on complete independence.

The United States can work toward these aims in several ways. First, it can take a more consistent line with Turkey. Over the past decade, the executive branch has signaled in ways large and small that Turkey's human-rights record does not fundamentally interfere with the U.S.-Turkish relationship while, at the same time, Congress has occasionally sought to punish Turkey for that record. Turkey's recent scorched-earth policies in Kurdistan may have dealt a major blow to the PKK, but they have not eliminated the Kurdish problem more generally and, in fact, may well have exacerbated it by radicalizing new segments of the Kurdish population. In the absence of a political solution, renewed conflict can be expected and will certainly have a negative impact on Turkey's quest to modernize and integrate itself into Western Europe. It is unrealistic to ask Turkey to cease all operations against the PKK, since this group does have many of the characteristics of a violent terrorist organization. But the United States is justified in demanding that Turkey avoid military operations that victimize civilians, that it eliminate laws and special measures that repress the Kurdish people, and that it work hard to find a political solution. U.S. aid should not be subsidizing some of the most egregious human rights abuses in the Middle East. The United States should make clear that Turkey's treatment of the Kurds will influence the overall tenor of U.S.-Turkish relations. High-level U.S. officials should consistently raise the issue in their meetings with Turkish leaders, and arms sales and military aid should be linked to better treatment of the Kurds. The United States should coordinate its message on the Kurds with those of its European allies, making clear that this issue will affect all aspects of Turkey's relations with the West.

While there is real hope that Turkey can be pushed and prodded over time to make peace with its Kurds, Iraq is a different story entirely. There can be no Kurdish participation in Iraqi political life as long as one-man rule prevails. The principal way for the United States to help the Kurds of Iraq is to keep up the pressure on Saddam Hussein's regime and to sustain its protection of Kurdish areas in the northern part of the country. It should make clear that any eventual settlement that removes the sanctions on Iraq must include guarantees of Kurdish human rights and cultural autonomy. In the meantime, the United States should use any influence it has with Iraq's Kurds—who are now notoriously fractious—to help them become a more unified and effective player in Iraq's internal politics.

As bleak as the situation in Kurdistan now is, there is potential for a peaceful resolution of this long-running ethnic conflict. Most Kurds in Turkey and Iraq have never shown the kind of implacable fanaticism that has characterized other minority groups in ethnic conflicts. The PKK has never spoken for a majority of Turkish Kurds, and with proper policies from Ankara, current support for the PKK could be expected to dwindle dramatically. Kurdish insurgents in Iraq have historically shown a willingness to compromise with Baghdad and settle for goals short of full independence. Given these realities, arrangements that provide for some measure of Kurdish autonomy—with the promise of more if initial efforts prove workable—would probably be acceptable to most Kurds. Despite recent bloody history, it is possible to imagine Kurdistan's becoming a future laboratory in which to experiment with the resolution of ethnic conflicts. The multiple instances in which problems in Kurdistan have demanded U.S. attention, money, and military force make it clear that the United States has a strong interest in devoting attention to finding a permanent solution to the agony of the Kurds.

ORGANIZING FOR ETHNIC CONFLICT

The United States entered the post–cold war era with a national-security establishment designed to handle the very particular challenges of waging a global struggle with Communism. That establishment has only slowly been reconfigured. In many crises policy makers have scrambled to adapt existing structures and procedures to meet new and unfamiliar demands. To cope more effectively with future ethnic conflicts, the lessons learned in these often bruising experiences must be applied to the ongoing process of organizational reform. There are at least four areas where this might be done: diplomacy, intelligence, propaganda, and planning for military intervention.

The diplomatic corps has two main limitations that affect its capacity to predict and prevent ethnic conflict. First, it lacks specialists in some of the regions where ethnic conflict has proved acute. Second, U.S. diplomats often lack an adequate understanding of emerging ethnic conflicts in the countries where they are stationed. Neither of these problems is easily solved.

During the cold war, the diplomatic corps developed great expertise at tracking developments in Moscow and other national capitals but far less knowledge of outlying areas. Soviet experts were mostly experts on Russia and, even more narrowly, on the Communist political and military establishment. The desire of some U.S. propagandists and intelligence leaders to exploit the ethnic fractures of the Soviet empire ensured that the fourteen non-

Russian republics that also made up the Soviet Union were not entirely ignored by the national-security bureaucracy, but overall there was little emphasis within the foreign service on developing the language skills and political expertise for monitoring events in these areas. There was scant prestige in this work, either. Becoming a specialist in, say, the Caucasus was not the path to career success for a young U.S. diplomat.

The conflicts in Georgia, Moldova, Nagorno-Karabakh, and Chechnya all caught the State Department without an adequate reserve of expertise. It was not until the first half of 1992—well after ethnic fighting had broken out in most of these places—that the United States established a serious diplomatic presence in Armenia, Azerbaijan, and Georgia. And when first opened, American embassies in these countries were poorly staffed and equipped. The half dozen Soviet republics in central Asia, with their complex ethnic politics, were also comparatively uncharted terrain for U.S. diplomats during the cold war, and here it took even longer than in the Caucasus for the United States to put in place a diplomatic presence. Similarly, while the United States had significant expertise on Yugoslavia when that country began to fragment, its expertise had historically focused on the central government in Belgrade and the government's external relationships. The United States did not, for example, have much knowledge about Macedonia or Kosovo.

Over the past several years, nearly twenty new countries have arisen in the former Communist bloc, and the U.S. diplomatic corps is still trying to develop new expertise and language skills for many of them. Following the collapse of the Soviet Union, the Foreign Service Institute added instruction in fifteen languages to its curriculum. Efforts have been made to increase the opportunities and incentives for junior foreign service officers to pursue intensive language training.[25] The pace of such work must be as quick as possible, especially in Central Asia, which has so far remained relatively stable. The United States must also commit to a long-term effort to provide sufficient expertise on Burundi and Rwanda and on Kurdistan. Finally, it is critically important that

U.S. diplomats who specialize in Asia's two great giants—China and India—look beyond the traditional geopolitical and economic issues that have long been the focus of U.S. policy deliberations and also understand the ethnic fracture lines that run through these countries.

It is a bitter irony that, at precisely the time when new resources are necessary to improve U.S. diplomacy, funding for the State Department is instead being cut. The international-affairs budget has been falling for years, and following the Republican takeover of Congress in 1994, that decline turned into a nosedive. The State Department has had to close consulates, leave embassies understaffed, and economize in a number of areas, including personnel training and reeducation. The department has, of course, traditionally been an easy target for isolationists in Congress, and most presidents, including Clinton, have shown no appetite for high-profile defenses of this institution. Some secretaries of state have also sought to distance themselves from their department. Such duck-and-cover politics has become an unaffordable luxury. In addition to personally defending the broad ideals of internationalism, the president must also stand behind the central institutions of U.S. foreign policy.

The State Department, in turn, must find ways to do its work better. It is an easy target not just because of what it represents but because of how poorly it functions. The State Department's bureaucracy is notoriously unwieldy and its policy products are infamous for their absence of acuity. Any institution that so consistently disappoints its natural allies will have a harder time keeping at bay its bitter enemies. Numerous studies have sought ways to fix the department's problems, but progress toward reform has been halting. The essential dilemma is that no secretary of state wants to spend time overhauling the department instead of working toward high-profile successes on the diplomatic circuit. While this is understandable, a high price is paid for neglecting the department's institutional problems.

One element of that price is evident in the hobbled capacity of foreign service officers in the field. Quite apart from staff cuts abroad that have left officers doing more paperwork, the culture of the diplomatic corps seems to discourage vigorous exploration beyond the embassy compound. It is not uncommon for U.S. personnel to lead ghettolike existences that seldom bring them in contact with the local populace. In addition, U.S. professional diplomats do relatively short tours of duty and change posts frequently—factors that make it harder to develop great depth of understanding about the countries in which they are stationed. As the veteran diplomat Monteagle Sterns writes, deep expertise in a country "requires passionate interest in a foreign culture, great intellectual discipline, and an extended period of time living among the people of the region and speaking their language. Not all diplomats are willing to plunge into another culture so deeply. Furthermore, the professional ethic that has been cultivated in the service since 1960 discourages it."[26]

When ethnic conflicts threaten in remote areas like northern Burundi, Turkish and Iraqi Kurdistan, and Chechnya, the leading experts are invariably local and international NGOs that are working in the affected regions and tracking developments related to human rights, refugees, and other humanitarian needs. Rarely will a U.S. diplomat gain a cutting-edge knowledge of a nascent ethnic conflict by doing what diplomats are wont to do: nurturing sources within the host government and talking with other diplomats in the capital city. Understanding emerging ethnic conflicts will often require a courageous search for information in remote areas and vigorous networking among local dissidents and unpopular outside observers. It requires the time and inclination to leave the familiar environs of the capital. It means being ready to alienate the host government with inconvenient snooping and uncomfortable questions. It may require relying on scathing critics of U.S. human-rights policy for information. This kind of work is not the norm for diplomats.

Also, while U.S. diplomats have often performed brilliantly in mediating full-blown wars, they have shown little capacity to engage in conflict resolution at early stages. By contrast, NGOs like Search for Common Ground and, to some extent, IGOs like the

United Nations, the OAU, and the OSCE have developed new conflict-resolution techniques and a new network of practitioners and scholars. But the U.S. diplomatic corps has yet to embrace these innovative approaches.

The culture of caution that affects nearly all the foreign service's activities abroad has been the source of much discussion by analysts, and various remedies have been proposed, from changing the ways officers are recruited and promoted to altering the procedures by which they are rotated and managed. Beyond addressing the deficiencies of political reporting from overseas, reform proposals have also suggested ways to improve the analytical and long-range planning capacities within the State Department's headquarters.[27] Those capacities—notably the Policy Planning Staff and the Bureau of Intelligence and Research—were once first-rate but have been in a state of decline for decades. Revitalizing them and better integrating them with other elements of the national-security establishment is essential if reporting from the diplomatic corps is to have a sharper edge and be of greater use to policy makers. Again, however, no agenda for such institutional reform is likely to succeed without a commitment from the highest levels of the State Department and from the White House.

Some of the problems that weaken the diplomatic corps can also be found in the intelligence establishment. Very much a product of the cold war, it has struggled to retarget its resources on the new threats to national security. The recent record of intelligence predictions in the realm of ethnic conflict has been mixed. The violent breakup of Yugoslavia was predicted, the Kurdish uprising after the Gulf War was not. Intelligence analysts overestimated the potential for ethnic violence in Ukraine, but they failed to see the potential gravity of the situation in Chechnya. The full scope of the Rwandan disaster was not anticipated, while, in the wake of that disaster, intelligence analysts did sound the alarm about Burundi.

The current intelligence establishment has several weaknesses that make it particularly ill-suited to predicting ethnic conflict. First, maintaining the vast apparatus of technical surveillance capabilities costs a huge amount of money and dominates the intelligence budget. In fiscal year 1996, more than 90 percent of the $29 billion budget was concentrated on information collection, with most of this money paying for high-technology surveillance and eavesdropping efforts.[28] This kind of intelligence is of limited use, however, for understanding emerging ethnic tensions. Typically, there are no big armies on the move or other large-scale activities that can be watched from above. Electronic eavesdropping can sometimes yield useful information—as it did, for example, on communications among commanders of the Burundian army or relations between the Serb leadership in Belgrade and Serb authorities in Kosovo. But this technique has obvious limitations for monitoring paramilitary groups, clandestine terrorist organizations, peasant insurgencies, and the like.

Human intelligence   agents abroad who cultivate local sources —is more effective for monitoring emerging ethnic conflicts, but it shares some of the same limits as diplomacy. American agents usually operate out of an embassy or consulate, and national capitals are their natural milieu. Like foreign service officers, they may find it difficult to spend extended periods of time in remote regions, especially dangerous or restricted ones. They may not know the local language and thus may have difficulty recruiting spies. Finally, avenues of communication between intelligence agents and local and international NGOs may be scarce because of suspicions on both sides.

There are no easy solutions to these problems. For years, if not decades, various reformers have suggested ways to enhance the intelligence establishment's capacity for better human intelligence. These efforts must continue. In the realm of ethnic conflict, this kind of intelligence is more likely than electronic surveillance to yield genuinely useful information. More generally, with the end of the cold war and the arms race, human intelligence has become increasingly important for tracking a number of new threats to international security.

At a time of declining intelligence budgets, ever-stricter priority will be given to monitoring the central threats to U.S. vital interests. As the slice of the intelligence pie left over for tracking threats to secondary interests grows smaller, it will be impossible to cover all the ethnic hot spots, and choices will have to be made about which ones deserve full attention. Some of these choices are obvious: major human intelligence efforts are clearly needed in Rwanda and Burundi, in the Caucasus, in Central Asia, and in Kurdistan. But some nascent crises will inevitably be overlooked, and others will be neglected because of the long lead time required for fostering language skills and cultivating spies.

Better analytical capabilities can compensate for some of the deficiencies in both electronic surveillance and human intelligence. Analysts can combine fragmentary information from these two sources with information gathered from other sources, including scholarship by area specialists, reporting in regional media outlets, dispatches by foreign journalists, and studies and firsthand accounts by NGOs and IGOs. An energetic analyst sitting in an office in Langley can probably get a more sophisticated picture of the overall situation in Burundi than an agent in Bujumbura. Also, a major strength of analytical intelligence is its surge capacity. It is far easier to assign more analysts to examine an emerging crisis than it is to increase the number of effective agents in the field. It is easier, as well, to make use of nongovernment consultants to aid intelligence agencies in the analytical process.

In recent years, the analytical capabilities of the U.S. intelligence establishment have been in decline as more resources have gone to information collection and as the military's share of the intelligence budget has risen. A 1997 congressional report concluded that the intelligence services had a "largely inexperienced work force" that lacked adequate language skills and expertise on the countries it analyzed.[29] Career incentives within the intelligence community have tended to encourage managerial experience and flexibility over depth of knowledge and analytical prowess. The growing fragmentation of the foreign policy process has weakened links between intelligence analysts and policy makers. Analysts unfamiliar with the needs of policy makers are less capable of providing useful intelligence products, while policy makers—particularly in the

State Department—have become less able to give direction and focus to the intelligence community. In addition, intelligence analysts are often too insulated because they have not been encouraged to cultivate contacts with outside specialists or with foreign intelligence agencies, ties that could greatly improve the quality and relevance of their work. These trends must be reversed.

Often when policy makers have been underinformed, the problem has been not a lack but a surplus of information and a failure by lower-level policy officials and analysts to effectively package and transmit analysis. Intelligence analysis that is not effectively executed and presented will have little chance of capturing the attention of policy makers. Bolstering the analytical prowess of the intelligence establishment is therefore essential. A 1996 report by a task force of the Twentieth Century Fund recommended that budgets for intelligence analysis be at least doubled, even if funds must be taken away from information collection.[30] Institutional problems must also be solved, as they hamper the coordination of analytical work, water down or politicize the final products of that work, prevent intelligence analysts from interacting with outside experts and foreign agencies, and weaken the links between analysts and policy makers. Ongoing efforts to reform the intelligence establishment have generally recognized these challenges. But again, as with reforming the State Department, active presidential leadership is an absolute prerequisite for the success of these efforts. Sustaining U.S. internationalism means not just paying attention to problems abroad but also fighting bureaucratic battles to change institutions at home.

There are areas besides the diplomatic and intelligence establishments where the government can enhance its capacity for dealing with ethnic conflict. Information was a major weapon in the cold war and it can play a role in defusing ethnic conflicts. In several recent ethnic conflicts, most notably in Rwanda, vitriolic messages of ethnic hatred have been widely broadcast on the radio and have helped incite violence. Less extreme nationalist broadcasts and writing have contributed to deteriorating ethnic relations in various parts of the former Communist bloc. The U.S. government has already taken some steps to harness its cold war propaganda organs to the task of countering such material, and this work should be expanded. American radio broadcasts can be an important source of nonchauvinist information in areas of ethnic tensions where political debate is hopelessly shrill and polarized or where only a single insidious viewpoint gets airtime. During the Rwandan genocide, Voice of America broadcasts counseled an end to the violence and sought to counter Hutu propaganda. According to Human Rights Watch and other groups, these broadcasts had some effect on the situation and saved lives.[31] In 1996, as the Burundian crisis escalated, the State Department and the National Security Council asked that the Voice of America increase its broadcasts to the region. In July, it began special language programs in Kirundi and Kinyarwanda. The U.N. experience in constructing a new political order in Cambodia yielded important lessons about the value of radio in facilitating the work of international peacekeeping forces.[32] These lessons have been applied in Bosnia, where U.S. broadcasts have been used in the post-Dayton period to inform citizens about the many complex aspects of the transition to peace.

In the Department of Defense, changes to enhance the military's ability to cope with ethnic conflict and other types of internal warfare have been under way for some time. These are informed by the experiences in Somalia, Haiti, northern Iraq, and Bosnia—the lessons of which have been the subject of considerable examination within the armed forces and the scholarly community. The changes include new attention to peacekeeping operations, increased capabilities for humanitarian intervention, closer examination of the limited use of force, particularly airpower, and the establishment of new links to the United Nations and to regional organizations.[33] This progress has come haltingly and will require energetic political effort to continue.

Operations other than war, even low-intensity warfare, have never been the military's favorite activities, for two main reasons. First, these missions cannot justify big-ticket weapons systems. Historically, major congressional and presidential pressure has been necessary to get the armed services to devote significant resources to special forces, and the military has traditionally resisted being cast in the role of relief worker or peacekeeper. Military leaders have often insisted that their job is to fight and win wars. Second, the legacies of Vietnam and Lebanon, reflected in the Weinberger principles and later in the Powell doctrine, have deeply influenced the current generation of military leaders and imbued them with an enormous sense of caution. In the political establishment as a whole, there has also been a perceived rise in the price to be paid for allowing U.S. military personnel to die overseas.

Much of this outlook is warranted. A central argument of this book, however, has been that some situations will demand that the United States commit limited power to defend limited interests, even when the outcome is uncertain. Bosnia and Rwanda are far more typical of the challenges that the United States will confront than Desert Storm—a war that could be fought and won with near-scientific precision. Policy makers in the national-security establishment cannot allow themselves to be paralyzed by the fact that U.S. involvement in ethnic conflicts, including military action, carries no guarantee of success. The armed services must be ready to present military options to policy makers in situations where vital interests are not at stake and where clear-cut outcomes cannot be assured. Political leaders, in turn, must educate the public about the realities of using military force in the post–cold war era, pointing out that sometimes U.S. personnel will die but that these people are professionals and know the risks of their work when they sign on. Internationally, U.S. leaders should seek to reduce their obsession with prestige. Occasional failed attempts to use military power do not necessarily call into question the credibility of U.S. power more broadly. There is no evidence that the failed mission in Lebanon or the pullout from Somalia had a lasting negative impact on U.S. credibility. Indeed, the country's prestige may be more likely to suffer if the United States fails to try any military action in the face of unchecked barbarism. Rogue state leaders and paramilitary extremists are more likely to fear a United States that uses its military power liberally, and at times unsuccessfully, than a United States that never uses its military power at all. Among democratic states, the United States will suffer if it fails to carry its fair share of global peacekeeping burdens.

The military-technical revolution now under way has yielded spectacular advances in the ability to use airpower in a limited manner against elusive targets. New surveillance technologies allow the military to pinpoint the location of camouflaged military equipment, command and control centers, and political-military leaders. Advances in air-defense suppression and stealth technology make it less risky than ever before to mount bombing missions. The ever-increasing speed with which battlefield intelligence can be processed and communicated to commanders in the field has radically enhanced the ability to destroy targets of opportunity. In many ethnic conflicts, armed forces are much more likely to be decentralized, and heavy equipment may not be crucial to combat operations. Terrain may also not be hospitable to the effective use of airpower. Military forces may intentionally mix themselves in with civilian populaces. Nevertheless, the overall capabilities of the United States to put at risk the military and political assets of any organized group on the planet have increased dramatically since the Vietnam War.

FEW THINGS COULD BE more damaging to U.S. foreign policy than unthinking engagement in the many conflicts that will always rage in areas peripheral to the country's core interests. Likewise, it would be disastrously shortsighted to dismiss such conflicts as irrelevant to the American people. In recent years, isolationists have proffered a false choice between a United States that squanders its prestige and treasure in Third World cesspools and a United States that keeps its powder dry, staying strong for the fights that really affect its vital interests. A central point of this book has been that, between the extremes of globalism and withdrawal, there exists a vast range of choices in dealing with the periphery and that nowhere is this more apparent than in the realm of ethnic conflict.

As a collective phenomenon, ethnic conflicts can damage U.S. vital interests by making the international system less stable and prosperous. Individually, however, these conflicts typically threaten only secondary national interests. They are limited threats most appropriately handled with limited responses, and a resounding lesson of the historical record is that early preventive action is the key to avoiding deeper commitments of U.S. power. Policies of prevention, of course, have never come easily to U.S. leaders. Beyond the fact that full-blown crises consume the attention of policy makers from the moment they take office until the day they leave, prevention is difficult because it requires officials to gamble with their time and resources. At any one moment a number of ethnic crises will be brewing throughout the world and there remains no exact formula for determining where an investment of U.S. attention will pay dividends. Preventive efforts by the United States may be crucial in a given crisis, but then again, it may subside by itself. Determined efforts may stop a crisis from escalating, but then again, escalation may be inevitable. For example, NATO airstrikes on Serb guns shelling Dubrovnik and Vukovar in fall 1991 might have deterred future aggression or might have achieved nothing. The deployment of a much larger U.N. force in Rwanda in early 1994 might have forestalled genocide or a larger force might have to withdraw just as quickly as the smaller force did.

Coping with ethnic conflict means living with this kind of uncertainty. Preventive action will always be a gamble, but ultimately the odds favor such action. If a half dozen preventive efforts forestall the need for a single major humanitarian operation, these efforts will more than pay for themselves. In budgetary terms, the money that the United States spends on foreign assistance, preventive diplomacy, and international organizations is small change compared to what it spends on its military. In fiscal year 1997, for example, the United States will spend more on research and development for a single fighter plane, the F-22, than it will spend on foreign-assistance programs in all of the former Soviet Union. It will spend more money on amphibious military forces like the marines than it will spend on foreign aid for the entire developing world. It will spend more money on new nuclear weapons systems than it will contribute to all international organizations.

The calculus of preventive action is not sold easily in U.S. politics. Americans prefer to tackle problems that seem to have obvious dimensions and self-evident remedies. The war on poverty appeared to be a straightforward battle, and when things proved otherwise, the public turned on it with a vengeance. In the war on drugs it has always been easier to get money for measures like intercepting smugglers and imprisoning dealers than for efforts to curb demand through prevention and rehabilitation. Environmental problems get addressed only when they become unbearable; a choking United States will pass clean-air legislation but is incapable of taking even modest measures to deal with the more distant threat of global warming. Similarly, vast expenditures on high-tech medicine and consistent underfunding of preventive medicine are typical of a societal ethos that champions heroic crusades over slogging long-term efforts.

There is no remedy for this national flaw, beyond an endless reiteration of the obvious virtues of preventive engagement. Such messages do, on occasion, result in policy changes. Real leadership in all parts of U.S. life means preaching preventive messages and forsaking the short-term political gains of embracing more spectacular efforts that focus on symptoms rather than causes. In foreign policy, internationalist leaders must now be willing to work harder despite the promise of fewer visible results. Addressing the causes of global instability is pick-and-shovel work compared with presiding at superpower summits or bloodying Moscow's nose in a proxy war. Secretaries of state do not win Nobel Peace Prizes or help get their bosses reelected by defusing mounting conflicts in countries that most Americans have never heard of. The quest for order in peripheral regions of the post–cold war world is the real "twilight struggle" of modern times.

If it is true that the world has now largely passed through the third great wave of imperial disintegration and state fragmentation, then the next decade or two may see relatively few new ethnic conflicts. Recently, too, a number of the worst ethnic war zones have quieted considerably. U.S. policy makers and scholars should not take these developments to mean that ethnic conflict was just a passing trend akin to, say, Marxist insurgencies. Instead, the current respite should be used as a time to study intensively the lessons of past ethnic conflicts, to formulate better policy responses to future crises, and to implement long-term strategies of prevention.

Despite all the uncertainty that now characterizes international affairs, there can be no doubt that the United States will inevitably face horrible new dilemmas abroad that arise from ethnic violence. In the best cases, good policy can eliminate some of these dilemmas altogether. More commonly, farsighted planning can give policy makers greater options for reducing the scope, intensity, and duration of ethnic conflicts. There is little glamour or excitement in much of this work, just the potential for steady progress toward a world with less killing.

Introduction

[1] Thomas Patrick Melady, *Burundi: The Tragic Years* (Maryknoll, N.Y.: Orbis Books, 1974), p. 15.

[2] David Ress, *The Burundi Ethnic Massacres* (San Francisco: Mellon Research University Press, 1988), p. 87.

[3] *Ibid.*, p. 81.

[4] Melady, *Burundi: The Tragic Years*, p. 27.

[5] *Ibid.*, p. 83.

[6] U.S. Congress, 93-1, House Foreign Affairs Committee, Hearings: *International Protection of Human Rights: The World of International Organizations and the Role of U.S. Policy* (Washington, D.C.: GPO, 1974), pp. 70–71.

[7] Ress, *Burundi Ethnic Massacres*, p. 1.

[8] U.S. Congress, 100-2, House Foreign Affairs Committee, Hearings: *Recent Violence in Burundi: What Should Be the U.S. Response?* (Washington, D.C.: GPO, 1988), p. 2.

[9] Crawford Young, *The Politics of Cultural Pluralism* (Madison: University of Wisconsin Press, 1976); Anthony D. Smith, *Nationalism in the Twentieth Century* (New York: New York University Press, 1979); Donald

Horowitz, *Ethnic Groups in Conflict* (Berkeley: University of California Press, 1985).

[10] For an exception, see Astri Suhrke and Lela Noble, eds., *Ethnic Conflict and International Relations* (New York: Praeger, 1977).

[11] "The New Tribalism: Defending Human Rights in an Age of Ethnic Conflict," *Los Angeles Times*, June 8, 1993, p. 8.

[12] U.S. Congress, 102-1, House Armed Services Committee, Hearings: *Potential Threats to American Security in the Post–Cold War Era* (Washington, D.C.: GPO, 1992), p. 8.

[13] David Binder with Barbara Crossette, "As Ethnic Wars Multiply, U.S. Strives for a Policy," *New York Times*, February 7, 1993, p. A1.

[14] U.S. Congress, 103-1, Senate Foreign Relations Committee, Hearings: *Nomination of Warren M. Christopher to Be Secretary of State* (Washington, D.C.: GPO, 1993), p. 72.

[15] Bohdan Nahaylo and Victor Swoboda, *Soviet Disunion: A History of the Nationalities Problem in the USSR* (New York: Free Press, 1989), p. xiii.

[16] For a full discussion, see Michael E. Brown, Sean M. Lynn-Jones, and Stephen E. Miller, *Debating the Democratic Peace* (Cambridge: MIT Press, 1996).

[17] For an inquiry into this issue, see Renee de Nevers, "Democratization and Ethnic Conflict," *Survival*, vol. 35, no. 2 (Summer 1993), pp. 31–48.

Chapter One

[1] For an excellent early study of U.S. policy responses, see Morton H. Halperin and David J. Scheffer with Patricia Small, *Self-Determination in the New World Order* (Washington, D.C.: Carnegie Endowment for International Peace, 1992).

[2] Felix Gilbert, *To the Farewell Address: Ideas of Early American Foreign Policy* (Princeton: Princeton University Press, 1961).

[3] Robert Lansing, *The Peace Negotiations: A Personal Narrative* (Boston: Houghton Mifflin, 1921), pp. 97–98.

[4] On the historical misfortunes of the Kurds, see David McDowall, *A Modern History of the Kurds* (New York: I. B. Touris/St. Martin's Press, 1996).

[5] Alexis Heraclides, *The Self-Determination of Minorities in International Politics* (London: Frank Cass, 1991), p. 21.

[6] *Ibid.*

[7] For a review of the scholarly arguments regarding self-determination, see *Ibid.*, pp. 27–37.

[8] Amitai Etzioni, "The Evils of Self-Determination," *Foreign Policy*, no. 89 (Winter 1992–93), pp. 34–35.

[9] *Ibid.*, pp. 29–31.

[10] See, for example, the ideas of Gideon Gottlieb, "Nations without States," *Foreign Affairs*, vol. 73, no. 3 (May/June 1994), pp. 100–12.

[11] Michael Lind, "In Defense of Liberal Nationalism," *Foreign Affairs*, vol. 73, no. 3 (May/June 1994), p. 90.

[12] See, for example, Human Rights Watch, *Playing the "Communal Card": Communal Violence and Human Rights* (New York: Human Rights Watch, 1995).

[13] Richard Rosecrance, *The Rise of the Trading States* (New York: Basic Books, 1986), p. 176.

[14] Halperin, Scheffer, and Small, *Self-Determination in the New World Order*, pp. 33–34.

[15] Gideon Gottlieb, "Nations without States," 106–07.

[16] *Ibid.*

[17] For an analysis of PD-25 and the policy debate that surrounded its drafting, see Testimony of Madeleine Albright, U.S. Congress, 103-2, House Appropriations Committee, Hearings: *Foreign Operations, Export Financing, and Related Program Appropriations for 1995*, part 4 (Washington, D.C.: GPO, 1995), pp. 584–88, and David Callahan, "Fall Back Troops: Clinton's New U.N. Policy," *Foreign Service Journal*, May 1994, pp. 20–28.

[18] Richard Halloran, "U.S. Will Not Drift into a Latin War, Weinberger Says," *New York Times*, December 10, 1984, p. A1.

[19] Robert W. Tucker, "The Purposes of American Power," *Foreign Affairs*, vol. 59, no. 2 (Winter 1980–81), pp. 241–74.

[20] Richard Haass, *Conflicts Unending: The United States and Regional Disputes* (New Haven: Yale University Press, 1990).

Chapter Two

[1] David J. Scheffer, "Use of Force after the Cold War: Panama, Iraq, and the New World Order," in *Right v. Might: International Law and the Use of Force* (New York: Council on Foreign Relations, 1991), pp. 146–48.

[2] Human Rights Watch, *Playing the "Communal Card": Communal Violence and Human Rights* (New York: Human Rights Watch, 1995).

[3] "Turkey: Human Rights Groups Say Abuses against Kurds Have Risen," *Inter Press Service*, March 18, 1993.

[4] Jonah Blank, "In Turkey, Kurds Fight to Preserve Their Identity," *Orlando Sentinel Tribune*, October 11, 1992, p. D8.

[5] For an overview of this conflict, see Richard Sisson and Leo Rose, *War and Secession: Pakistan, India, and the Creation of Bangladesh* (Berkeley: University of California Press, 1990).

[6] Human Rights Watch, *Playing the "Communal Card*," pp. 80–96.

[7] Stephen Van Evera, "Hypotheses on Nationalism and War," *International Security*, vol. 18, no. 4 (Spring 1994), p. 18.

[8] David Ress, *The Burundi Ethnic Massacres* (San Francisco: Mellon Research University Press, 1988).

[9] Human Rights Watch, *Playing the "Communal Card*," pp. 1–17.

[10] Philip Gourevitch, "After the Genocide," *New Yorker*, December 18, 1995, p. 80.

[11] Ress, *Burundi Ethnic Massacres*, p. 25.

[12] Ronald H. Bailey, *Partisans and Guerrillas* (Alexandria: Time-Life Books), p. 87.

[13] Barry R. Posen, "The Security Dilemma and Ethnic Conflict," *Survival*, vol. 35, no. 1 (Spring 1993), p. 40.

[14] For a lengthy discussion of this issue, see Van Evera, "Hypotheses on Nationalism and War," pp. 16–22.

[15] U.S. Congress, 100-2, House Foreign Affairs Committee, Hearings: *Recent Violence in Burundi: What Should Be the U.S. Response?* (Washington, D.C.: GPO, 1988), p. 42.

[16] *Ibid.*, p. 14.

[17] *Ibid.*, p. 42.

[18] See testimony of Assistant Secretary of State George Moose, U.S. Congress, 103-2, House Foreign Affairs Committee, Hearings: *The Crisis in Rwanda* (Washington, D.C.: GPO, 1995), p. 5.

[19] Holly Burkhalter, "The Genocide Question: The Clinton Administration and Rwanda," *World Policy Journal*, vol. 11, no. 4 (Winter 1994–95), p. 45.

[20] Nik Gowing, "Behind the CNN Factor," *Washington Post*, July 31, 1994, p. C1.

[21] Joseph E. Thompson, *American Policy and African Famine: The Nigeria-Biafra War, 1966–1970* (New York: Greenwood Press, 1990), p. 8.

[22] "U.S. Sees Internal Stresses," *New York Times*, January 16, 1966, p. A25.

[23] Terrence Lyons, "Keeping Africa Off the Agenda," in Warren I. Cohen and Nancy Bernkopf Tucker, eds., *Lyndon Johnson Confronts the World: American Foreign Policy, 1963–1968* (New York: Cambridge University Press, 1994), p. 272.

[24] Henry Kissinger, *Years of Upheaval* (Boston: Little, Brown, 1982), p. 788.

[25] U.S. Congress, 94-1, Senate Foreign Relations Committee, Report: *The Middle East* (Washington, D.C.: GPO, 1975), p. 18.

[26] U.S. Congress, 94-1, Senate Foreign Relations Committee, Report: *Peace and Stability in the Middle East* (Washington, D.C.: GPO, 1975); U.S. Congress, 94-1, Senate Foreign Relations Committee, Report: *Realities of the Middle East* (Washington, D.C.: GPO, 1975).

[27] James Rupert, "Ukraine Marks 4th Anniversary as a Stable and Unified State," *Washington Post*, August 27, 1995, p. A25.

[28] Michael Kelly, "Surrender and Blame," *New Yorker*, December 19, 1994, p. 45.

[29] Warren Zimmerman, "The Last Ambassador: A Memoir of the Collapse of Yugoslavia," *Foreign Affairs*, vol. 74, no. 2 (March/April 1995), p. 6.

[30] Morton H. Halperin and David J. Scheffer with Patricia Small, *Self-Determination in the New World Order* (Washington, D.C.: Carnegie Endowment for International Peace, 1992), p. 33.

[31] David Binder, "CIA Doubtful on Serbian Sanctions," *New York Times*, December 22, 1993, p. A3.

[32] U.S. Congress, 99-2, House Foreign Affairs Committee, Hearings: *Persecution of the Albanian Minority in Yugoslavia* (Washington, D.C.: GPO, 1987).

[33] U.S. Congress, 102-2, Senate Foreign Relations Committee, Hearings: *Civil Strife in Yugoslavia: The United States Response* (Washington, D.C.: GPO, 1991).

[34] Henry Kissinger, *The White House Years* (Boston: Little, Brown, 1979), p. 842.

[35] *Ibid.*, p. 851.

[36] *Ibid.*, p. 851–52.

[37] Zimmerman, "Last Ambassador," p. 2.

[38] For an overview of this issue, see Alexander DeConde, *Ethnicity, Race, and American Foreign Policy: A History* (Boston: Northeastern University Press, 1992). See also Paul Y. Watanabe, *Ethnic Groups, Congress, and American Foreign Policy: The Politics of the Turkish Arms Embargo* (Westport: Greenwood Press, 1984).

[39] Joseph S. Nye, Jr., "Peering into the Future," *Foreign Affairs*, vol. 73, no. 4 (July/August 1994), p. 91.

[40] Robert S. McNamara, *In Retrospect: The Tragedy and Lessons of Vietnam* (New York: Times Books, 1995), p. 273.

[41] Don Oberdorfer, "A Bloody Failure in the Balkans," *Washington Post*, February 8, 1993, p. A1.

[42] Zimmerman, "Last Ambassador," p. 12.

[43] James A. Baker, III, *The Politics of Diplomacy: Revolution, War, and Peace, 1989–1992* (New York: Putnam, 1995), p. 637.

[44] U.S. Congress, 104-1, Commission on Security and Cooperation in Europe, Hearings: *The Crisis in Chechnya* (Washington, D.C.: GPO, 1995), p. 29.

[45] Thompson, *American Policy and African Famine*, p. 9.

[46] Kissinger, *Years of Upheaval*, p. 445.

[47] On the strengths and weaknesses of U.S. intelligence analysis, see Loch K. Johnson, "Smart Intelligence," *Foreign Policy*, no. 89 (Winter 1992–93), p. 53.

[48] Oberdorfer, "Bloody Failure in the Balkans," p. A1.

[49] Patrick Glynn, "See No Evil: Bush-Clinton and the Truth about Bosnia," *New Republic*, October 23, 1993, p. 25.

[50] James Rupert, "Ukraine Marks 4th Anniversary," p. A25.

Chapter Three

[1] Joseph E. Thompson, *American Policy and African Famine: The Nigeria-Biafra War, 1966–1970* (New York: Greenwood Press, 1990), p. 9.

[2] Lloyd Garrison, "Revolts Cripple Army in Nigeria," *New York Times*, August 9, 1966, p. 7.

[3] Lloyd Garrison, "Political Breakup Looms in Nigeria as Ibos Challenge Regime," *New York Times*, August 3, 1966, p. A6.

[4] Terrence Lyons, "Keeping Africa Off the Agenda," in Warren I. Cohen and Nancy Bernkopf Tucker, eds., *Lyndon Johnson Confronts the World: American Foreign Policy, 1963–1968* (New York: Cambridge University Press, 1994), p. 272.

[5] Thompson, *American Policy and African Famine*, p. 22.

[6] *Ibid.*

[7] Lloyd Garrison, "Eastern Region Quits Nigeria, Lagos Vows to Fight Secession," *New York Times*, May 31, 1967, p. 1.

[8] U.S. Congress, 90-2, House Committee on Foreign Affairs, Hearings: *Africa Briefing—1968* (Washington, D.C.: GPO, 1968), pp. 14–16.

[9] Lyons, "Keeping Africa Off the Agenda," p. 275.

[10] House Committee, *Africa Briefing*, p. 14.

[11] "Support for Lagos Affirmed by U.S.," *New York Times*, February 6, 1968, p. A3.

[12] Thompson, *American Policy and African Famine*, p. 29.

[13] Henry Kissinger, *The White House Years* (Boston: Little, Brown, 1979), pp. 180–81.

[14] *Ibid.*, p. 849.

[15] Seymour Hersh, *The Price of Power: Kissinger in the Nixon White House* (New York: Summit Books, 1983), p. 448.

[16] *Ibid.*; Kissinger, *White House Years*, p. 852.

[17] Kissinger, *White House Years*, p. 852.

[18] *Ibid.*, p. 853.

[19] *Ibid.*, p. 914.

[20] For the best account of political developments in Burundi over the past thirty years, see René Lemarchand, *Burundi: Ethnic Conflict and Genocide* (Cambridge: Cambridge University Press, 1996).

[21] Interview with author, May 12, 1996.

[22] Thomas Patrick Melady, *Burundi: The Tragic Years* (Maryknoll, N.Y.: Orbis Books, 1974), p. 15.

[23] Testimony of Roger Morris, U.S. Congress, 93-1, House Committee on Foreign Affairs, Hearings: *International Protection of Human Rights: The Work of International Organizations and the Role of U.S. Policy* (Washington, D.C.: GPO, 1974), p. 65.

[24] Testimony of Herman Cohen, *Ibid.*, p. 71.

[25] Testimony of Charles Gladson, U.S. Congress, 100-2, House Foreign Affairs Committee, Hearings: *Recent Violence in Burundi: What Should Be the U.S. Response?* (Washington, D.C.: GPO, 1988), p. 42.

[26] On Buyoya's reform agenda, see Lemarchand, *Burundi: Ethnic Conflict and Genocide*, pp. 118–20.

[27] House Committee, *Recent Violence in Burundi*, pp. 15–16.

[28] *Ibid.*, p. 42.

[29] *Ibid.*, p. 43.

[30] James A. Baker III, *The Politics of Diplomacy: Revolution, War, and Peace, 1989–1992* (New York: Putnam, 1995), p. 636. See also David C. Gompert, "The United States and Yugoslavia's Wars," in Richard H. Ullman, ed., *The World and Yugoslavia's Wars* (New York: Council on Foreign Relations, 1996), pp. 127–28.

[31] Ralph Johnson, "U.S. Efforts to Promote a Peaceful Settlement in Yugoslavia," *U.S. Department of State Dispatch*, October 21, 1991, p. 783.

[32] Michael Kelly, "Surrender and Blame," *New Yorker*, December 19, 1994, p. 45.

[33] *Ibid.*

[34] Don Oberdorfer, "A Bloody Failure in the Balkans," *Washington Post*, February 8, 1993, p. A1.

[35] "U.S. Policy toward Yugoslavia," *U.S. Department of State Dispatch*, June 3, 1991, p. 395.

[36] Warren Zimmerman, "The Last Ambassador: A Memoir of the Collapse of Yugoslavia," *Foreign Affairs*, vol. 74, no. 2 (March/April 1995), p. 11. For Baker's account, see his *Politics of Diplomacy*, pp. 479–81.

[37] Baker, *Politics of Diplomacy*, p. 481.

[38] *Ibid.*, p. 483.

[39] Zimmerman, "Last Ambassador," p. 11.

[40] Kelly, "Surrender and Blame," p. 45.

[41] Zimmerman, "Last Ambassador," p. 14.

[42] Alan Cowell, "War on Kurds Hurts Turks in U.S. Eyes," *New York Times*, November 17, 1994, p. A3.

[43] Celestine Bohlen, "In Turkey, Open Discussion of Kurds Is Casualty of Effort to Confront War," *New York Times*, October 29, 1995, p. A20.

[44] Graham E. Fuller, "The Fate of the Kurds," *Foreign Affairs*, vol. 72, no. 2 (Spring 1993), p. 116.

[45] See, for example, U.S. State Department, *Country Reports for Human Rights Practices for 1993* (Washington, D.C.: GPO, 1994), pp. 1086–107.

[46] Duygu Bazoglu Sezer, *Turkey's Political and Security Interests and Policies in the New Geostrategic Environment of the Expanded Middle East* (Washington, D.C.: Henry L. Stimson Center, 1994), p. 30.

[47] U.S. Congress, 103-1, House Foreign Affairs Committee, Hearings: *Developments in Europe and the Former Yugoslavia* (Washington, D.C.: GPO, 1993), p. 29.

[48] *Ibid.*, p. 28.

[49] Commission on Security and Cooperation in Europe, *Reports on the U.S. Helsinki Commission Delegation to Bosnia-Herzegovina, Albania, and Turkey* (Washington, D.C.: GPO, 1994), p. 21.

[50] Thomas W. Lippman, "U.S. Steps Up Warnings to Turkey over Rights," *Washington Post*, December 14, 1994, p. A30.

[51] Bruce D. Porter and Carol R. Saivetz, "The Once and Future Empire: Russia and the 'Near Abroad,' " *Washington Quarterly*, vol. 17, no. 3 (Summer 1994), p. 89.

[52] On the U.S. response to the crackdown, see testimony of James Collins, U.S. Congress, 104-1, Commission on Security and Cooperation in Europe, Hearings: *Crisis in Chechnya* (Washington, D.C.: GPO, 1995), pp. 52, 109.

[53] *Crisis in Chechnya*, p. 41.

[54] "The Russian Federation: Independence Issues in Chechnya," background brief, British Information Services, New York, April 1995, p. 4.

[55] *Crisis in Chechnya*, pp. 59–60.

[56] *Ibid.*, p. 60.

[57] *Ibid.*, p. 109.

[58] *Ibid.*

[59] *Ibid.*

[60] *Ibid.*, p. 64.

[61] Steven Greenhouse, "U.S. Says Russian Move Is 'An Internal Affair,' " *New York Times*, December 12, 1994, p. A13.

[62] Michael Gordon, "U.S. Stays Aloof from Russia's War Within," *New York Times*, December 25, 1994, p. A10.

[63] *Crisis in Chechnya*, p. 58.

[64] R. Jeffrey Smith, "U.S. Interests Seen Allied with Russia in Chechnya," *Washington Post*, December 25, 1994, p. A27.

[65] Strobe Talbott, "U.S.-Turkish Leadership in the Post–Cold War World," *U.S. Department of State Dispatch*, April 24, 1995, p. 361.

[66] Human Rights Watch, *Playing the "Communal Card": Communal Violence and Human Rights* (New York: Human Rights Watch, 1995), p. 6.

[67] *Ibid.*

[68] U.S. Congress, 103-1, House Foreign Affairs Committee, Hearings: *Peacekeeping and Conflict Resolution in Africa* (Washington, D.C.: GPO, 1994), pp. 51–52.

[69] *Ibid.*, pp. 60–61.

[70] See testimony of Assistant Secretary of State George Moose, U.S. Congress, 103-2, House Foreign Affairs Committee, Hearings: *The Crisis in Rwanda* (Washington, D.C.: GPO, 1995), p. 5.

[71] "Rwanda Peace Agreement," *U.S. Department of State Dispatch*, August 16, 1993, p. 504.

[72] Nik Gowing, "Behind the CNN Factor," *Washington Post*, July 31, 1994, p. C1.

[73] For an explanation of this legislation, see Bob Dole, "Peacekeeping and Politics," *New York Times*, January 24, 1994, p. A15.

[74] Philip Gourevitch, "After the Genocide," *New Yorker*, December 18, 1994, p. 91.

[75] Gowing, "Behind the CNN Factor," p. C1.

[76] U.S. Congress, 99-2, House Foreign Affairs Committee, Hearings: *Persecution of the Albanian Minority in Yugoslavia* (Washington, D.C.: GPO, 1987); U.S. Congress, 100-2, House Foreign Affairs Committee, Hearings: *Developments in Europe, 1988* (Washington, D.C.: GPO, 1988).

[77] Zimmerman, "Last Ambassador," p. 3.

[78] *Ibid.*, p. 8.

[79] "U.S. Policy toward Yugoslavia," p. 396.

[80] Lawrence Eagleburger, "London Conference to Galvanize International Action," *U.S. Department of State Dispatch Supplement*, September 1992, p. 9.

[81] Paul Iredale, "Kosovo Seen as Possible Balkan Flashpoint," Reuters Library Report, January 11, 1993.

[82] Don Oberdorfer, "A Bloody Failure in the Balkans," *Washington Post*, February 8, 1993, p. A1.

[83] *Ibid.*

[84] Craig Hines, "U.S. Plan Would Draw a Line in the Balkans," *Houston Chronicle*, May 12, 1993, p. 1.

[85] "300 U.S. Troops in Macedonia to Try to Contain Balkan War," *New York Times*, July 13, 1993, p. A10.

[86] "U.S. Warns Yugoslavia against Spillover of Conflict," Reuters, October 22, 1993.

[87] Llazar Semini, "Macedonia Using Shameful Old Serbian Plot, Albania Says," Reuter Library Report, November 12, 1993.

[88] David Binder, "CIA Doubtful on Serbian Sanctions," *New York Times*, December 22, 1993, p. A3.

[89] Yigal Chazan, "Albania Urged to Rein in Radicals amid Fears of Greater Balkan Bloodbath," *Guardian*, May 30, 1994, p. 8; Chazan, "Tempering the Dream of a 'Greater Albania,' " *Christian Science Monitor*, July 20, 1994, p. 7.

[90] Suzanne M. Schafer, "Perry Opens Talks on Military Assistance to Albania," AP Worldstream, July 20, 1994.

[91] George E. Condon, Jr., "Clinton Opens Summit Trip to Latvian Cheers," *San Diego Union-Tribune*, July 7, 1994, p. A1.

[92] Ted Hopf, "Managing Soviet Disintegration: A Demand for Behavioral Regimes," *International Security*, vol. 17, no. 1 (Summer 1992), p. 55.

[93] Martin Sieff, "Latvia Fears Foment of Ethnic Russian Hard-Liners," *Washington Times*, April 10, 1993, p. A7.

94 Jonathan Broder, "U.S. Quietly to Mediate Russia's Baltic and Border Problems," *Ethnic NewsWatch*, August 22, 1993, p. 1.

95 Martin Walker, "Clinton's Secret Successes: In Ireland and Latvia, the President Gets on Track," *Washington Post*, September 4, 1994, p. C1.

96 Alessandra Stanley, "Divided Latvians Awaiting Clinton," *New York Times*, July 6, 1994, p. A1.

97 U.S. Department of State, *Country Reports on Human Rights Practices for 1994* (Washington, D.C.: GPO, 1995), pp. 870–73.

98 "Burundi: U.S. Lifts Suspension of Aid," *U.S. Department of State Dispatch*, December 20, 1993, p. 879.

99 Lemarchand, *Burundi: Ethnic Conflict and Genocide*, p. xiii.

100 Human Rights Watch, *Playing the "Communal Card,"* p. 17.

101 House Committee, *Crisis in Rwanda*, p. 14.

102 Townsend Friedman, "Update on Developments in Rwanda and Burundi," *U.S. Department of State Dispatch*, April 17, 1995, p. 335

103 R. Jeffrey Smith, "Demand for Humanitarian Aid May Skyrocket," *Washington Post*, December 17, 1994, p. A22.

104 Friedman, "Update on Developments," p. 336.

105 *Ibid.*

106 The groups were the African-American Institute, the Center for Preventive Action of the Council on Foreign Relations, Refugees International, and Search for Common Ground.

107 "U.N. Envoy to Burundi Says Massacres Are Rife," *New York Times*, January 10, 1996, p. A5.

108 "U.S. Warns Tutsi Army against Coup," *Boston Sunday Globe*, January 21, 1996, p. 4.

109 Barbara Crossette, "U.N., Pressing for Restraint, Delays Its Action on Burundi," *New York Times*, January 30, 1996, p. A2.

110 Barbara Crossette, "In About-Face, U.S. Proposes Standby Force for Burundi," *New York Times*, February 22, 1996, p. A6.

111 *Ibid.*

112 *Ibid.*

113 "Security Council Urges Diplomacy in Burundi," *New York Times*, March 6, 1996, p. A5.

114 Barbara Crossette, "To Quell Violence in Burundi, an International Force Is Urged," *New York Times*, May 9, 1996, p. A13.

115 Thomas W. Lippman, "Burundi at Risk, Ex-Ambassador Warns," *Washington Post*, May 25, 1996, p. A21.

[116] Donald G. McNeil, Jr., "Burundi Army Stages Coup, and New Fighting Is Feared," *New York Times*, July 26, 1996, p. A3.

[117] Barbara Crossette, "U.N. Hears Conflicting Views on What to Do about Burundi," *New York Times*, August 22, 1996, p. A7.

[118] Thomas W. Lippman, "U.S. Officials Fear Violence in Burundi Will Escalate," *Washington Post*, August 25, 1996, p. A23.

[119] John Shattuck, "More than Words Are Needed to Stop Terror in Burundi," *Christian Science Monitor*, June 24, 1996, p. 19.

[120] Chris Tomlinson, "Hutu Rebels Shell Burundi City," AP Online, September 3, 1996.

Chapter Four

[1] For broad discussions of intervention, see Robert Cooper and Mats Berdal, "Outside Intervention in Ethnic Conflicts," in Michael E. Brown, ed., *Ethnic Conflict and International Security* (Princeton: Princeton University Press, 1993), pp. 181–205, and Charles William Maynes, "Containing Ethnic Conflict," *Foreign Policy*, no. 30 (Spring 1993), pp. 3–21.

[2] Benjamin Welles, "U.S. Scores Soviets on Arming Nigeria," *New York Times*, August 22, 1967, p. A7.

[3] Joseph E. Thompson, *American Policy and African Famine: The Nigeria-Biafra War, 1966–1970* (New York: Greenwood Press, 1990), p. 29.

[4] "Support by Lagos Affirmed by U.S.," *New York Times*, February 6, 1968, p. A3.

[5] *New York Times*, September 1, 1967, p. A3.

[6] Roger Morris, *Uncertain Greatness: Henry Kissinger and American Foreign Policy* (New York: Harper and Row, 1977), p. 121.

[7] Henry Kissinger, *The White House Years* (Boston: Little, Brown, 1979), p. 914.

[8] *Ibid.*, p. 853.

[9] Seymour Hersh, *The Price of Power: Kissinger in the Nixon White House* (New York: Summit Books, 1983), p. 444.

[10] Benjamin Welles, "Nations Muting Comment on Pakistan to Avoid Inflaming the Trouble There," *New York Times*, April 7, 1971, p. 3.

[11] Benjamin Welles, "U.S. Urges Pakistan Seek Peaceful Accommodation," *New York Times*, April 8, 1971, p. 3.

[12] *Ibid.*

[13] *Ibid.*

[14] Hersh, *Price of Power*, p. 445.

[15] *Ibid.*

[16] Kissinger, *White House Years*, p. 854.

[17] "Transcript of the President's News Conference on Foreign and Domestic Matters," *New York Times*, August 5, 1971, p. 16.

[18] Thomas Patrick Melady, *Burundi: The Tragic Years* (Maryknoll, N.Y.: Orbis Books, 1974), p. 15.

[19] Benjamin Welles, "Burundi Reported Continuing Executions and Reprisals against Ethnic Minority," *New York Times*, June 25, 1972, p. 2.

[20] Kathleen Teltsch, "Killings Go On in Burundi, U.N. Statement Suggests," *New York Times*, July 29, 1972, p. 1.

[21] Welles, "Burundi Reported Continuing Executions," p. 2.

[22] *Ibid.*

[23] "Zaire Says Troops Will Help Burundi Put Down Disorders," *New York Times*, May 4, 1972, p. 5.

[24] U.S. Congress, 93-1, House Foreign Affairs Committee, Hearings: *International Protection of Human Rights: The Work of International Organizations and the Role of U.S. Policy* (Washington, D.C.: 1974), p. 71.

[25] Melady, *Burundi: The Tragic Years*, p. 22.

[26] "Statements on Bosnia-Hercegovina," *U.S. Department of State Dispatch*, April 20, 1992, p. 311.

[27] "Situation in Bosnia-Hercegovina," *U.S. Department of State Dispatch*, May 11, 1992, p. 373.

[28] John C. Kornblum, "Continued Aggression in Bosnia-Hercegovina," *U.S. Department of State Dispatch*, May 11, 1992, pp. 374 75.

[29] "Chronology: Developments Related to the Crisis in Bosnia, March 10–September 22, 1992," *U.S. Department of State Dispatch Supplement*, September 1992, p. 15.

[30] Edward J. Perkins, "Aggression by the Serbian Regime," *U.S. Department of State Dispatch Supplement*, September 1992, p. 22.

[31] Patrick Glynn, "See No Evil: Bush-Clinton and the Truth about Bosnia," *New Republic*, October 23, 1993, p. 25.

[32] *Ibid.*

[33] Lawrence Eagleburger, "Detention Centers in Bosnia-Hercegovina and Serbia," *U.S. Department of State Dispatch*, August 10, 1992, p. 618.

[34] *Ibid.*

[35] George Bush, "Containing the Crisis in Bosnia and the Former Yugoslavia," *U.S. Department of State Dispatch*, August 10, 1992, p. 617.

[36] Michael Kelly, "Surrender and Blame," *New Yorker*, December 19, 1994, p. 47.

[37] Warren Christopher, "The CSCE Vision: European Security

Rooted in Shared Values," *U.S. Department of State Dispatch*, December 13, 1993, p. 860.

[38] Glynn, "See No Evil," p. 23.

[39] Stephen A. Oxman, "Status of Bosnian Peace Negotiations," *U.S. Department of State Dispatch*, October 18, 1993, p. 735.

[40] Kelly, "Surrender and Blame," pp. 47–48.

[41] U.S. Congress, 103-2, House Foreign Affairs Committee, Hearings: *The Crisis in Rwanda* (Washington, D.C.: GPO, 1995), p. 4.

[42] *Ibid.*, p. 5.

[43] Philip Gourevitch, "After the Genocide," *New Yorker*, December 18, 1995, p. 91.

[44] Douglas Jehl, "Officials Told to Avoid Calling Killings 'Genocide,' " *New York Times*, June 10, 1994, p. 8.

[45] Steven Greenhouse, "U.S. Support for Turks' Anti-Kurd Campaign Dims," *New York Times*, March 29, 1995, p. A8.

[46] *Ibid.*

[47] *Ibid.*

[48] Douglas Jehl, "U.S. Again Urges Turkey to Pull Out of Iraq," *New York Times*, April 20, 1995, p. A5.

[49] Strobe Talbott, "U.S.-Turkish Leadership in the Post–Cold War World," *U.S. Department of State Dispatch*, April 24, 1995, p. 361.

[50] Jim McGee, "U.S., Russian Officials Stress Mutual Interests despite Recent Tensions," *Washington Post*, January 2, 1995, p. A16.

[51] Alessandra Stanley, "Yeltsin Orders Bombing Halt on Rebel City," *New York Times*, January 5, 1995, p. A1.

[52] Ann Devroy, "Clinton Offers Yeltsin 'Friendly Suggestions,' " *Washington Post*, January 7, 1995, p. A17.

[53] Elaine Sciolino, "U.S. and Allies to Press Russia for Chechnya Peace Settlement," *New York Times*, January 6, 1995, p. A8.

[54] William Drozdiak, "Christopher Hints Aid Cuts for Russians if War Goes On," *Washington Post*, January 18, 1995, p. A11.

[55] Douglas Jehl, "Struggle in Russia: In the U.S. Clinton Exhorts Russians to Halt War in Russia," *New York Times*, January 14, 1995, p. A1.

[56] Steven Greenhouse, "U.S., in Shift, Says Russia Breaks Pacts," *New York Times*, January 12, 1995, p. A3.

[57] William Drozdiak, "Russia Gives U.S. Pledges on Chechnya Aid, Voting," *Washington Post*, January 19, 1995, p. A15.

[58] Steven Greenhouse, "Christopher Says Russia May Pay High Price for Chechen War," *New York Times*, March 23, 1995, p. A5.

⁵⁹ Steven Greenhouse, "U.S. Sharply Rebukes Russia for Its Offensive in Chechnya," *New York Times*, April 12, 1995, p. A16.

⁶⁰ Kimberly Ann Elliott and Gary Clyde Hufbauer, " 'New' Approaches to Economic Sanctions," in Arnold Kanter and Linton F. Brooks, eds., *U.S. Intervention Policy for the Post–Cold War World* (New York: American Assembly/W.W. Norton, 1994), pp. 132–58. For a comprehensive study of sanctions in 116 cases, see Gary Clyde Hufbauer, Jeffrey J. Schott, and Kimberly Ann Elliott, *Economic Sanctions Reconsidered* (Washington, D.C.: Institute for International Economics, 1990).

⁶¹ U.S. Congress, 91-1, Part 1, Senate Judiciary Committee, Hearings: *Relief Problems in Nigeria-Biafra* (Washington, D.C.: GPO, 1969), p. 27.

⁶² Tad Szulc, "Nixon Is Criticized by Senator Church on Aid to Pakistan," *New York Times*, July 8, 1971, p. 2.

⁶³ Tad Szulc, "U.S. Says It Will Continue Aid to Pakistan despite Cutoff Urged by Other Nations," *New York Times*, May 29, 1971, p. 2.

⁶⁴ "Transcript of the President's News Conference," p. 16.

⁶⁵ House Foreign Affairs Committee, *International Protection of Human Rights*, pp. 65–69.

⁶⁶ Jeff Lang, "Slaughter of Hutu," Letter to the Editor, *New York Times*, September 6, 1972, p. 44.

⁶⁷ House Committee, *International Protection of Human Rights*, p. 71.

⁶⁸ U.S. Congress, 100-2, House Foreign Affairs Committee, Hearings: *Recent Violence in Burundi: What Should Be the U.S. Response?* (Washington, D.C.: GPO, 1988), p. 17.

⁶⁹ *Ibid.*, p. 48.

⁷⁰ On Buyoya's reforms after the 1988 massacres, see Rene Lemarchand, *Burundi: Ethnic Conflict and Genocide* (Cambridge: Cambridge University Press, 1996), pp. 131–39.

⁷¹ U.S. Department of State, *Country Reports on Human Rights Practices for 1989* (Washington, D.C.: GPO, 1989), p. 37.

⁷² U.S. Department of State, *Country Reports on Human Rights Practices for 1992* (Washington, D.C.: GPO, 1993), p. 24.

⁷³ U.S. Congress, 95-2, House International Relations Committee, Hearings: *Foreign Assistance Legislation for Fiscal Year 1979* (Washington, D.C.: GPO, 1978), p. xv.

⁷⁴ *Ibid.*, p. 5. See also Testimony of Morris Draper, U.S. Congress, 95-2, House Appropriations Committee, Hearings: *Second Supplemental Bill, 1978* (Washington, D.C.: GPO, 1978), p. 6.

⁷⁵ U.S. Congress, 98-1, House Armed Services Committee, Report:

Lebanon: Limited Interest, Limited Involvement, Frequent Accounting (Washington, D.C.: GPO, 1983), p. 5.

[76] David Callahan, "Failure of Vision: Behind the U.S. Tilt toward Iraq," *Foreign Service Journal*, January 1991, p. 24.

[77] U.S. Congress, 100-2, House Foreign Affairs Committee, Markup: *Legislation to Impose Sanctions against Iraqi Chemical Use* (Washington, D.C.: GPO, 1988), p. 20.

[78] Ralph Johnson, "U.S. Efforts to Promote a Peaceful Settlement in Yugoslavia," *U.S. Department of State Dispatch*, October 21, 1991, p. 784.

[79] U.S. Congress, 102-2, House Foreign Affairs Committee, Hearings: *Developments in Europe—June 1992* (Washington, D.C.: GPO, 1992), p. 2.

[80] James A. Baker III, *The Politics of Diplomacy: Revolution, War, and Peace, 1989–1992* (New York: Putnam, 1995), p. 648.

[81] Bill Clinton, "Additional Measures Tighten Embargo against the Federal Republic of Yugoslavia (Serbia and Montenegro)," *U.S. Department of State Dispatch*, May 3, 1993, p. 308. On U.S. support for monitoring the enforcement of the sanctions, see Stephen A. Oxman, "Containment of the Bosnian Conflict," *U.S. Department of State Dispatch*, August 9, 1993, p. 575.

[82] Aleksa Djilas, "A Profile of Slobodan Milosevic," *Foreign Affairs*, vol. 72, no. 3 (Summer 1993), p. 95.

[83] David Binder, "CIA Doubtful on Serbian Sanctions," *New York Times*, December 22, 1993, p. A3.

[84] John Stremlau, *Sharpening International Sanctions: Toward a Stronger Role for the United Nations* (New York: Carnegie Corporation of New York, 1996), p. 29.

[85] Lawrence Eagleburger, "Detention Centers in Bosnia-Hercegovina and Serbia," *U.S. Department of State Dispatch*, August 10, 1992, p. 618; Thomas M. T. Niles, "U.S. Position and Proposed Actions Concerning the Yugoslav Crisis," *U.S. Department of State Dispatch Supplement*, September 1992, p. 26.

[86] Lawrence Eagleburger, "The Need to Respond to War Crimes in the Former Yugoslavia," *U.S. Department of State Dispatch*, December 28, 1992, p. 923.

[87] "Identifying Yugoslav War Criminals," *U.S. Department of State Dispatch*, December 28, 1992, p. 924.

[88] Madeleine Albright, "Bosnia in Light of the Holocaust: War Crimes Tribunals," *U.S. Department of State Dispatch*, April 18, 1994, pp. 209–11.

[89] Thomas W. Lippman, "U.S. Troop Withdrawal Ends Frustrating Mission to Save Rwandan Lives," *Washington Post*, October 3, 1994, p. A11.

[90] For an overview of mediation issues related to ethnic conflict, see Jeonne Walker, "International Mediation in Ethnic Conflict," in Brown, *Ethnic Conflict and International Security*, pp. 165–80.

[91] On the importance of ripeness, see Richard Haass, *Conflicts Unending: The United States and Regional Disputes* (New Haven: Yale University Press, 1990).

[92] Dana Adams Schmidt, "Nigerians to Meet Biafran on Peace," *New York Times*, May 3, 1968, p. A1.

[93] Joseph E. Thompson, *American Policy and African Famine: The Nigeria-Biafra War, 1966–1970* (New York: Greenwood Press, 1990), p. 49.

[94] Benjamin Welles, "Biafra Study Unit Is Set Up by U.S.," *New York Times*, November 27, 1968, p. A8.

[95] Benjamin Welles, "Katzenbach Asks Peace in Nigeria," *New York Times*, December 4, 1968, p. A7.

[96] Benjamin Welles, "U.S., in Shift, Maps $20 Million Plan to Relieve Biafra," *New York Times*, December 15, 1968, p. A1.

[97] Morris, *Uncertain Greatness*, p. 123.

[98] Hersh, *The Price of Power*, p. 142.

[99] Morris, *Uncertain Greatness*, p. 129.

[100] U.S. Congress, 91-1, Part I, Senate Judiciary Committee, Hearings: *Relief Problems in Biafra* (Washington, D.C.: GPO, 1969), p. 27.

[101] Morris, *Uncertain Greatness*, p. 124.

[102] For background on efforts to end the Lebanese war and on Carter initiatives, see Hani A. Fari, "The Failure of Peacemaking in Lebanon, 1975–1989," in Dierdre Collings, ed., *Peace for Lebanon? From War to Reconstruction* (Boulder: Lynne Rienner Publishers, 1994), pp. 17–30.

[103] See testimony of Joseph Sisco, U.S. Congress, 94-2, Senate Judiciary Committee, Hearings: *Humanitarian Problems in Lebanon* (Washington, D.C.: GPO, 1976), p. 21.

[104] U.S. Congress, 94-2, Senate Foreign Relations Committee, Hearings: *Middle East Peace Prospects* (Washington, D.C.: GPO, 1976), p. 167.

[105] David Binder, "Envoy Says U.S. Erred in Beirut Policy," *New York Times*, May 27, 1976, p. A3.

[106] See testimony of Morris Draper, U.S. Congress, 95-2, Senate Foreign Relations Committee, Hearings: *Lebanon* (Washington, D.C.: GPO, 1978), p. 32.

[107] Jimmy Carter, *Keeping Faith: Memoirs of a President* (New York: Bantam Books, 1982), p. 369.

[108] Alexander M. Haig, Jr., *Caveat: Realism, Reagan, and Foreign Policy* (New York: Macmillan, 1984), pp. 317–18.

[109] For a scathing account of this policy, see Scott Shuger, "What America Hasn't Learned from Its Greatest Peacekeeping Disaster," *Washington Monthly*, October 1989, p. 40.

[110] *Ibid.*

[111] Thomas L. Friedman, *From Beirut to Jerusalem* (New York: Farrar, Straus and Giroux, 1989), p. 197.

[112] Robert C. McFarlane, *Special Trust* (New York: Cadell and Davies, 1994), pp. 244–45.

[113] Robert Fisk, *Pity the Nation: The Abduction of Lebanon* (New York: Atheneum, 1990), p. 454; Friedman, *From Beirut to Jerusalem*, p. 197.

[114] McFarlane, *Special Trust*, p. 245.

[115] Shuger, "What America Hasn't Learned," p. 40.

[116] *Ibid.*

[117] Madeleine K. Albright, "Current Status of U.S. Policy on Bosnia, Somalia, and UN Reform," *U.S. Department of State*, April 5, 1993, p. 208.

[118] Stephen A. Oxman, "Status of Bosnian Peace Negotiations," *U.S. Department of State Dispatch*, October 18, 1993, p. 734.

[119] *Ibid.*

[120] U.S. Congress, 103-1, House Foreign Affairs Committee, Hearings: *Developments in Europe and the Former Yugoslavia* (Washington, D.C.: GPO, 1993), p. 13.

[121] U.S. Congress, 103-2, House Foreign Affairs Committee, Hearings: *The NATO Summit and the Future of European Security* (Washington, D.C.: GPO, 1994), p. 10.

[122] House Foreign Affairs Committee, *Developments in Europe and the Former Yugoslavia*, p. 16.

[123] "Signing of a Framework Agreement for Peace in Bosnia," *U.S. Department of State Dispatch*, March 14, 1994, p. 137; Bill Clinton, "Bosnia and Croatia: The Challenge of Peace and Reconstruction," *U.S. Department of State Dispatch*, April 4, 1994, p. 181.

[124] John J. Mearsheimer and Stephen Van Evera, "When Peace Means War," *New Republic*, December 18, 1995, p. 18.

[125] Holbrooke commented in April 1995 that "the Bosnian Serbs have refused categorically to accept the Contact Group plan as the standing

point for negotiation" (U.S. Congress, 104-1, Commission on Security and Cooperation in Europe, Hearings: *The United Nations, NATO, and the Former Yugoslavia* [Washington, D.C.: GPO, 1995], p. 7). Even more than Muslim intransigence, this inflexibility seemed to Holbrooke the principal obstacle to peace.

126 Roger Cohen, "Taming the Bullies of Bosnia," *New York Times Magazine*, December 17, 1995, p. 78.

127 Martin Walker, "Clinton's Secret Successes," *Washington Post*, September 4, 1994, p. C1.

128 "Northern Ireland: Contacts with Sinn Fein Party Leaders," *U.S. Department of State Dispatch*, October 10, 1994, p. 686.

129 "Supporting Peace in Northern Ireland," *U.S. Department of State Dispatch*, November 7, 1994, p. 755.

130 Richard C. Holbrooke, "A Framework for Peace and Justice in Northern Ireland," *U.S. Department of State Dispatch*, April 3, 1995, p. 279.

131 James F. Clarity, "Clinton's Role for Northern Ireland Talks: Restoring the Focus on the Big Picture," *New York Times*, December 5, 1995, p. A4.

132 Bill Clinton, "The U.S. and Ireland: Dedication to a Future of Cooperation and Prosperity," *U.S. Department of State Dispatch*, May 29, 1995, p. 443.

133 Morris, *Uncertain Greatness*, p. 42.

134 Terrence Lyons, "Keeping Africa Off the Agenda," in Warren I. Cohen and Nancy Bernkopf Tucker, eds., *Lyndon Johnson Confronts the World: American Foreign Policy, 1963–1968* (New York: Cambridge University Press, 1994), p. 275.

135 Morris, *Uncertain Greatness*, p. 19.

136 "Aid Is Snarled for Starving Millions in Biafra," *New York Times*, July 3, 1968, p. A1.

137 Thompson, *American Policy and African Famine*, p. 60.

138 Benjamin Welles, "Rusk Urges Both Sides in Nigeria War to Show Restraint," *New York Times*, July 31, 1968, p. A4.

139 Welles, "Biafra Study Unit Is Set Up by U.S.," p. A8.

140 Welles, "U.S., in Shift, Maps $20 Million Plan to Relieve Biafra," p. A1.

141 "Lagos Warns U.S. on Aid to Biafra," *New York Times*, December 31, 1968, p. A1.

142 Kissinger, *White House Years*, p. 417.

[143] Morris, *Uncertain Greatness*, p. 122.

[144] Human Rights Watch, *Human Rights and U.N. Field Operations* (New York: Human Rights Watch, 1993), p. 167.

[145] *Ibid.*, pp. 167–68. For a full analysis of Resolution 688, see David J. Scheffer, "Use of Force after the Cold War: Panama, Iraq, and the New World Order," in *Right v. Might: International Law and the Use of Force* (New York: Council on Foreign Relations, 1991), pp. 145–48.

[146] Scheffer, "Use of Force," p. 147.

[147] Baker, *Politics of Diplomacy*, pp. 648–49.

[148] George Bush, "Containing the Crisis in Bosnia and the Former Yugoslavia," *U.S. Department of State Dispatch*, August 10, 1992, p. 617.

[149] Elaine Sciolino, "For West, Rwanda Is Not Worth the Political Candle," *New York Times*, April 15, 1994, p. 3.

[150] Thomas W. Lippman, "U.S. Troop Withdrawal Ends Frustrating Mission to Save Rwandan Lives," *Washington Post*, October 3, 1994, p. A11.

[151] Paul Lewis, "Security Council Votes to Cut Rwanda Peacekeeping Force," *New York Times*, April 22, 1994, p. A1.

[152] Holly J. Burkhalter, "The Question of Genocide: The Clinton Administration and Rwanda," *World Policy Journal*, vol. 11, no. 4 (Winter 1994–95), p. 46.

[153] Paul Lewis, "U.N. Council Urged to Weigh Action on Saving Rwanda," *New York Times*, April 30, 1994, p. A1.

[154] Paul Lewis, "U.S. Examines Way to Assist Rwanda without Troops," *New York Times*, May 1, 1994, p. A1.

[155] Paul Lewis, "U.S. Opposes Plan for U.N. Force in Rwanda," *New York Times*, May 12, 1994, p. A9.

[156] Paul Lewis, "Security Council Agrees on Plan to Send Peace Force to Rwanda," *New York Times*, May 14, 1994, p. A1.

[157] Paul Lewis, "U.N. Backs Troops for Rwanda but Bars Any Action Soon," *New York Times*, May 17, 1994, p. A1.

[158] *Ibid.*

[159] Stephen Kinzer, "European Leaders Reluctant to Send Troops to Rwanda," *New York Times*, May 24, 1994, p. A1.

[160] Paul Lewis, "Boutros-Ghali Angrily Condemns All Sides for Not Saving Rwanda," *New York Times*, May 26, 1994, p. A1.

[161] Paul Lewis, "3 African Lands Offer Troops for Rwanda," *New York Times*, May 25, 1994, p. A12.

[162] Michael R. Gordon, "U.S. to Supply 60 Vehicles for U.N. Troops in Rwanda," *New York Times*, June 16, 1994, p. A12.

[163] Michael R. Gordon, "U.N.'s Rwanda Deployment Slowed by Lack of Vehicles," *New York Times*, June 9, 1994, p. A10.

[164] Gordon, "U.S. to Supply 60 Vehicles," p. 1.

[165] Lewis, "U.N. Council Urged to Weigh Action," p. 12.

[166] "200 U.S. Troops to Assist Relief Mission in Rwanda," *Baltimore Sun*, July 30, 1994, p. A1.

[167] Gilbert A. Lewthwaite, "Larger U.N. Force for Rwanda," *Baltimore Sun*, May 5, 1994, p. 12.

[168] Brian Atwood, "Responding Further to the Plight of the Rwanda Refugees," *U.S. Department of State Dispatch*, August 1, 1994, p. 524.

[169] Cooper and Berdal, "Outside Intervention in Ethnic Conflicts," p. 201.

[170] Friedman, *From Beirut to Jerusalem*, p. 191.

[171] See testimony of Nicholas A. Veliotes, U.S. Congress, 98-1, House Foreign Affairs Committee, Hearings: *Developments in the Middle East, February 1983* (Washington, D.C.: GPO, 1983), p. 7.

[172] House Committee, *Lebanon: Limited Interest, Limited Involvement, Frequent Accounting*, pp. 3–4.

[173] Colin Powell, *My American Journey* (New York: Random House, 1995), p. 291.

[174] *Ibid.*

[175] Baker, *Politics of Diplomacy*, p. 651.

[176] U.S. Congress, Senate Armed Services Committee, Hearings: *Situation in Bosnia and Appropriate U.S. and Western Responses* (Washington, D.C.: GPO, 1992), pp. 16–47.

[177] Powell, *My American Journey*, p. 558.

[178] *Ibid.*, p. 562.

[179] *Ibid.*, p. 576.

[180] *Ibid.*

[181] U.S. Congress, 103-1, Senate Appropriations Committee, Hearings: *Department of Defense Appropriations, Fiscal Year 1994, Part I* (Washington, D.C.: GPO, 1993), pp. 213–14. See also Elizabeth Drew, *On the Edge: The Clinton Presidency* (New York: Touchstone Books, 1994), p. 154.

[182] Drew, *On the Edge*, p. 96.

[183] *Ibid.*, p. 213.

[184] Michael R. Gordon, "Pentagon Is Wary of Role in Bosnia," *New York Times*, March 13, 1994, p. A6.

[185] U.S. Congress, 103-2, Senate Armed Services Committee, Hearings: *Briefing on Bosnia and Other Current Military Operations* (Washington, D.C.: GPO, 1994), p. 17.

[186] *Ibid.*
[187] Kelly, "Surrender and Blame," p. 50.
[188] Cohen, "Taming the Bullies of Bosnia," p. 78.
[189] *Ibid.*
[190] *Ibid.*

Chapter Five

[1] John Ikenberry and Dan Deudney are the authors of this term.
[2] See *Inalienable Rights, Fundamental Freedoms: A U.N. Agenda for Advancing Human Rights in the World Community* (New York: United Nations Association, 1996), pp. 55–58.
[3] Carl Conetta and Charles Knight, *Design for a 15,000-Person UN Legion* (Cambridge: Project on Defense Alternatives, 1995).
[4] Interview with author. See David Callahan, "Fall Back, Troops: Clinton's New U.N. Policy," *Foreign Service Journal*, May 1994, p. 21.
[5] Barbara Crossette, "Experts' Study Says Attacking U.N. Hurts the U.S.," *New York Times*, August 20, 1996, p. A6.
[6] Testimony of Madeleine Albright, U.S. Senate Appropriations Committee, *Hearings*, May 23, 1996, Federal News Service.
[7] Barbara Crossette, "At the U.N., a Proposal to Speed Aid during Crises," *New York Times*, July 20, 1996, p. 7.
[8] Howard W. French, "U.S. Wins Liberians' Pledge to Back Truce," *New York Times*, April 26, 1996, p. A3.
[9] On the background and activities of the high commissioner, see Rob Zaagman, "Minority Questions, Human Rights and Regional Instability: The Prevention of Conflict," in Robert L. Pfaltzgraff, Jr., and Richard H. Shultz, Jr., eds., *Ethnic Conflict and Regional Instability: Implications for U.S. Policy and Army Roles and Missions* (Washington, D.C.: Strategic Studies Institute, 1994), pp. 217–28.
[10] See, for example, Michael Mandelbaum, *The Dawn of Peace in Europe* (New York: Twentieth Century Fund, 1996).
[11] Diana Chigas, with Elizabeth McClintock and Christophe Kamp, "Preventive Diplomacy and the Organization for Security and Cooperation in Europe: Creating Incentives for Dialogue and Cooperation," in Abram Chayes and Antonio Handler Chayes, eds., *Preventing Conflict in the Post-Communist World: Mobilizing International and Regional Organizations* (Washington: Brookings Institution, 1996), p. 61.
[12] *Ibid.*, p. 74.

[13] For research and policy recommendations on this subject, see Jeffrey Boutwell, Michael T. Klare, and Laura W. Reed, *Lethal Commerce: The Global Trade in Small Arms and Light Weapons* (Cambridge: Academy of Arts and Sciences, 1995).

[14] Steven Erlanger, "U.S. Report Says Bosnia Peace Is Fragile," *New York Times*, May 17, 1996, p. A6.

[15] *Ibid.*

[16] Jane Perlez, "Serbs in Pragmatic Pullout from Albanian Region," *New York Times*, July 22, 1996, p. A10.

[17] For discussion, see Center for Preventive Action, *Toward Comprehensive Peace in Southeast Europe: Stabilizing the South Balkans* (New York: Council on Foreign Relations/Twentieth Century Fund, 1996).

[18] Martin Sieff, "Clinton, Yeltsin Have Common Cause: Ending War Could Help Reelection," *Washington Times*, March 26, 1996, p. A12.

[19] For a review of these efforts, see John Herbst's statement before the House International Relations Committee, July 30, 1996, Federal News Service.

[20] Jarat Chopra and Thomas G. Weiss, "The United Nations and the Former Second World: Coping with Conflict," in Chayes and Chayes, *Preventing Conflict in the Post-Communist World*, pp. 532–33.

[21] Thomas P. Melady, "To Stop the Killing, Partition Burundi," *New York Times*, September 1, 1988, p. A25.

[22] See "Saving Failed States," Gerald B. Helman and Steven R. Ratner, *Foreign Policy*, no. 89 (Winter 1992–93), pp. 3–20.

[23] *Ibid.*, pp. 13–21.

[24] For the lessons of Cambodia and some analysis of Somalia, see Janet E. Heininger, *Peacekeeping in Transition: The United Nations in Cambodia* (New York: Twentieth Century Fund, 1994).

[25] Monteagle Stearns, *Talking to Strangers. Improving American Diplomacy at Home and Abroad* (Princeton: Princeton University Press, 1996), p. 131.

[26] *Ibid.*, pp. 64, 162.

[27] See, most notably, U.S. Department of State Management Task Force, *State 2000: A New Model for Managing Foreign Affairs* (Washington, D.C.: U.S. Department of State, 1992).

[28] *In from the Cold: The Report of the Twentieth Century Fund Task Force on the Future of U.S. Intelligence* (New York: Twentieth Century Fund, 1996), p. 6.

[29] Tim Weiner, "House Panel Says C.I.A. Lacks Expertise to Carry Out Its Duties," *New York Times*, June 19, 1997, p. A20.

[30] *In from the Cold*, p. 8.

[31] See the congressional testimony of Geoffrey Cowan, director of Voice of America, July 9, 1996, Federal Document Clearing House.

[32] Janet E. Heininger, *Peacekeeping in Transition: The United Nations in Cambodia* (New York: Twentieth Century Fund, 1994), pp. 110–11.

[33] For examinations of these developments, see Barry McCaffrey, "Military Support for Peacekeeping Operations," and Steven L. Arnold, "Operations Other than War in a Power Projection Army," in Pfaltzgraff and Shultz, *Ethnic Conflict and Regional Instability*, pp. 241–48, 281–98. See also Antonio Handler Chayes and George T. Raach, *Peace Operations: Developing an American Strategy* (Washington, D.C.: National Defense University Press, 1995).

INDEX